Charles Loring Brace

The unknown God

Inspiration among pre-Christian races

Charles Loring Brace

The unknown God
Inspiration among pre-Christian races

ISBN/EAN: 9783337221607

Printed in Europe, USA, Canada, Australia, Japan

Cover: Foto ©Lupo / pixelio.de

More available books at **www.hansebooks.com**

THE
UNKNOWN GOD

OR

INSPIRATION AMONG PRE-CHRISTIAN RACES

BY

C. LORING BRACE

AUTHOR OF "GESTA CHRISTI," "RACES OF THE OLD WORLD," ETC.

New York
A. C. ARMSTRONG AND SON
1890

(ALL RIGHTS RESERVED)

PREFACE.

WHAT may be called the "modern method" in studying ethnic or heathen religions is not, as was once the case, merely to search for their defects, or to show their inferiority to the highest religion, but to find what good there was in them; to see how the man of other races and times regarded the problems of the universe. We wish to know what was his conception of the primeval Cause, what he considered his relation to be to that strange power, and how far that relation affected his daily life and practical morals. We would gladly know how he regarded the great darkness beyond life, and what thoughts he conceived of another life and of the beings there. We eagerly seek to learn what moral ideals and conceptions he transferred to another existence, and how far he succeeded in lifting the great veil which hangs before it. We try to stand in his footsteps and to see the great mystery as he endeavored to see it. We do not feel it necessary to laugh at his vagaries or sneer at his imaginations; we merely seek to gaze at the universe as he gazed at it.

And in doing this we have a still further object; we expect to find with man in all ages and races some evidences of the inspiration of the Divine Spirit, and to discover traces of God and higher inspirations in the remotest annals and records of mankind.

In this volume the writer has taken for his special theme the words used by Saint Paul in his sermon on Mars Hill, "The Unknown God," — words which the great Apostle applied also to the spiritual Zeus of the ancient Greeks. The effort of the writer is to show the ancient belief of mankind in the Unknown God, and that the great Father of all has granted his inspirations to many of very different countries and tribes and races. This volume is in some respects a search for the footprints of the Divine Being on the shifting sands of remote history.

The first chapters deal with the Hamitic and Semitic races. Fortunately the latest investigations in the early inscriptions of Egypt show that there was a period (not the earliest) in which a profound belief in the One God existed in the minds of the scholars and priests of that ancient country. From this field the student is conducted to the Semitic tribes in the valley of the Euphrates. There among an ancient race — probably Semitic — called

Akkadian, are found remarkable penitential psalms and devout prayers stamped with a religious spirit which had seemed peculiar to another Semitic tribe, the Jews; they certainly bear evidence of inspiration from the Unknown God.

The investigation then turns to the Aryan races, and evidence is adduced from the remarkable associations which existed, like secret churches, among the Greeks, called the Mysteries. From the rites of these secret societies the belief in God and a future judgment is discovered, and shown to have been held in secret by a certain number of believers. The investigation then enters the field of the early Greek poetry, and presents the faith in a spiritual God, or Zeus, before the idea had been degraded by the myth-making fancy. The evidence from the Greek dramatists and many of the ancient writers is here overwhelming that one spiritual God was at certain periods adored by considerable numbers of the Greek race.

The religion of Plato and Socrates and the faith of the Stoics are then examined for evidences of pure monotheism and of genuine religion. Copious extracts are given from the Stoical writers, to show what their genuine religious belief was.

The course of the inquiry then turns to the Oriental Aryan races; and the Zoroastrian religion is investigated, to show the purity of its character and its elevated views on truth and moral purity, and on the character of Ormazd.

From the Persians the study passes to the Hindus; and the old Vedic hymns furnish the proof of Hindu monotheism in the worship of Varuna, the Heaven-God. In both these chapters extracts are given from the Persian and Hindu religious writings. The fullest description in the book is devoted to the Buddhist faith, with copious extracts from the Dhammapada and other sacred writings of that religion. The author regards Buddha as in a high degree inspired, and as an instrument in the hands of Providence for the elevation and purification of Asia. A contrast is drawn between the Buddhistic and Christian faiths, and the causes which have impeded the success of Buddhism are traced. The final chapter is on the Biblical argument for the inspiration of the heathen; and suggestions are given as to the principles which should guide the missionary in his religious teachings, especially among the Buddhists.

The work, it should be remembered, is not designed as a critical attack on the heathen religions, or as a defence of Christianity, by contrasting its superior truths with those of other faiths. The object is rather to show what great truths have inspired the pious heathen of the past, and how far the influences of the Divine Spirit have reached remote and separated tribes of men and revealed to them the nature of God, and their duties to their fellow-men. It is an effort to make manifest the ways of God to men in a field not hitherto much traversed. It is believed the most devout disciple of Christianity will find little to shock his faith in these presentations, but will rather be strengthened by this broader view of the providence of God to men.

C. LORING BRACE.

CHESKNOLL, DOBBS FERRY, N. Y.
    December, 1889.

CONTENTS.

CHAPTER		PAGE
	Preface	v
I.	Egyptian Monotheism	1
II.	The Jews and Egyptians	41
III.	Akkadian Penitential Psalms	51
IV.	The Greek Mysteries	78
V.	Zeus as Spiritual God	90
VI.	The Religion of Socrates and Plato	106
VII.	The Faith of the Stoics	120
VIII.	The Faith of the Stoics. — Seneca	133
IX.	Stoical Writings. — Epictetus	144
X.	Stoical Writings. — Marcus Aurelius	152
XI.	Review	167
XII.	Zoroastrianism	182
XIII.	Hinduism	198
XIV.	Buddhism	224
XV.	Sacred Writings of Buddhism	255
XVI.	Review	290
XVII.	Heathen Inspiration and the Scriptures	299
XVIII.	The Conversion of Non-Christian Nations	309
XIX.	Conclusion	317
	Appendix	321
	Index	323

*Ye whose hearts are fresh and simple,
Who have faith in God and Nature,
Who believe that in all ages
Every human heart is human,
That in even savage bosoms
There are longings, yearnings, strivings
For the good they comprehend not,
That the feeble hands and helpless,
Groping blindly in the darkness,
Touch God's right hand in that darkness,
And are lifted up and strengthened,—
Listen!*

       LONGFELLOW'S HIAWATHA.

THE UNKNOWN GOD;

OR,

INSPIRATION AMONG PRE-CHRISTIAN PEOPLES.

―――・―――

CHAPTER I.

EGYPTIAN MONOTHEISM.

I AM HE THAT IS AND WAS AND SHALL BE.
Inscription on the Temple of Isis.

THE only conception of the moral action of the Divine Being on the human soul which is *a priori* defensible and philosophical, is of a continued and impartial influence, limited to no time, or age, or race. It should be like the great physical forces, — like gravity, magnetism, or electricity, forever acting in all particles of matter, but not always manifesting themselves, sometimes resisted, often unseen, but eternally working toward definite ends.

Religion, if it be the binding of human beings to the Unseen Power of the universe, and Revelation, or the manifestation of his nature to men, must have been realities and phenomena through all ages of human history, and as definite and sustaining to the first savage who sharpened his flints in the tertiary period, or the first cave-dweller whose mental faculties had grasped the idea of a cause, as to the saint of the middle ages or the religious philosopher of the nineteenth century. The conceptions of the "fossil savage" and of the modern thinker would not be the same, but they would have great elements in common. Both would bow in unspeakable awe before the vast and incomprehensible Mystery behind the things seen; both would depend utterly on this Infinite and Unknown Power, whether manifested in one being or many beings; both would bend their wills to the eternal Will, or wills; and both would seek to guide their lives by what had been revealed to them of the qualities and purposes of the tremendous Being, or beings, unseen yet ever felt. The man of the flint ages would undoubtedly be capable of grasping but few, and those the simplest, truths; but as his race gradually rose in the scale, its members would be open more and more to the higher divine influences which were ever acting around them, and attaining thus to purer and grander conceptions. Then, from reasons which we cannot always explain, — perhaps connected with the freedom of the human will, — some branch or descendant of the savage race would arise which was peculiarly sensitive to these unseen influences, which became inspired with moral and spiritual truths, and was especially open to inspiration from above.

This tribe or nation has become inspired with religion,

and seems at once to make a great bound in spiritual growth. Truths are revealed to it that move men through all succeeding time; and lives appear in such a people, so controlled by these inspirations and so animated by moral and unseen powers, that the memories and the legends of them survive all other traditions, and never cease to console or elevate or purify mankind. On the other hand, other races appear in history — why, we cannot say — less open to the divine influences, and thus manifesting them less, and tending toward a lower and more selfish animal life. Yet among such races there are probably far more humane, sympathetic, and spiritual lives, passed in obscurity, than human records ever describe. We know but little of the morals or religion of the remote past. What we do know, we judge of by tests entirely inapplicable, and interpret an ancient poetic symbolism by a modern and exact glossary.

It is a side evidence of the spiritual inspiration of ancient or barbarous races that so many tribes of men in all ages have a tradition or legend of a moral Benefactor of their race, who came from above, bore human ills, sought to scatter happiness and enlightenment among men, and perhaps perished at last in the struggle with evil on earth, to appear again among the stars, or to await his faithful followers in the region of the blessed. Even "sun-myths," subsequently attached to such traditions, would not disprove the substantial historical truth of the original story;

nor would the tendency of the human mind to frame its ideals in legends demonstrate that no such ideal benefactors had arisen. The strength and purity of the feelings and practices which gather around such memories are perhaps the best test of their reality. Under a continuity of spiritual influences through all ages, such lives are natural and to be expected. And even if some of these be imagined, the ideal shows the moral forces working on the hearts of men, and the truths which had here and there dawned on them.

The highest forms of spiritual thought and the purest ideals of religion would probably be developed in connection with a certain advancement of civilization or of intellectual life; and yet they would not necessarily follow mental progress. To the savage and unreflecting mind the conception of one Power behind the universe comes later than the thought of many powers, though even with the earliest religious beliefs will be a faith in one unseen Being who is greater than other similar beings. And it is perfectly possible that a healthful, independent, roving tribe, — like some branch of the Semitic race, — much in contact with Nature and not corrupted by luxury, might be more open to the unseen spiritual influences, and thus reach a grander conception of the mystery of the universe, than some races much more developed intellectually and materially.

If we search human records for the most ancient

civilization, we unquestionably come at once upon the Egyptian. To the student among the Greek and the Roman races in their prime, the founders of the magnificent temples and gigantic tombs in the valley of the Nile seemed as remote as they do to us. Indeed, it may with truth be said that the modern European and American student of archaeology knows more of that antique civilization than did Herodotus or Plutarch. Whatever doubts may linger about the exact numbers of the Egyptian chronology, whether certain lines of kings were synchronous or successive, the general conclusion can hardly be questioned by scholars, that far back in the shadowy ages of the past, thousands of years before the first dawn of Greek culture, centuries before Moses or Abraham or the received dates of the Flood, a remarkably organized civilization and highly developed religion existed in the lower Nile valley, shut apart from the world, though destined to influence all countries and all succeeding ages.

EGYPTIAN RELIGION.

Till comparatively recent years the modern student was under the double misfortune of knowing the Egyptian religion only through a symbolism utterly foreign to our mental habits, and then through Greek and Roman interpreters. If the reader will imagine so strange a calamity as that the Christian religion had utterly perished from the earth in the fifth or sixth century, and that its documents had been hidden or destroyed, and it could only be known through its symbolism and art, and through Greek and Latin historians, he will have some slight appreciation of our relation to the Egyptian religion.

In such a case as we have supposed, we would have learned from the noblest and purest Roman historian that this dead religion was a "detestable superstition;" from another that its followers indulged in shameful orgies of lust, and resorted to human sacrifice; from others among the Greeks of apparently the highest moral sympathies, living within fifty or sixty years of the death of its founder, we would not hear a word of its doctrines, or its marvels, or the wonderful life of its originator. From its symbolism and art, students of archæology would have inferred as to this extinct faith that its central deity was an aged man with flowing locks, of noble and venerable countenance, that it worshipped also a goddess of fair appearance with a wonderful child, that it believed in a marriage of this divinity with a higher deity, and also that it adored a sad man of suffering who had been executed as a criminal. They would also discover animal worship in the adoration of the lamb and the dove, and in the figures of gods with the heads of the lion, the eagle, the bull, and the pigeon. They would detect, besides, the struggles of the good and evil principles in the pictures of gods of frightful aspect contending with gods of benignant countenance, and they would find pictures of heaven which were merely the continuance of the familiar pastoral scenes of Italy and Germany.

No doubt, too, as time passed away and the facts and traditions connected with the life of the great founder of this religion had become vague and shadowy, solar myths would attach themselves to its incidents; the twelve apostles would become the twelve months, the day of nativity would be the day of the sun's return northward, his death would be an eclipse, the name which this supposed god gave himself, the "Light of the World," would indicate the solar origin of the story, and his resurrection would be the emerging of the sun from the deep shadow, and the life and light which follow it.[1] It would require but a brief time and little imagination to attach a solar myth to the Gospel narrative, provided the facts had become obscured.

When Herodotus visited Egypt in the third century before Christ, or when Diodorus wrote of it about the time of Christ, or Plutarch gathered the legend of Osiris from Egyptian sources within seventy or eighty years after, the Egyptian religion was a thing of the remote

---

[1] The Christmas chant is well known, "Sol novus oritur," and the midsummer festival of bonfires to Saint John the Baptist. The words, "He must increase but I must decrease," might well have a solar interpretation.

past, at a greater distance from Herodotus or Plutarch than these are from us. The ancient faith had degenerated into extreme polytheism, or idol worship, except among those initiated in its "mysteries," and there was only a tradition or vague impression among other peoples of the purity and grandeur of the belief of the early Egyptians. The excessive and peculiar symbolism of this race served also both to hide their real conceptions from foreign races and gradually to degrade their own beliefs. Close observers, like Herodotus, saw clearly that they believed in the immortality of the soul, and others that they looked forward to a coming moral judgment. Their faith in this great moral reckoning of mankind in a future life no doubt influenced some of Plato's ideals pictured in his myths. The Jews may have derived certain spiritual conceptions and portions of ritual from them, and no doubt through Alexandria and the platonizing Jews some of their most ancient beliefs reached the apostles, and through them have come down to modern times. But in general it may safely be said that we know much more of the ancient Egyptian religion than did the Greeks or Romans.

In the remotest ages of human history certain dwellers in the Nile valley, perhaps gazing into the solemn depths of the tropical night, or watching the majestic courses of the stars, or seeing the sudden and resplendent rising of the glorious orb of the sun over the silent desert sands, received in awe-struck wonder the grandest inspiration which can come to the human soul from the unseen: even the thought of a Power, illimitable, incomprehensible, eternal, behind all the phenomena of the universe, above and behind the varied personalities of mythology and polytheism; the One awful beyond expression, enduring while all things change, filling immensity and eternity, self-created, the one original, before whom was nothing, and in whose presence the earth and heavens are but as a morning cloud; "living in truth,"[1] "truth itself," the essence of "righteousness," terrible to evil-doers, yet merciful, beneficent, full of love. Here to the ancient Egyptian was a Being, vast beyond imagination to conceive, and yet inspiring and directing each believer, — a being who lived in righteousness, and demanded righteousness, or "truth," of all those worshipping and loving him. Their wills must be submitted to his will. He guided and blessed them in life, and the happiness of eternity was to be in union with him.[2]

This dread invisible "concealed" Being manifests himself through various persons or divinities. He creates through "Thoth," his spirit, or "word." Thoth is his manifestation as word, or truth. He creates from himself through the word. Without Thoth is nothing made, and Thoth is God.[3]

[1] Words often used in the Book of the Dead.
[2] Book of the Dead.
[3] Brugsch, p. 58. "Of his own will he brought us forth by the *word* of truth" (James i. 18). "I call to witness the *word* of the Father

Saint John (i. 1-3) precisely describes the oldest Egyptian faith. "In the beginning was the Word, and the Word was with God, and the Word was God. The same was in the beginning with God. All things were made by him, and without him was not anything made that is made."

The word used for the original source of all things, Xoper,[1] according to Brugsch, means the cause of all being and becoming. This creates from himself through the word, or Thoth, not from any " stuff " or things existing. " Hail to thee, creator, body of God who buildeth his own body when heaven was not and earth was not."[2] Thousands of prayers are addressed to Xoper: " Thou wert first; nothing was then. Thou makest what is there." " Nothing was before thee, the Only or Self-born." " He was from the beginning, when nothing was." " The heart which he first spoke when he established the universe by his will " (Orpheus's words, quoted by Justin Martyr, Orat. ad gentes). It should be said here that the word " Truth," of such frequent and remarkable use in Egyptian religious writings, is expressed by a sign, meaning *rule* or *measure*, like our word righteousness. It means what is straight, conformed to rule, and true ; what is enduring and harmonious and real; what is good forever. The triumph of truth is the triumph of goodness. Truth is the end of man. The " justified " is the man held true and good. God is truth. Plutarch describes the amulet which protects Isis as the φωνή ἀληθής, " Voice of truth " (Isis and Osiris, lxviii.), as if that were the favorite phrase of the Egyptians.

[1] Religion und Mythologie der alten Aegypter, p. 51 ; H. Brugsch, 1885. See also De Rougé.

[2] Brugsch, p. 58.

of Rā, the tongue of Tum, the throat of the god (Ammon) whose name is hidden," says Brugsch,[1] "all mean one God;" and Thoth is the manifestation of that god as Word.

An inscription on the Temple of Dendera proclaims the "revelation of the light-god, Rā, being from the beginning [through] Thoth, who rests in truth; what flows from his heart works on, and what he has spoken stands for eternity."[2]

When these ancient inscriptions were chiselled in the granite near the Nile, before Moses or Abraham, the culture and religion of the Egyptians had passed from their low condition. Mighty buildings had been erected, demanding a remarkable knowledge of mechanical principles, a complex society was created, and the faith of this race was developed from a belief in the heavens as god to a heaven-god, and again from a sun-god to one who said to the sun, "Come unto us!"[3]

Philosophers note that these ancient Egyptian titles of deity do not in general take their origin from the heavens or the light, or from sensual images, as with the Aryan and other races, but are derived from deeper and more philosophic ideas of cause and origin and independent eternal being. In this they seem nearer the ancient Semitic

---

[1] Brugsch, p. 50.
[2] Ibid., E. Meyer: Set. Typhon. 1875.
[3] Book of the Dead, v. 21: Words of creative power.

Hebrew name of the Self-existent.[1] They are such as Xoper, (Being), Ammon (the Concealed), Rā (the Original), Ptah (artist), Xnum (builder or potter), Sebák (contriver), etc.

Only Osiris[2] (*os* or *us*, periodic force) seems to relate to the sun. But behind all these separate gods is the One, unnamable, eternal, infinite. They all seem only forms, or manifestations, of the original being.[3] Before they could express it in language, the Egyptians possessed the intuition or felt the power of this boundless creator and father. From innumerable of the oldest documents it is clear, says Brugsch, that to the ancient Egyptians God and the universe were as soul and body. God was a spirit dwelling in his cosmic house which he had furnished and built.[4]

In analyzing the ancient belief of the priests and thinkers and artists of the Nile valley, we find everywhere the statements that God is One and alone, and no other near him, the one who has made all. A Theban inscription

---

[1] Jahveh, — I AM THAT I AM.

[2] Brugsch.

[3] He is the holy spirit who begets gods; who takes on forms, but who remains unknown (Book of the Dead, xv. 46). The substance of the gods is the body of God (xvii. 75).

[4] Brugsch. The Egyptians frequently group these manifestations of the Original One in triads. Thus, Xoper (Being), Tum (the Unknown), and Rā make a triad. In the Boston Art Museum (No. 634) may be seen two sets of triad Egyptian figures, — Ptah, Horus, and Keph; and Ptah, Horus, and Thoth. A stéle of the nineteenth dynasty speaks of God as " Father and Son," at Thebes and Memphis (Rev. Arch., p. 357. 1860).

says of God in his form of Ammon: "The concealed spirit, a mystery for him whom he hath created, is Ammon the ancient of days, who is from the beginning, the creator of heaven, earth, the depth, and the mountains."

A remarkable hymn to Ammon Rā thus invokes him:

"Author of the pastures which feed the beasts and the plants which nourish man; he who feedeth the fishes of the river and the fowls of the air; he giveth the bread of life to the germ yet concealed in the egg; he feedeth the flying and creeping insects; he provideth food for the mouse in his hole and the birds in the forests. Homage to thee, author of all forms, the One who is alone, whose arms extend and multiply everywhere, thou who watchest over rulers when they repose, who lookest for the good of thy creatures! God Ammon who preservest all that is! Homage to thee because thou abidest in us [or because of thy *immanence* in us]! We prostrate ourselves before thy face because thou hast produced us. Homage to thee, by all creatures! Praise to thee in every region, — in the heights of the heavens, in the spaces of the earth, in the depths of the seas! The gods bow before thy majesty and exalt the soul of him who produced them, happy that their creator abideth in them (or at the *immanence of their generator* in them). They say to thee: 'Be in peace, O Father of the fathers of the gods, who hast hung the heavens and planted the earth. Author of things! Creator of blessings! Prince supreme! Chief of gods! We adore thy majesty at the moment in which thou producest us. Thou begettest us, and we cry out to thee to dwell in us.'"[1]

Or again, take this ancient and lofty inscription of praise to Ammon Rā:[2] —

[1] Translated by Grébaut; Museum of Boulaq.
[2] Chabas, Pap Hav.; Records of the Past; Trad. pap. Mag., Harris.

"Vast in his largeness without limit. Virtue supreme, in mysterious forms! Soul mysterious! Author of his fearful power, life holy and strong, created by himself; brilliant, illuminating, dazzling! Soul more soul than the gods, thou art concealed in great Ammon! Old man renewed! Worker of ages! Thou who hast designed the world! O Ammon, with the holy transformations! He whom no man knoweth, brilliant are his forms, his glory is a veil of light! Mystery of mysteries! Mystery unknown! Hail to thee in the bosom of Nun (celestial abyss)! Thou who hast truly begotten the gods! The breath of truth is in thy mysterious sanctuary. . . . Thou art adored upon the waters. The fertile land adores thee; the entrails of the wild animals are moved when thy bark [the sun] passeth by the hidden mountain. The spirits of the east congratulate thee when thy light shineth on their faces."

All the principal gods in the early faith are but manifestations of this original Spirit.

Besides being "One," he is a Spirit, as we see from these ancient hymns: he is from the beginning; the Original One; he was when nothing was, the father of beginnings; he is eternal; he stands from everlasting ages, and will be for eternity; he is concealed, and his form hath no man known, his face hath no man seen; he is hidden from gods and men, a mystery to his creatures; no mortal can name him; his name a mystery, countless are his titles.[1] God is Truth; he lives through Truth, he is nourished on Truth, he is King of Truth, and Truth he erects over the world. He is Life, and men live through him; he is Father and Mother of all crea-

---

[1] Book of the Dead, xlii., xliv. 4; Gr. pap., Harris, iii.

tures; he begets, and is not begotten; he is the creator, and not created, the creator of his own form and builder of his own body,—the universe; the Maker of all that was, and is, and is not yet; the original Framer (weaver) of the world, of heaven and earth and the depths. He hung the heavens and founded the earth; he let water (or moisture) come forth, and built the mountains. He is Being itself, the enduring One, who increaseth and is never lessened, the One who multiplies himself million-fold, the many-formed. He is Father of the gods; gods come forth from the word of his mouth; the great Master, the original potter who moulds men and gods. He is the weaver of the universe on the loom of life. Heaven rests on his head, and earth bears his feet; heaven conceals his spirit, earth his form, and the depth covers his mystery. God is merciful to his worshippers: he heareth him who calleth upon him, and protecteth the weak from the strong; he heareth the cry of him bound in chains; he guardeth the humble against the haughty, and is Judge between the powerful and the miserable. God acknowledgeth him who confesseth him, rewardeth him who serveth him, and guardeth him who followeth him.

The revelation of light is the most elevated expression of this divine original Power. The various gods, Rā, Ptah, Xnum,[1] Thoth, Osiris, are in inner being the same, and all manifestations of this original One.

[1] Brugsch.

To such a conception the worshipper might well say: "Hail to thee, thou King of the stars! Thou who art one with the heaven's arch! Thee the heavens and the lamps on heaven's arch do praise."[1]

"Hail to thee, our lord of truth, Ammon! whose shrine is hidden, Lord of gods, Creator sailing in thy boat [the sun], at whose command the gods were made; Tum, the maker of men, who supporteth their works, who giveth them life, who knoweth how one differeth from another, who listeneth to the poor that is in distress, who art gentle of heart when a man crieth unto thee; thou who deliverest the fearful from the violent, who judgest the poor and oppressed; Lord of wisdom, whose precepts are wise, at whose pleasure the Nile overfloweth her banks; Lord of mercy, most loving, at whose coming men live, opener of every eye, proceeding from the firmament, causer of pleasure and light, at whose goodness the gods rejoice, their hearts rejoicing when they see thee."[2]

"Bringer of food, great lord of all things nourishing,
Lord of all terrors and of all choicest joys.
 .   .   .   .
He filleth all granaries, he enricheth all the storehouses,
He careth for the estate of the poor.
 .   .   .   .   .   .
He is not beheld by the eye,
He hath neither ministers nor offerings,
He is not adored in sanctuaries.
 .   .   .   .
He wipeth away tears from all eyes,
He careth for the abundance of his blessings."[3]

[1] Inscription in Temple of Esne; Brugsch, p. 194.
[2] Brugsch, and Records of the Past. ii. 131.
[3] Hymn, Records of the Past; Birch, iv. 108.

As we have stated, in our condensed résumé of the Egyptian belief, Truth was held to be the essence and life of the divine being, as if only the Eternal and the Just could be true. God is held to be the author of truth, and more than once it is said in the "Book of the Dead" that "the society of divine persons [meaning the divine manifestations] subsists by truth every day." But even with this austere idea of divinity, the Egyptian's heart melts when he thinks of the all-pervading love of the unseen deity. "His love is in the south," he says in impassioned prayer, "his grace is in the north, his beauty taketh possession of all hearts, his love maketh the arms grow weak. His creatures are beautiful enough to paralyze the hands; hearts break in seeing him; by his will he hath produced the earth, gold, silver, stone, and the like."[1]

The sun especially is worshipped as a manifestation of this unknown Being. "Thy rays," says the worshipper, "come from a face not known; thou marchest unknown, thou shinest upon us and we know not thy form; thou presentest thy face to ours and we do not know thy body."[2]

That this exalted being was equally exalted in purity and spirituality is evident from a thousand inscriptions and documents. What is called the oldest manuscript

[1] A Hymn to Ammon Rā, v. 7; Records of the Past.
[2] Denkmäler, vi. 116.

in the world, "The Teachings of Prince Ptahhotep," gives this instruction: "Be good to thy people, for that is well pleasing to God.... Be not proud of riches, for the giver of fulness is God.... To obey, meaneth to love God; not to obey, to hate God." On the doors of the Temple of Edfu it is said: "God findeth his satisfaction in truth; he is propitiated by it, and he finds his pleasure in the most perfect purity.... God hath purity dearer than millions of gold and silver offerings."

These exalted conceptions lasted even into later times, when a Cyprian king, Nikokreon, asked the oracle of Serapis, "What is he among the gods?" and the reply was, "Heaven's space is my head, my body the sea, the earth my feet; my ears are in the upper ether, and my eye the wide-shining, glorious sunlight;" and of this same deity, Osiris-Serapis, an early papyrus says: "O Lord, no god is equal to thee; heaven bears thy spirit, earth thy image, and the depth is furnished with thy mysteries."[1] Of Rā, the god of light, it is said: "He is the invisible god, the mysterious spirit, whose form no man hath seen, whose being no man hath understood; the soul lightens from his eyes."[2]

The inscription on the Temple of Dendera speaks of God as having made all beings and things: "All that lives hath been made by God himself. He is creator of

[1] Papyrus of the Dead, British Museum; Brugsch.
[2] Brugsch, p. 197.

all that hath been formed, but he hath not been formed."[1] God is adored under his eternal name of "Furnisher of souls for forms."[2] He traverses eternity, is Master of infinity, Author of eternity, traversing millions of years in his existence. He is the Master of eternity without limits.[3] He is omnipresent, commanding at once at Thebes, Heliopolis, and Memphis.[4] He is unnamable, and abhorreth to have his name pronounced.[5]

OSIRIS.

But the manifestation of the Infinite Spirit dearest to the hearts of all Egyptians, and which gained an extraordinary power over the whole people, was that of Osiris. That most ancient of human documents, the "Book of the Dead," which is a collection running through many centuries, of prayers, invocations, and protecting spells, deposited with the mummy to guard the dead in his perilous journey through Amenti, is almost one long prayer or ascription of praise to this gentle and blessed Being. "He was appointed to reign over the gods in the presence of the supreme lord on the day of the constitution of the world."[6] He is Truth itself; he is

---

[1] Pantheon Eg.; P. Pierret, 1881, p. 168.
[2] Chabas, Maximes d'Ani.
[3] Book of the Dead. lxii. 3.
[4] Aegyptische Denkmäler, iii. 246.
[5] Book of the Dead, xliv. 4.   [6] Ibid.. xvii. 70.

Love. "*His heart is in every wound.*"[1] His especial name is Ounnofer,— the essence of goodness. He is Lord of life, Lord of eternity, yet a human mother hath begotten him. "Oh, Osiris, thy mother hath begotten thee in the world. She hath called thee with a beautiful name. Osiris is thy name in the bosom of the spirit; Goodness thy name in the lower heaven; Lord of life thy name among the living; . . . but thy [true] name is God."[2]

From assimilation with him comes the perfection of being.[3] He destroys the great serpent, Apap, the embodiment of evil, "the devourer of souls."[4] There appears through innumerable inscriptions and records in lower Egypt an extraordinary feeling of affection and reverence for this remarkable being. "Gold is nothing compared to thy rays," says an impassioned worshipper; "Thy transformations are like those of the celestial ocean. Grant that I arrive at the country of Eternity, and the region of the justified; that I be reunited to the fair and wise spirits of Kerneter (Hades), and that I appear with them to contemplate thy beauties in the morning of every day."[5] But

---

[1] Book of the Dead, xvii. 69. This may be rendered, "His heart is in every bloody sacrifice," but the idea is the same. The sacrifice of Osiris gives him sympathy with every human sacrifice. See De Rougé.

[2] Pap. 3148; Cat. des Man. Egypt.
[3] Book of the Dead, viii 2.
[4] Ibid., xxxix. 9; xv. 7.
[5] Stéle of Boulaq, Mus. No. 72; Mariette.

though subsequently becoming the sun-god, at that early period he was above and behind the great luminary. He created it. "He saith to the sun, Come unto us!" is the remarkable expression of the "Book of the Dead" (v. 21). "When the sun riseth," says another inscription, "it is by his will; when it goeth down, he contemplates its splendors. Hail to thee, whom thy name of Goodness maketh so great; thou, the eldest son, the risen from the dead! There is no god can do what he hath done. He is lord of life, and we live by his creation; no man can live without his will."[1]

The received myth of Osiris, it should be remembered, was gathered by a fair-minded and judicious Greek author several thousand years after the probable date of these early inscriptions and funereal records. And yet, if we strip Plutarch's narrative of its mythical and fanciful features, it presents a remarkable basis of probable fact.

At the birth of this extraordinary being, there were the omens which often precede in reality or imagination the birth of the earth's benefactors. A voice was heard announcing that the lord of all things had stepped into light[2] (ὡς ἁπάντων κύριος εἰς φῶς πρόειδεν). As king of Egypt he raised up his subjects from a wild and miserable mode of life, taught them agriculture and the arts of civilization, accustomed them to laws, and taught them

[1] Mariette: Not. et prin. man., p. 304.
[2] Plutarch: Isis and Osiris.

of the Divine Being who had created and who sustained them. His presence was a continual charm to men, and his influence was not exerted through violence but by persuasion, music, and oratory. His sweetness and goodwill carried him beyond the bounds of nationality, which then held people so widely from one another, and the story is related that he went from one country to another, calming passions, softening savagery, bringing the good news of human brotherhood and devotion to God. War ceased in his presence, there was no need of arms ('Ἐλάχιστα μὲν ὅπλων δεηθέντα), and his sweetness and the persuasion of his words and music turned all hearts. These benevolent expeditions weakened his power at home, and on returning to his kingdom he was defeated by the spirit of evil (Typhon) and killed, though not yet thirty years old, but rose again, became the "first-born of mummies,"[1] and was made judge of quick and dead in the divine Amenti, or lower world.

The classical historian saw even at that late day that there were mysteries in this narrative which the myth did not explain, and which were known only to the Egyptian priests. He notes that they feel a certain horror at the Greek and Roman interpretation that Osiris is a kind of Pluto, and only reigns over the dead in the shadowy

---

[1] "First of mummies" is a not uncommon title of Osiris in Egyptian inscriptions.

region of Hades. This feeling, of which the vulgar do not know the true motive, throws many people into trouble, and makes them believe that Osiris, that god so lovely, so pure, lives really in the bosom of the earth and the abode of the dead. But on the contrary he is as far as it is possible to be from that land; always pure and without stain, he has no kind of communication with the substances which are subject to corruption and death. Human souls, while united to bodies and subject to their passions, can have union with the god only by feeble images which philosophy traces for their intelligence, and which resemble obscure dreams. But when, disengaged from their earthly bondage, they have passed to that abode, pure, holy, and invisible, exposed to no change, then this god becomes their chief and king. They are, as it were, planted in him, contemplating without weariness that ineffable beauty which cannot be expressed or uttered by any language of men.[1]

Plutarch holds Osiris to be the embodiment of love in the Egyptian religion, as Seti, or Typhon, was of the evil principle.

The ancient Egyptian litanies dwelt especially on Osiris as having come forth from darkness to light, as having risen from the sombre dwelling, from the mysterious underworld, from the night. Others speak of him as one having gone forth from heaven, to offer a special

[1] Plutarch: Isis and Osiris, civ.

sacrifice for sin.¹ A symbolic liturgy recalled all his sufferings and death; the whole land was in lamentation and mourning; and then, with the representation of his resurrection, came songs and shouts of joy. "Adoration to Osiris, who lives in Amenti!" says an ancient inscription, "to Ounnofer [Goodness], king of eternity, great god, manifested over the celestial abysses, and king of gods, lord of souls; he is the great one of heaven, king of hell, creator of gods and men. When we observe the duties he commandeth, we reign over sin, know evil, know ourselves."²

Another expresses the almost passionate love of the people for this great ideal:—

"He judgeth the world, . . . the crescent of the sun is under him, — the winds, the waters, the plants, and all growing things. . . . He giveth all seeds and the abundance of the ground, he bringeth plentifulness and giveth it to all the earth. All men are in ecstasy, hearts in sweetness, bosoms in joy, every one is in adoration. Every one glorifies his goodness, mild is his love for us; his tenderness environs our hearts, great is his love in all bosoms. . . . His foe falleth under his fury, and the evil doer at the sound of his voice. . . . Sanctifying, beneficent is his name; . . . respect immutable for his law. . . . Both worlds are at rest; evil flies, and earth becomes fruitful and peaceful under its lord."³

[1] I am he who killed for thee the sacrifice of the ram of sins in the land of light (Book of the Dead, Uhlemann, p. 158).

[2] Mariette: Not. et prin. man., p. 386.

[3] Records of Past, Birch, ii. 131, 408.

"Homage to Thee, Ounnofer! Goodness itself," says an ancient prayer, "Lord of Time, who conductest Eternity, God benevolent from heart, greatest of forms, most holy of laws; he is beloved by the lower heaven; he is the One, fair of face, the great of crown, who rulest the elements which he hath created.

"Hail to thee, Osiris, elder son of Father Rā, Father of Fathers, he who sittest near Rā, the King of immense times and the Master of Eternity. . . . No man knoweth his name: innumerable his names in all towns and provinces."[1]

"Praise to thy countenance!" says the "Book of the Dead," "Creator of the fulness of the Universe, Osiris, Lord of all that has breath, thou who hast fastened the universe together. Grant that I praise the Builder, the Originator of the fulness of the universe, who once called into being all things that are on earth or beyond; he hath contrived them for me."

"I praise thee, the Father, the well-doer, the Just One. I serve the Lord whom all lands of the world honor, Osiris, in the Land of Light. I sing of the works of the Lord, which refresh my soul so long as I wander in the house of the Lord. . . . Bring fear on those who hate thee, cause thine enemies to blush, Lord and Prince of

---

[1] Pap. 3292, Louvre MSS. Devéria: Cat. d. man. Eg. Mariette: Not d. prin. man. p. 304. Handbuch d. ges. Aeg. Alterth.; Dr. M. Uhlemann, 1858, iv. 138.

the very brilliant star-house who hast planned thy planting. Thou who seest the murder of the righteous ... let me come to thee! Unite me with thee, that I see thy sunlight, King of the Universe! Praise to Thy countenance, streaming Light in the firmament, the glorious Lord of thy heavenly bark [the sun], the creator and ruler who distributes righteousness to all men that delight themselves in seeing thee wandering in thy shining web."[1]

"Praise to thy countenance, the Powerful, the Elevated One, thou who causest thy enemies to blush, thou who overthrowest their dwellings. Thou destroyest the schools of the liar, thou hatest the dwellings of the tyrants."[2]

"Praise to thee, Lord of the thunder (trumpet), maker (weaver) of the divine dwelling, Lord of heaven's clouds and heaven's darkness. Let me approach thee, my Prince; cleanse my hands of sin. Thou unitest thyself to me. Thou enlightenest those who are united with thee."[3]

The dream of union with Osiris was the dying hope of all Egyptians. Almost every grave-inscription speaks of the deceased as having "passed over to union with Osiris, the high and holy." Though the sun-god, he is not identified with the sun. "He hath brought on the years of the sun-god: he lighteneth the day. He made the glory

---

[1] Book of the Dead, cxv. 3.
[2] Ibid., cxv. 29–33.   [3] Ibid., c. 21.

of the sun." "I have kindled the light," it is said of Osiris, in the "Book of the Dead," "I have woven the star-strewn path."

The Day of Account of Words. — The symbolism of the last great judgment for men, the "day of accounts of words," as the ancient inscriptions call it, is well known on the Egyptian monuments. The dead, the accused, is brought before the great Judge of quick and dead, Osiris, who is clad in mummy clothes to indicate his having risen from the grave. His face is sweet and grave, and he bears the shepherd's crook and the scourge, to express his twofold character. The heart of the deceased is weighed against an image of truth by Anubis, "the director of the balance," who declares the balance satisfied by the deceased. Thoth (or *Logos*) registers the sentence, and the virtuous dead is acquitted, and united to his Lord. So intimate is this union that he is called by the name of the merciful judge;[1] he is Osiris "N.," or whatever was his name in life, and is henceforth one with the Lord of Eternity.

The justified one says to the forty-two accusers or assessors, representing before the Judge forty-two different sins: —

"Oh gods, dwellers of the divine underworld, hear the voice of Osiris N.! He has arrived near you. There is no fault found in

---

[1] "He is called by my name." "For me to live is Christ." "I am Christ's."

him, no sin against him, no witness against him. He lives in truth, nourishes himself on truth. The heart of the gods is satisfied with what he has done; he has given bread to the hungry, water to the thirsty, clothing to the naked. . . . There is no witness against him before any god." [1]

Then follows the well-known negative defence: —

"I have guarded myself from holding godless speeches. I have committed no revenge in act or in heart; no excesses in love; I have injured no one with lies; have driven away no beggars, committed no treacheries, caused no tears. I have not taken another's property, nor committed murder, nor ruined another, nor destroyed the laws of righteousness. I have not aroused contests, nor neglected the creator of my soul. I have done no robbery. I have not disturbed the joy of others. I have not passed by the oppressed, sinning against my creator, or the Lord, or the heavenly powers." [2]

"I am pure, pure! . . . He hath reconciled God by his love [charity]. . . . He is with the perfect spirit; he is lord of eternity." [3]

To his Judge and Saviour his prayer is, "Allow to the dead a quiet dwelling-place, Osiris, thou heavenly Lord! Elevated One, open the doors of glory for the heart of thy glorified servant that he come to thee, Lord and Judge of worlds, Osiris, ruler of the life of men." [4]

"Reverenced by me, beloved one, thou openest the doors of the firmament. Thou madest the valleys of the

---

[1] Book of the Dead. [2] Ibid., cxxv. 14–34.
[3] Ibid., c. xiii. [4] Ibid.

earth, the Holy One who sendeth flames of lightning on the earth, the twofold Judge of men who delightest in men bringing burnt offering."

The "day of the account of words" is, above all, a day of moral reckoning and purifying. "The destruction of the faults of the dead is made by the hands of the master of truth," says the ritual, "when he has wiped away the stain in him. Evil unites itself to divinity in order that truth should expel this bad element. The god who chasteneth becomes the god who strengthens superabundantly."[1]

To his Judges the deceased says, "O ye who bring justice to the universal Lord, judges of my punishment and my triumph, ye who reconcile with the gods by the fire of your mouths, ye who receive the offerings to the gods, and gifts destined for the manes, ye who live on justice, who nourish yourselves on a truth without error, and who abhor iniquities, wash away all my stains, do away with all my sins! Ye who bear no stain, grant me . . . to traverse the mysterious gates of Amenti."[2]

Resurrection.—The Egyptians above all things believed in the resurrection of the body. It was for this that loving hands laid so many million human bodies, preserved by careful art from decay, in the rock-tombs on the Nile, and in thousands of unknown graves. It

[1] Book of the Dead, cxiv.
[2] Ibid. cxxv. 1–3. De Rougé: Rev. Arch., 1860, p. 364.

was for this that "the kings and counsellors of the earth built solitary piles for themselves" (Job iii. 14), made difficult of access, and trusted thus to bid defiance to time and change, and to permit the beloved ones to carry their vital organs into the shadowy land of Amenti.

But despite this literal belief, it was not in the Egyptian faith the same corporeal frame as in life which the departed would take with him into the divine lower world. The divine spirit or word (Thoth) breathed new life and vigor into the body of the dead. He clothed it in the garment of truth, — in external transformation. The body is purified and restored by the gods; it is no longer the old body, nor is it a new soul. The justified soul is restored to a purified body. This is clearly shown in the ancient book, "The Breaths of Life."[1] The dead has passed through the same fate as Osiris, and now rises like him. "Thy word is truth, O Osiris, against thy enemies. . . . The word of Osiris N. is truth before the great gods."[2]

"I place myself before thee, Lord of eternity. I have no sin, I have no accuser . . . what I have done, gods rejoice at. Hail to the dwellers of Amenti! Grant me a passage on the road of darkness, that I re-

---

[1] Trans. by De Horrack, Record of Past, iv. 119. See for amulets to preserve dead, Rev. Arch., 1862, p. 130.

[2] Book of the Dead; Set. Typhon, E. Meyer, 1875, p. 14.

join thy servants, dwellers of the underworld." When he is acquitted, he can say with joy, "I do not penetrate to the cell of the murderer in the lower world; they do not unto me as to those whom the gods detest."[1] "My soul is not carried to the hall of immolation; it is not destroyed. ... It is saved from the devourer of souls [Apap] in the lower world."[2]

The souls of the wicked are tortured or become immovable for millions of years. They are in gulfs of fire where are seen their dissolving heads; lion-headed goddesses are executioners who "live on the cries of the impious" and feed on the groans of the souls of the wicked, who stretch unavailing hands from the depths of the gulfs. The saddest of all sentences to those under the "second death" is, "Ye shall not see those upon earth any more, never!"

The good spirit will not perish. It rejoins his body. "I arrive; having made my body embalmed, my flesh is not dissolved. I am complete as my Father Osiris."[3] "The earth hath not gnawed me; the sun hath not eaten me."[4]

The dead arises: "I raise again my heart after weakness; I fly to heaven; I descend on earth every day. I

---

[1] Book of the Dead.
[2] Pierret, p. 63; Book of the Dead.
[3] Book of the Dead.   [4] Ibid.

raise myself and begin among the gods."[1] He[2] is renewed and begins his life for millions of years.

The soul again addresses the mighty Judge: "I am Osiris N. . . . Hail to thee, great God, Lord of justice! I come near thee to see thy beauties, I know the name of the great God, and of those with thee in the hall of the double justice, . . . in the day of account of words."[3] And to the spirit charged with the office of punishment he says: "Receive in peace this Osiris N., justified! Open to him thy gates! . . . Let me not be repulsed by thy guards! Let me see God in his beauties! Let me serve him in the place where he is!"[4] Then to Osiris: "I arrive near thee, I am with thee to see thy face every day.[5] Let me not be imprisoned, let me not be repulsed; let my limbs renew themselves to contemplate thy glory, as one of thy chosen ones, for I am one of

---

[1] Book of the Dead.

[2] The persons are constantly confused in the Egyptian hieroglyphics.

[3] Pap. N. Devéria, pl. vii.

[4] Cat. d. man. Eg., 39–92.

[5] Hear Job, who has evidently known something of the early Egyptian faith: "For I know that my Goel (Vindicator) liveth, and that he shall stand up at the last upon the earth; and after my skin has been destroyed, this shall be, — even from my flesh shall I see God; whom I shall see for myself, and my eyes shall behold and not another" (Job xix. 25–27).

Angessi has brought out the correspondence in a most interesting manner between Job's thoughts and expression and the ancient Egyptian writings, in his charming work, "Job et L'Égypte."

those consecrated to thee on the earth. I reach the land of Eternity; I rejoin the eternal country, and it is thou who hast ordained this for me who am (henceforth) in Râ and every god."[1]

These ancient liturgies — the "Book of the Dead" — from which we have quoted so much call the day of death the "day of birth."[2] The soul becomes master of fear and terror in the heart of men, of gods, spirits, and the dead. It liveth for eternity. It doth not suffer "the second death" in Hades. No ill is done it in the day of account of words.[3] The dead seeth with his eyes, heareth with his ears. He is truth.[4] "Living; living is he who dwelleth in darkness; all his grandeurs live; living is Osiris N., who dwelleth among the gods."[5] The dead will suffer no harm. He will be in the state of the original God. No bad thing will destroy him; he will not see the second death; he will eat and drink every day with Osiris; he will be living; he will be like god.[6] The mouth of no worm shall devour him.[7]

A Spiritual Body. — A new growth of life begins in his body, he is for eternity, and his flesh has vigor in

---

[1] Book of the Dead, xv. 7.
[2] Seneca perhaps borrows his expression, "dies natalis eterni," from Egyptian inscriptions.
[3] Book of the Dead, cxxx. 28, 29.
[4] Ibid., cxxxiii. 8.
[5] Louvre; Pap. No. 3071, Devéria.
[6] Book of the Dead, cxxxv. 13, 14.
[7] Ibid., clxiv. 16.

the divine lower world through Thoth, who has done this for Osiris.[1] "My limbs are renewed every day to contemplate thy splendor."[2] "Thy rays, O Osiris, in my face, pure gold is eclipsed. Incomprehensible is thy glory. Give me a new heart in place of my heart, . . . give me my mouth to speak, my legs to walk,"[3] etc. "The dead is in peace, in peace!"[4]

At the close of the "Book of the Dead" it is said of him: "He shall be deified among the gods. . . . He shall not be rejected. His flesh and bones shall be healthy as one who is not dead. He shall plunge in the stream of the heavenly river. . . . It shall be granted to him to shine like a star forever in heaven. . . ."[5]

"His body is complete"[6] "He seeth God with his flesh."[7] "I have come to see the gods."

"I have come to thee, O Lord! I present myself to contemplate thy glory. I know thee, I know thy name."[8] "The spirit of the dead is living for eternity. He does not pass through the second death."[9] Chapter lxxxix. of this Ritual treats of uniting the soul to its mummy, that its body be not injured, or destroyed forever.[10]

---

[1] Book of the Dead, ci. 8.   [2] Ibid., xv. 61.
[3] Ibid., xv. 8, 9.   [4] Ibid., cxx. 27.   [5] Ibid., clxv.
[6] Book of the Dead, clxv. 6.
[7] Compare Job xix. 25-27: "Whom I shall see for myself, and my eyes shall behold, and not another."
[8] Book of the Dead, cxxv. 1.   [9] Ibid., cxxx. 27.
[10] Ibid., lxxxix. 27.

Amenti (Hades). — As the dead traverses Amenti, the Ritual says: " Osiris N. hath come; he seeth his father Osiris. It is he who loveth Osiris; he hath made the journey."[1] " I arrive at the shore of eternity. I rejoin the land of eternity."[2] " Protect Osiris N. in the region of the divine lower world; grant that he conquer evil; place thyself as protector between him and his sins; place him among the august; let him join himself to the spirits of the divine lower world; let him rove in the fields of heaven; in fine, let him journey with gladness of heart."[3] " Hail to ye, Masters of the Truth, exempt from evil, who art living for eternity and perpetuity of ages! Make me to penetrate into this heavenly country."

In his passage through Amenti the dead meets Apap, the great serpent, " the devourer of souls," the spirit of evil, who attacks him as he had attacked his Lord, Osiris.[4] As he reaches the heavenly land, the sore-driven spirit hears the welcome, " Appear thou in heaven ; be not thy appearance hindered. Thou diest not; thou renewest life; thou wilt not be destroyed; thou makest thyself young. Nothing evil is in thee; thou renewest thyself. No sin is in thy nature. . . . Eternity be to thy name. Thou must be in the mouth of those on earth indestructible, like the sun."[5]

[1] Book of the Dead, ix. [2] Ibid., xv. [3] Ibid., xiv.
[4] Cat. MSS. Eg., p. 177. [5] Miramar, p. 14.

The Entrance into Heaven. — A prayer to the sun-god: "I am united with the radiant, noble, and wise spirits of the underworld. I step with them to behold thy glories at thy rising in the early morn, and in the evening by thy setting, when thy mother embraces thee with her arms. When thou turnest thy face to the west country,[1] I praise thee with raised hands at thy union with the Land of Life."[2] "I have come into the world of radiant spirits, and I have appeared in the door of this lordly land. What is it, this world of radiant spirits, of gods near the sun-dwelling? The door of the lordly land is the door-opening [of the sun]."[3] "Open stands the hidden kingdom of the dwellers of the lower world, and there unveil themselves those who belong to the enlightened. Open stands the hidden kingdom of the air-spaces, and I step out to my seat in the ship [the sun] of the God of Light."[4]

"Osiris N. wanders on his feet, the justified, the holy; he finds out him who hateth righteousness, and in like manner the hidden dwellings of the pious, — him who beareth manifold cares for the good of many men, who arouseth other men to worship. He discovereth him who honors the holy on earth, who loves the care of thy creatures."

The dead, as he feels himself purified, and freed from inherited evil, makes the passionate exclamation: "No

---

[1] Hades, the underworld of life.
[2] Book of the Dead, xv. 15.
[3] Ibid., xvii. 20.
[4] Ibid., lxiii.

more stain from my mother! I am delivered [from sin]."[1] "All the stains which I keep are what I have done against the Masters of Eternity since I went forth from my mother's womb."[2]

The sinners, after the great judgment, are some of them sentenced to punishment, as we have before described, and some are compelled to enter the bodies of animals. But some of them are even then forgiven by the merciful Judge. "He, the powerful, pities the begging sinners who call upon the gods. He raises the slaves of his race, the begging sinners, to himself."

Heaven. — The pictures of heaven to the Egyptian are such as would be most grateful to a dweller in that hot climate, — deep shades of over-branching sycamores, cool waters, the fresh north wind, and fruitful fields, forever watered, and rich in never-ceasing harvests. The departed still busy themselves in the pursuits of a happy, peaceful agriculture, where the harvest is a hundred-fold. There is a tree of immortal life in this blessed garden, and a heavenly river.

But the happiness of eternity, as we have abundantly shown, is for the Egyptians in spiritual life and in union with their Lord.

One of the more material though imaginative glories of the future is in embarking with the sun-god in his radiant bark, and thus each day surveying the universe.

---

[1] Book of the Dead, lxiv. 7.   [2] Ibid., xvii. 37.

But the Egyptian's conception of religion had reached the highest point: it regarded sympathy and morality as the flower and fruit of faith in invisible beings. The spirits or gods unseen, the One God over all, were in harmony with the highest moral ideas of the race. God was the Law of righteousness, embodied in spiritual form. A burial inscription on the stéle of Beka[1] says: "I myself was just and true, having put God in my heart, and having been quick to discern his will. I reach the city of those who dwell in eternity. I have done good upon the earth. I have harbored no prejudice. I have not been wicked. I have not countenanced any offence or iniquity. I have taken pleasure in speaking the truth. . . . My sure defence shall be to speak truth in the day when I reach the divine judges, the skilful interpreters, the discerners of sins. Pure is my soul. I have spent my lifetime in the life of Truth."

Such was the picture, drawn in a few strokes of light over a dark background, which the ancient Egyptian drew in his imagination of the shadowy Unseen that surrounded him as it surrounds us. He peered into the darkness which infolded the unseen life then even as now; he bade farewell to his beloved as he laid their bodies in the rocky tombs with the same agony, and anxiously questioned them, even as we do now, and like us he received

---

[1] Trans. Chabas.

no sensible whisper from the unseen. He gazed at the majestic and orderly course of Nature sixty centuries ago as we still gaze, and prayed as we pray for light from the source of all this.

More than the members of any modern race, the Egyptian lived in the life invisible. His grandest dwellings were for the dead. And we now know that his deep religious hunger and thirst were rewarded. The divine inspiration was admitted to the souls of many among that ancient people. It gained, in part at least, the grandest conception known to man of the Unknown God. It sought to serve him by lives of mercy, justice, and truth. It believed in a "day of the account of words." It trusted in a merciful Being, even though a shadowy person, a manifestation of God's goodness, who had lived and died for the good of men. As this "Son of God," as he is called, rose again and became "the first-born of the dead," so would the dead arise and meet him as Judge. To be like him, and to be united to that sweet and perfect being, was to be the joy of eternity.

This faith, too, was in harmony with man's highest ideals. The purest morality and highest human sympathy were only the natural fruits of his relation to "the concealed" God and to Osiris.

Is not this ancient faith, then, a faint reflection of the light in a great darkness, shining to all men ages ago in the youth of mankind from the eternal Light, even as now, but not received of men, for men knew it not? Is it not a precursor of the brighter Light forty centuries later in Galilee?

This great light which gilds the morning dawn of human history, and was so rich a blessing to so many millions of men, has completely faded away. We can merely trace its faint reflections in the papyri which the dead bore with them into the tomb, and on the inscriptions — unread for centuries — upon broken shafts and crumbling pyramids.

Its truth alone lives in higher forms, and, in the words of the "Book of the Dead," "is indestructible as the sun."

NOTE. — The "Book of the Dead," or, more literally, the "Book of the Soul's Transformation," has been frequently quoted in these pages. Different translations have been used, the preference being given to those of Pierret and De Rougé; but it is clear that considerable uncertainty attaches to any one exact rendering. There are varying texts, and, as might be expected in a writing to be placed in unseen tombs and to be read only by invisible spirits, many mistakes and omissions, and much carelessness by the original scribes.

Then the highly symbolic language is easily mistranslated. Still, enough comes forth to prove the elevated monotheism of the early Egyptians, and their faith in resurrection and a moral judgment. De Rougé states that the British Museum possesses a copy of this Ritual written before Moses, in the time of Seti I., father of Ramses II. The monuments of the First Empire reveal several chapters of these writings (Rev. Arch., p. 357. 1860).

Most of the prominent Egyptologists affirm the monotheistic belief of the ancient Egyptians. See the writings of De Rougé, Brugsch, Chabas, Maspero, Pierret, Renouf, Uhlemann, and others.

CHAPTER II.

THE JEWS AND EGYPTIANS.
JAHVEH.

"I AM THAT I AM."

ONE of the singular facts of history is that a people like the Jews should have lived for so many years under the rule of a nation like the Egyptians, and have carried away after their emancipation so few mental and religious influences. The Egyptians were the pre-eminently cultivated and religious race of antiquity. Their achievements in the arts and sciences far surpassed those of any people of early times, and are the admiration of all succeeding ages. They were luxurious, refined, and overflowing with riches. Their society was artificial and elaborate in the extreme. They showed, no doubt, the conservatism and pride of opinion and habit belonging to a nation and civilization of immemorial antiquity. All their characteristics were such as would stamp themselves deeply on a race of inferior culture and less ancient existence among nations. Then they were peculiarly filled, as we have seen, with the convictions of a future life for the soul, of a coming judgment, and a resurrection of the body. Many classic writers speak of them as the earliest people who believed in the immortality of the soul. Their daily life was crowded with emblems and reminders of their religious faith, such as scarcely any race, ancient or modern, has presented. Their grandest structures were tombs to preserve the bodies of their kings from the gnawing tooth of time, or the wanton destruction of man, until the great "day of the account of words." The very soil has become filled with the embalmed remains of those whom their friends hoped thus to prepare for the great journey through the shadowy Amenti. Never, certainly, was a people so deeply inspired with the belief in a future life.

Among this people, too, were profound thinkers and philosophers, to whom had been revealed the grandest truths and inspirations of religion. These beliefs, indeed, were concealed from the masses, and held as esoteric or inside faiths of the learned. But they existed, as abundant proofs show, and even influenced the classic ages. This race, so powerful and so religious, held under their subjection for a considerable period — perhaps several centuries — a race of semi-barbarous Semitic herdsmen from the plains of Asia. The relation was perhaps somewhat like that of the African slaves in this country to the Anglo-Americans during a century.

The foreign Semitic laborers worked under their Hamite task-masters, and brought up their offspring amid this splendid civilization, and then revolted and fled from the country to the wilds of the mountainous region east of Egypt. Their leader and emancipator, one of the grandest figures on the stage of history, had been educated by the Egyptian priestly caste, and was familiar with their most sacred and concealed beliefs. Yet if one studies carefully the succeeding history of this roving people, one finds marvellously few evidences of any mental influence from their masters. The Jewish people in their early history seem singularly little inspired with the belief in a future life or a coming judgment. It is as if the African slaves and their descendants had been freed and removed from this country after a century, and had carried with them into their new homes no trace, or only the slightest, of a belief in a Christian heaven and hell, or of the resurrection of the body. The voices of hope and consolation which brought sweet comfort to so many millions of dying Egyptians, telling of a loving Judge and Deliverer at the great Day, of the journey through the shadowy Amenti, and the blessed life of the departed, did not apparently for centuries touch the ears of the dying Hebrews. Probably hundreds and thousands said with Hezekiah: "For sheol cannot praise thee, death cannot celebrate thee: they that go down into the pit cannot hope for thy truth. The living, the living, he shall praise thee, as I do this day."[1] Or with the author of Ecclesiastes:

[1] Isaiah xxxviii. 18, 19.

"For the living know that they shall die: but the dead know not anything, neither have they any more a reward; for the memory of them is forgotten, as well their love as their hatred; and their envy is now perished."[1] There are indeed some evidences of Egyptian influence on the mode of garments worn by the Jewish priests, their sacrifices of atonement, and the ornaments of the Tabernacle;[2] but of the faith of the followers of Osiris in a continued existence there is the least possible trace. Egyptian mythology has touched the people, as we see in the story of the golden calf and the hidden teraphim; but ancient Egyptian religion in its own peculiar spirituality or its faith in a future Divine judgment did not penetrate the Hebrew masses.

But it was not so with their great leader, Moses. From childhood he had undoubtedly been in intercourse with the earnest and religious thinkers who belonged to the Egyptian priestly class. He heard their secret beliefs, which were not to be divulged to the crowd. Amid the multitude of deities worshipped by the masses, the deifying of animals and reptiles, the disgusting superstitions into which the Egyptian religion had degenerated, he heard from these solitary thinkers of One, by name Xoper, who was before all, over all, and in all,— the Self-existing, the All-beginning, the Source of all life and action, the Eternal, Immortal, and Invisible; he

[1] Ecclesiastes iv. 5, 6.   [2] Angessi: L'Égypte et Moïse.

learned, doubtless, that the other so-called gods were only manifestations of this Infinite One, or were spirits beneath him.

It is possible that he read on the pediment of the Temple of Isis that wonderful ancient inscription, "I am he that is, and was, and shall be." It is not probable that these ancient and secret faiths were adopted in all respects by Moses, for he belonged to a race visited by higher inspirations; but they made a background in his mind, over which future inspirations could play. As the teachings of a Christian childhood will in this age sometimes open the soul later to the highest inspiration, so Egyptian monotheism perhaps prepared Moses for his wonderful revelation.

The history of this momentous event in the inner life of the great Jewish emancipator is given with distinctness. God has been especially worshipped and communed with, in all ages, on the tops of mountains. Moses had withdrawn to the grand heights and sublime granite peaks of the ridge where Mount Horeb appears in the southern extremity of the Sinaitic peninsula. It is a region still known for the grandeur of its outlines and the wonderful beauty of its coloring, especially under evening and sunset lights. There, in those almost inaccessible solitudes, the lower earth shut out by a sea of white clouds, this leader of men sought communion with the unseen Source of life. Perhaps while gazing into the dark-blue depths of the vault above, or at night following the paths of the clear orbs of light, there came to the soul of Moses the grandest inspiration granted to man, — the revelation of a personal Being who came not from any birth, who was when all things were void, who is now, and shall be when all worlds have ceased to be. He is revealed, not as the son of Kronos and Chaos, of Gēa and Ouranos, of Eros and Pneuma; he is no creature of mythology; he has the reverend name Jahveh, the I am that I am, the Self-existent. He is behind all time and space, and all matter and spirit; the One, so awful that his name was to be the most revered of all possible things; the Self-containing, All-embracing, Eternal. And yet to Moses, not a brute force, but a Spirit, a person of righteousness, punishing evil by the laws of heredity, and in like manner showing compassion and tender mercy. This inspiration of Jahveh carried with it future revelation, and coming moral progress for the world; the moral code, or Ten Commandments, supported by infinite power and wisdom; the widening revealing of the sympathy and love of this Spirit, and the final perfecting of humanity through union with him, by means of his highest manifestation in later ages. But this profound monotheism had already become rooted among the Jewish people. They lived in Egypt during the decadence of its ancient faith, when its most disgusting and degrading idolatry and superstition prevailed. The idea of the one God, which had been the inspiration of early Egyptian thinkers, had died out among the masses. The statues and figures of innumerable divinities represented what remained of that sublime and ancient faith. Only the learned and the spiritual-minded among the chosen and secret circles of the priests believed in that God whom so many prayers and inscriptions represented as having existed in all past ages and as to exist in all future.

Probably the thoughtful and the initiated among the people still considered the various divinities as local manifestations of the Infinite and Unnamable, but the masses of the nation had fallen into the lowest forms of idolatry. The Jews, though so much inferior to their task-masters in learning and civilization, were inspired with profound faith in Jahveh, and probably felt an intense abhorrence for the superstitions of the race who held them in bondage. The natural result was, that even the grand truths believed in by this ancient people of the Nile did not anywhere touch the minds of these Semitic herdsmen. They did not spend a moment's thought on the "day of account" and the future life revealed to the Hamitic thinkers; they classed them all together under "the worship of the dead gods,"[1] as idolatry was called at a later period of the same people. And under the higher inspiration of Moses, it is possible that the new conception of Jahveh, the self-existent and

[1] See Teachings of the Twelve Apostles: θεῶν νεκρῶν.

awful, the one Person who is and was and is to be, and who holds the power of righteousness in the world, so filled their thoughts and hearts that they did not dwell on what might be their future condition in the unseen life. It was enough for them that Jahveh lived, and that all men and all things were in his hands. This at least seems to us the most probable explanation of the singularly slight influence of the Egyptian dogmas upon the religion of the Hebrews.

The faith in Jahveh as a Being of righteousness, and a constantly higher conception of him as a compassionate Father and loving Creator, carried with it naturally the belief in a continued existence of union with him. In very early ages the tradition of Enoch as being united with Jahveh without passing through the pangs of death, showed what lay at the bottom of this faith as among the possibilities of the future; and in the Book of Job, and among the Psalms of David and other singers, and in the utterances of the Prophets, this hope of a future life with God comes forth clear and distinct. But it cannot be said that the faith in immortality among the Hebrews is in any way derived from the faith of the Egyptians. It is true the famous passage in Job, wherein the resurrection of the body is so clearly set forth, bears very evident marks of Egyptian influence.[1] Such an influence would naturally be expected from the wandering nomad Semitic

[1] See Angessi.

chieftain, whose genius under a higher inspiration framed that sublime drama.

But it should be remembered that in those early ages, as in the present, the air was full of certain thoughts and ideals peculiar to separate races, and the grand conceptions and imaginings of one people inevitably floated over into the intellectual atmosphere of another. The Egyptian faith in immortality and a coming judgment was scattered far beyond the borders of the Nile, and the intense and profound Hebrew conviction of an Eternal Being who led the world toward righteousness, reached thinkers in every country who otherwise despised the half-savage tribe that held this belief. There was a considerable commerce in those early days, movements of large caravans, the sailing of little vessels from one coast to another, and the wanderings here and there of eager and curious travellers. The secrets of one nation gradually became known to the thinkers of another, and the great truths which had inspired solitary leaders among distant tribes slowly diffused themselves to far-away scholars in other lands. The mysteries and inner truths held by the priests of one nation finally became the property of the ordinary citizens of another; and the divine inspirations which had been granted to a few in remote ages were thus conveyed to the many in distant times and places. It is true that these inspirations were soon over-flooded by tides of worldliness and animalism, yet they left here and there in the human mind seeds of a divine life.

The principal influence of the secret Egyptian religion on the Jews is no doubt seen in the profound monotheistic faith of Moses, and in his connection of religion with a high morality.

The experience of ages, and among peoples far more cultivated than either Egyptians or Jews, shows how difficult it is for the human mind to grasp and retain the inspiration of a " God of righteousness."

Moses was granted that sublime conviction, and through that inspiration has moved all succeeding ages. To a less degree some ancient Egyptian thinkers had reached a like point of moral progress. The devout Hamitic believer in the " negative defence " of the sinner before Osiris (so often quoted), and the Jew uttering the code of the Ten Commandments, both trusted in a God who loved righteousness, and who demanded righteousness of his creatures.

NOTE. — Schrader derives the name Jahveh from the Assyrian god Jahon (Cuneif. Inscr., p. 23), and Renan, in his History of Israel (p. 70), follows him. The Aramaic word *Hawa*, which seems allied to these names, means *breath*, or *life*, or *being*. The version given in our Bible of Self-Existence, seems perfectly consistent with this derivation.

The Genesis narrative (iv. 26) indicates an ancient period when men began to call the Infinite One by the name of Jahveh.

CHAPTER III.

AKKADIAN PENITENTIAL PSALMS.

God my Creator, stand by my side!
Keep thou the door of my lips, guard thou my hands,
O Lord of light!   AKKADIAN PRAYER.

THE investigations of the last few years in the cuneiform inscriptions of Babylonia have brought forth remarkable results, both as regards an ancient faith and a forgotten people. In northern Babylonia existed probably three thousand years before Christ a race who attained a considerable degree of cultivation, and who are supposed to have invented the cuneiform mode of writing. They have been called "Akkadians,"[1] or Mountaineers, from the mountainous region on the northeast, whence they probably issued. They were long thought to be of stock foreign to the Semitic-Assyrian race who inhabited this region, and were believed to be Turanian, or connected in language with such races as the Finns, Turks, and Mongols. But closer investigation[2] makes it probable that they were mainly Semitic in blood, though perhaps with strong Turanian mixture. The language of their inscrip-

[1] Sayce. Akkad, or Agade, their city, is mentioned in Genesis.
[2] La prétendue Langue d'Accad. J. Halévy. Also Delitzch, and Professor Lyon's paper before the American Oriental Society in 1887.

tions and tablets may have been a kind of classical or sacred dialect of the Semitic-Assyrians. This ancient people had made a considerable progress in civilization even two thousand years before Christ, and possibly nearly four thousand years.[1] They had founded great libraries; their scholars had written treatises on astrology, magic, and certain branches of mathematics; they possessed various histories of the wars and exploits of the Assyrian kings, and had constructed temples and many public buildings, and (to judge from the cuneiform tablets) seem to have carried on elaborate commercial affairs. This race or people is deeply interesting to the student of religions, because it manifestly drew its religious traditions from the same source as the Hebrews. And from the region inhabited or influenced by the Akkadians came forth one of the great figures of history, — Abraham, the father of monotheism. It seems to have been a people with a deep sense of the mysterious and supernatural. The Chaldean magic became known to all Oriental races. It was in that stage of development in which it especially worshipped the elemental powers, or the spirits of earth and storm, and sky and sun, and dreaded the evil powers of the universe.

A very ancient and remarkable invocation to "The Seven Evil Powers" of the world has been dug out from the

[1] A date now given to Sargon the Great is 3800 B. C., supposed to be derived from his tablets.

cuneiform. It is the product of the genius and reverence of this people, — the Akkadians. The mysterious significance attached to the number seven is common to them with many Oriental races. .

The Seven Evil Spirits.[1]

I.

Seven are they! Seven are they!
In the sea's depths are they seven!
In the heaven's heights are they seven!

II.

In the sea deep down their birth;
Not men are they; not women they;
Wives take they not, sons have they not,
Order and good-will know they not,
Prayers and wishes hear they not.

III.

Seven are they! Seven are they!
Seven *adi si-na* [evil spirits][2] are they.[3]

---

[1] Schrader's translation. Die Höllenfahrt von Istar.
[2] Others translate *adi si-na* as a numeral, or twice seven.

[3] Man they are not, nor womankind;
For injury, they sweep from the main,
And have wedded no wife but the wind,
And no child have begotten but pain;
Man they are not, nor womankind.

Fear is not in them, nor awe,
Supplication they heed not, nor prayer,
For they know no compassion nor law,
And are deaf to the cries of despair;
Fear is not in them, nor awe.
Professor Dyer's Translation.

In the following hymn the conception of a Heaven-God has come forth, one who struggles with the elemental, mysterious spirits of evil.

Hymn to the Fire-God.

O Fire-god, supreme on high, the first-born, the mighty, supreme
    enjoiner of the divine commands of Anu !
The fire-god enthroneth with himself the friend that he loveth ;
He bringeth forth the enmity of those seven evil spirits. . . .
O Fire-god, how were those seven begotten, how were they nurtured?
Those seven in the mountain of the sunset were born,
Those seven in the mountain of the sunrise grew up. . . .
As for them, in heaven and earth they have no dwelling ;
Hidden is their name.
Among the sentient gods they are not known.[1]

This ancient invocation also has been preserved: —

> "From the curse, O Spirit of heaven, protect us !
> O Spirit of earth, protect !
> O Spirit of the Lord of lands, protect !
> O Spirit of the Lord of light, protect !"[2]

In later development the same reverent spirit is directed towards both their own gods and the gods of the Assyrians, and we find this prayer: —

> "May Bel, the King, my Creator, pardon !
> May Hea, Spirit of earth, pardon !
> May Merodach, King of angels, pardon !
> May Istar, Goddess of love, pardon !
> In the days of sin may they cleanse him,
> Whoever he be !"[3]

---

[1] Sayce: Hibbert Lectures, 1887, p. 180.
[2] Biblical Archæology, vi. 539.   [3] Ibid.

In their mixture with a Semitic people, the Akkadians undoubtedly felt some touches of that inspiration which has glorified one humble Semitic tribe, the Hebrews, — an inspiration which sent forth from this region Abraham, and caused him to abandon the polytheism of his kindred,[1] and which a thousand years later made a wild barbaric chieftain of the same race, David, the mouthpiece of the prayers and aspirations of all succeeding ages. The resemblance of these Akkadian prayers to those of David and to the Psalms is truly remarkable; they show a form of expression so moulded in the furnace of intense feeling as to pass down among these races for a thousand years as the truest human words to set forth man's highest feelings. Some ancient Akkadian had risen out of his bondage to elemental powers and

[1] "And Joshua said unto all the people, Thus saith Jahveh, the God of Israel: Your fathers dwelt of old time beyond the river [Euphrates], even Terah, the father of Abraham, and the father of Nahor; and they served other gods. And I took your father Abraham from beyond the river, ... Now, therefore, fear Jahveh and serve him in sincerity and in truth: and put away the gods which your fathers served beyond the river, and in Egypt; and serve ye Jahveh" (Joshua xxiv. 2, 3, 14).

"This people [the Hebrews] are descended of the Chaldeans, and they sojourned heretofore in Mesopotamia because they would not follow the gods of their fathers which were in the land of Chaldea. For they left the way of their ancestors and worshipped the God of heaven, the God whom they knew; so they cast them out from the face of their gods, and they fled into Mesopotamia and sojourned there many days. Then their God commanded them to depart and to go into the land of Canaan" (Judith v. 6-9).

his dread of magical incantations, and had received a vision of a Being who loved righteousness and hated iniquity, and who was best served by purity of heart; he grasped the idea of sin and of moral purity; he felt that all in life and the future depended on this God of righteousness; he alone could save from sin and death. Apparently the human mind in its highest flights of devotion cannot attain a more perfect view of God, and of our moral relation to him, than did this ancient heathen from the valley of Mesopotamia two thousand years before the advent of Christ.

Akkadian Penitential Psalms.[1]

The heart of my Lord was wroth, to his place may he return.
The transgression that I commit, my God knoweth it.
The water of my tears do I drink.
O my Lord, my transgression is great, many are my sins.
The forbidden thing did I eat.
My Lord in the wrath of his heart hath punished me.
I cried aloud; there was none that would hear me.
I am in darkness and trouble; I lifted not myself up:
To my God my distress I referred, my prayer I addressed.
How long, O my God, shall I suffer?
O Lord, thy servant thou dost not restore.
In the waters of the raging floods seize his hand!
The sin that he hath sinned, to blessedness bring back!
The transgressions he hath committed, let the winds carry away!
My transgressions are before me; may thy judgments give me life.

---

[1] Translated by A. H. Sayce: Records of Past. vii. 153. This prayer must be anterior to the seventeenth century B. C. See Schrader: Höllenfahrt, p. 90.

Another Psalm.

O my Lord, my sins are many, my trespasses are great,
And the wrath of the gods hath plagued me with disease,
And with sickness and with sorrow. I fainted, but no one stretched
 forth his hand;
I groaned, but no one drew nigh;
I cried aloud, and no one heard.
O Lord, do not abandon thy servant!
In the waters of the great storm seize his hand!
The sins which he hath committed, turn thou to righteousness.
O my God, my sins are seven times seven![1]

Akkadian Prayer.

God my Creator, stand by my side.
Keep thou the door of my lips, guard thou my hands,
O Lord of light![2]

These prayers come from the depths of the human soul. They are filled with the sense of God and of sins as an evil to him.

Prayer for the King.

Length of days,
Long lasting years,
Strength of sword,
Long life,
Extended years of glory,
Pre-eminence among kings,
Grant ye to the king, my Lord,
Who hath given such gifts to his gods.
May he attain to gray hairs
And old age,
And after the life of these days,

---

[1] Records of Past, iii. 136.   [2] Ibid., iii. 137.

> In the feasts of the silvery mountains, the heavenly courts,
> The abode of blessedness,
> And in the light of the happy field,
> May he dwell a life
> Eternal, holy,
> In the presence of the gods
> Who inhabit Assyria.[1]

In all the ancient Hebrew annals there is scarcely one passage which conveys so distinct a belief in a future life as do the following prayers. Yet the faith in one God has not the simplicity which made the Jews such a power in the world's history.

Prayer for a Soul.

> Like a bird may it fly to a lofty place;
> To the holy hands of its God may it ascend.
> The man who is departing in glory,
> May his soul shine as radiant as brass.
> To that man may the sun give life!
> Grant him an abode of happiness!

This picture which follows, of the death of "the strong man" ages ago, has all the pathos and nature of a scene of yesterday. So died our father or friend; he who had been so strong and brave lay as one to whom "his strength doth not return;" and to him as to the old Akkadian came a divine messenger of love, bringing "a goblet from the heavenly treasure-house;" and by faith we behold the weak made strong, and the righteous man "shining as a silver goblet" in the celestial mansions.

[1] Records of Past, iii. 133.

Death of a Righteous Man.

Bind the sick man to heaven, for from the earth he is being borne away.
From the brave man who was so strong hath his strength departed.
To the righteous servant the force doth not return;
In his bodily frame he lieth dangerously ill.
But Istar, who in her dwelling is grieved concerning him,
Descendeth from her mountain unvisited of men;
To the door of the sick man she cometh.
The sick man listeneth:
"Who is there, who cometh?"
"It is Istar, daughter of the Moon-god."
They approach the body of the sick man;
They bring a goblet from the heavenly treasure-house.
That righteous man may now be risen high,
May shine like that goblet.
Like pure silver may his garment be shining white!
Like brass may he be radiant!
To the sun, greatest of the gods, may he ascend!
And may the sun, greatest of the gods, receive his soul into his holy hands![1]

After Death.

Wash thy hands! purify thy hands!
Let the gods, thy elders, wash their hands, purify their hands,
Eat sacred food from sacred platters,
Drink sacred water from sacred vessels.
Prepare thyself for the kingdom of the just![2]

Sense of Sin. — From the days of my youth am I bound fast to the yoke of my sin.[3]

---

[1] Records of Past, iii. 134. 135.
[2] Ibid., xi. 161.
[3] Budge: Babylonian Life, p. 148.

There is in the following that sense of moral obligation to man which usually only follows the highest stage of religious faith.

A Defence. — Have I estranged father and son, brother and brother, or friend and friend? Have I not freed the captive, released the bound, and delivered him who was shut in prison? Have I resisted my god? ... Have I taken land not my own, or entered with wrong desires the house of my fellow? Have I shed man's blood, or robbed one of his clothing?[1]

Among the remarkable features of human belief is a faith in a divine Mediator. The Akkadians and Assyrians embodied this in a being called Silik-khi, and later Merodach or Marduk.

Prayers to the Mediator.[2]

O Benefactor, who can escape thy hail?
Thy will is the sublime sword with which thou rulest heaven and earth.
I commanded the sea, and the sea became calm;
I commanded the flower, and the flower ripened to grain;
I commanded the circuit of the River [Euphrates], and by the will of the Benefactor I turned its course.
How sublime art thou!
What transitory being equal to thee!
O Benefactor amongst all the gods,
Thou art the rewarder! ...

---

[1] Budge: Babylonian Life, p. 148.
[2] *Silik-khi*, the Benefactor of man, Mediator between God and man Lenormant, Chald. Mag., pp. 192, 193), and the One who raises the dead.

O Lord of battles!
Merciful One amongst the gods!
Generator who bringest back the dead to life!
Beneficent King of heaven and earth! . . .
To thee is the life of life,
To thee belong death and life!

Another Invocation.

Thine the depth of the ocean!
Thine are all human beings, all who breathe, all who bear a name and exist on the earth's surface,
The whole of the four regions of the world, the archangels of the legions of heaven and earth, how many soever, —
These are thine.
Thou art the life-giver!
Thou art the Saviour!
The Merciful One among the gods!
Cure thou this plague![1]

This god, Merodach the Mediator, raises the dead to life, and combats the great dragon[2] and the powers of evil. He was first worshipped as the Sun-god, and later as Bel, or Baal, the Lord. It is interesting that in the inscriptions of Cyrus (circ. 549 B.C.) illustrating his reign, he (Cyrus) is spoken of as "governing in justice and righteousness," and Merodach is described as "beholding with joy the deeds of his vicegerent, who is righteous in hand and heart."[3]

[1] Lenormant.
[2] This struggle is represented on a well-known tablet.
[3] Sayce: Ancient Monuments, p. 156.

"Merodach," says the inscription, "who in his necessity raised the dead to life, who blesseth all men praying in need, hath in goodness drawn nigh to him, hath made strong his name." The prophet Isaiah (or his successor) uses like words of the same Cyrus: "I [God] have raised him up in righteousness."[1] "For Jacob my servant's sake, and Israel mine elect, I have even called thee by thy name; I have surnamed thee, *though thou hast not known me.*"[2]

"I am Jahveh, and there is none else; there is no god beside me. I girded thee though thou hast not known me." The inspired prophet of Israel evidently believed that the Unknown God was guiding and strengthening the Persian or Elamite conqueror, though he knew him not.[3]

Psalm to God.

(*Akkadian.*)

In heaven who is great? Thou alone art great!
On earth who is great? Thou only!
When thy voice soundeth in heaven, the gods fall prostrate.
When thy voice soundeth on earth, the spirits kiss the dust
O Thou, thy words who can resist?
Who can rival them?
Among the gods, thy brothers, thou hast no equal.
God, my Creator, may he stand by my side!
Keep thou the door of my lips!

---

[1] Isaiah xlv. 13.   [2] Ibid., xiv. 4, 5.
[3] Sayce has brought out this thought strikingly in his "Ancient Monuments."

Guard thou my hands, O Lord of light![1]
O Lord, who trusteth in thee, do thou benefit his soul![2]

To the ancient worshipper the sun embodied the highest manifestation of the Unnamable. It came forth from the great darkness, bringing light and life and gladness. It was the Unknown God showing himself to the world. To the Akkadian and Assyrian he was not alone light, radiant and glorious, but truth itself; he made lies to vanish.

To the Sun-God.

O Lord, at thy command
Will his sins be atoned,
His transgressions be removed.[3]

O Sun, I have called unto thee in the bright heavens!
In the shadow of the (holy) cedar art thou!
Thy feet are on the summits.
The lands have longed for thee;
They have longed for thy coming, O Lord!
Thy radiant light illuminates all countries;
Thou makest lies to vanish;
Thou destroyest the noxious influence of portents, omens, spirits, dreams, and evil apparitions;
Thou turnest wicked plots and evil apparitions to a happy issue.[4]

---

[1] Records of Past, iii. 136, 137. Schrader: Höllenfahrt, p. 100.
[2] Ancient tablet of Babylon. Budge: Babylonian Life, p. 145.
[3] Schrader, p. 96.
[4] Quoted by Ragozin. Story of Chaldea, p. 171.

Another Psalm to the Sun-God.

O Sun-god, king of heaven and earth, director of things above and below,
O Sun-god, thou that clothest the dead with life, delivered by thy hand,
Judge unbribed, director of mankind,
The mercy is supreme of him who is lord over trials. . . .
Creator of all the universe, the Sun-god, art thou. . . .
O Father supreme, I am debased, and walk to and fro,
With scourges and in expiation I beat myself;
My littleness I knew not, the sin I have committed I knew not;
I am small, and he is great, the walls of my god may I pass.[1]

Original Sin. — One peculiarity of the deep sense of sin among this ancient people was shared by the Jews, and perhaps with both was a Semitic transmission, — the profound belief in the inheritance of sinful desires, in transmitted depravity. Says one psalm: —

> "Against the evil spirit, disturber of his body,
> Whether it be the sin of his father,
> Or whether it be the sin of his mother,
> Or whether it be the sin of his elder brother,
> Or whether the sin of some one unknown,
> We pray."[2]

The following prayer to the supreme god of "Ur of the Chaldees," which is so stamped by monotheism that it might almost have been uttered to Jahveh himself, was

---

[1] Höllenfahrt, p. 321. This prayer then changes into a magical incantation, showing a mixture of the old Akkadian superstition with the Semitic monotheism.

[2] Records of Past, iii. 141.

possibly listened to by Abraham, and was perhaps fervently uttered by Terah his father, who worshipped the gods of that country.

Prayer to the God of Ur.

Lord and prince of gods, who in heaven and earth alone is supreme,
Father, Lord of the firmament,
Lord of the gods, . . .
Merciful one, begetter of the universe, who foundeth his illustrious seat among living creatures,
Father, long-suffering and full of forgiveness, whose hand upholdeth the life of all mankind,
Lord, thy divinity, like the far-off heaven, filleth the wide sea with fear. . . .
Father, begetter of gods and men, who causeth the shrine to be founded, who establisheth the offering, . . .
First-born, omnipotent, whose heart is immensity, and there is none whom he discovereth,
Lord, the ordainer of the laws of heaven and earth, whose command may not be broken,
Thou holdest the rain and the lightning; defender of all living things, there is no god who at any time hath discovered thy fulness.
In heaven, who is supreme? Thou alone, thou art supreme.
On earth, who is supreme? Thou alone, thou art supreme.
As for thee, thy will is made known in heaven, and the angels bow their faces.
Thy will is made known upon earth, and the spirits below kiss the ground. . . .
Thy will hath created law and justice, so that mankind have established law. . . .
King of kings, whose divinity no god resembleth, look with favor on this thy city, Ur.[1]

[1] Hibbert Lectures, p. 192.

Another Akkadian Psalm.

Whoso feareth not his God will be cut off even like a reed.
Whoso honoreth not the gods, his bodily strength shall waste away;
Like a star of heaven his light shall wane;
Like waters of the night he shall pass away.[1]

> If evil thou doest,
> To the eternal sea
> Thou shalt surely go.[2]

These outcries of human sorrow and repentance, it must be remembered by our readers, are among the most ancient of the prayers and litanies of mankind. When they were stamped in strange characters on the bricks and cylinders and tablets of Chaldean buildings, Abraham had not been long separated from his idolatrous kindred,[3] and from the people of the plains, being called by the divine voice within him.[4] They preceded by a thousand years, probably, the like impassioned utterances of David and the singers of the psalms of the Jews. They are the cry of a soul feeling what a pure God is and what human sin is. They are still the language of

---

[1] Schrader: Höllenfahrt, p. 97.
[2] Ragozin: Chaldea, p. 210. This utterance is believed to go back to 3800 B.C.; it is from Sargon's inscriptions. (See Records of the Past, xi. 154.) [3] Joshua xxiv. 2, 14.
[4] Acts vii. There seems good reason from the cuneiform inscriptions, to put Chedorlaomer, King of Elam, mentioned Genesis xiv., as connected with the Elamite invasion of Canaan, about 2000 B.C., which gives an approximate date for Abraham. (See Budge and Sayce.) Hommel places the date for Abraham at about 2170 B.C. Semitische Völker, p. 131.

man when he measures his life by the standard of perfect goodness. The Chaldean cuneiform psalms might be uttered by all men in every age of the world. It will seem strange to the reader that such exalted and pure thoughts could be expressed among a people such as the Chaldean Akkadians, given up to the worship of the powers and demons of Nature, and every kind of superstition, among whom human sacrifice prevailed, and whose public records on the tablets are a horrible history of murders, tortures, and brutalities. But it must be remembered that the divine inspiration called a man from this very region, the son of an idolater, under the same Semitic influences as were the Akkadians, and he left his polytheistic kindred, and founded the purest monotheism of history. This divine voice, no doubt, sounded in the ears of these ancient Akkadians. The horrible rite of human sacrifice was practised by all the tribes related to the Jews, and probably at times by the Jews themselves. The bloody cuneiform records of Chaldea are no worse than those of all ancient countries. They relate the exploits of great captains and kings. But during all these terrible wars and times of oppression people must have planted and sown, and quiet domestic histories of affection and piety must have been lived, and the "still small voice" listened to in the cameldriver's tent or under the shepherd's booth, even as it is now in the humblest places.

It would not be fair to judge of the Christianity of the nineteenth century from the records of Napoleon's campaigns or the battle-pictures of Versailles. History and art give but a fragment of human life.

The Akkadians were naturally deeply influenced by the Semitic Assyrians, and perhaps were mingled in blood with them. The Assyrians were polytheistic, yet many scholars maintain that their national god, Assur, was in his original form the first and source of all gods, the One, the Good. He was called Ilou,[1] and no temple was erected to him in Chaldea,[2] but Babylon (Babel, gate of God) is called from him. He is not always distinguished from his manifestations, such as Anu, the heaven, and later the heaven-god. Assur is spoken of as the "Father of all gods," the "King of all gods," "he who ruleth supreme over all;" his people are the "servants of Assur," and his enemies the "enemies of Assur." He placeth kings on their thrones, making their reigns glorious and lengthening their years; they ask him for victory and to grant all their wishes. He is the "Lord of hosts," that is, of all spirits.

Prayer to Assur.

Pray thou! Pray thou!
Before the couch pray!
Before the throne; before the canopy!

---

[1] The kindred word to *El*, or God, in all the Semitic races.
[2] Lenormant.

Before the dawn's light, pray!
By the tablets and books, pray!
By the hearth,
By the threshold,
At the sun-rising,
At the sun-setting, pray![1]

As we have seen in the psalms, the ancient Akkadians and Assyrians believed in a future life of blessedness for the righteous; and in the famous legend of Istar's descent into Hades there is an allusion to a place of punishment. The description of Hades in the cuneiform tablets is highly poetic, and has a tone as of Dante.

Istar's Descent.

To the land of no return, to the far-off, to regions of corruption,
Istar, the daughter of the Moon-god, her mind set
To the house whose entrance is without exit,
To the road whose way is without return,
To the house whose entrance is bereft of light;
A place where much dust is their food, their meat mud,
Where light is never seen, where they dwell in darkness;
Ghosts like birds whirl round and round the vaults;
Over the doors and wainscoting there lieth thick dust.[2]

One of the forms of manifestation of Ilou was as Sun-god.

Prayer to the Sun-God.

Lord, illuminator of the darkness,
Who piercest the face of darkness!
Merciful God, who settest up those that be bowed down,

---

[1] Biblical Archæology. vi. 540.
[2] Budge: Babylonian Life, p. 140.

Who sustainest the weak!
Towards thy light the great gods turn their glances.
The archangels of the abyss, every one of them, contemplate gladly thy face.
The language of praise is one word;
Thou directest it.
The host of their heads seek the light of the sun in the south;
Like a bridegroom thou risest joyful and gracious.
In thy lightnings thou dost reach afar to the boundaries of heaven.
Thou art the banner of the wide earth.
O God, the men who dwell afar off contemplate thee, and rejoice![1]

A peculiar interest, as we have said, follows the Akkadians and the Assyrians, because not only were they touched by these divine inspirations, but their traditions were in many forms closely similar to those of the Jews. They had a like history of the creation, an allusion to the temptation, a narrative of the flood as a moral punishment, and of the confusion of tongues, and they practised a similar observance of the Sabbath. But the Akkadian history of creation is immeasurably behind the Jewish in grandeur and simplicity, and is stamped by polytheism. Neither tradition seems likely to have been derived from the other, but both, as might easily happen, from a common Semitic source of great antiquity.[2]

One very curious legend, however, to which there is allusion only in the Scripture,[3] the "revolt in heaven,"

---

[1] Budge: Babylonian Life, p. 136.
[2] Dr. Dillman especially holds to this view, as do others.
[3] Rev. xii. 7-9; Isa. xxiv. 21, 22; Jude i. 6-9.

which must be a very ancient Semitic tradition, describes the "God of Life divine" as sitting supreme and beneficent amid thousands of adoring angels (or gods, *Ili*), who were chanting his praises in celestial songs, when a loud cry of discord broke up that holy harmony, "spoiling, confusing, and confounding the hymns of praise."

"Then he of the bright crown sounded a powerful blast on his trump, such as might wake the dead, and prohibited return, and stopped the service to those rebel angels and sent them to the gods, his enemies. In their place he created mankind.[1] The first who received life dwelt along with him. To them he gave strength never to neglect his word, following the serpents whom his hand had made. And may the God of divine speech expel from the whole assembly (the five thousand) those wicked (the one thousand) who in the midst of his heavenly chorus had shouted evil blasphemy,—the God Assur, who had seen the malice of those who had deserted their allegiance, to raise a rebellion."[2]

This ancient inscription clearly bears the stamp of monotheism as once existing in Chaldea.

---

[1] See Milton's similar thought, Paradise Lost, i. 184-191:—

> "Glory to him whose just avenging ire
> Had driven out the ungodly from his sight,
> And the habitations of the just; to him
> Glory and praise, whose wisdom had ordained
> Good out of evil to create, instead
> Of spirits malign a better race to bring
> Into their vacant room, and thence diffuse
> His good to worlds and ages infinite."

[2] Biblical Archæology, iv. 349; Talbot's translation.

Each year now increases the discoveries in regard to this ancient people. No doubt much light will be thrown on the Bible by future investigations in this field. But each new fact makes plainer the wonderful superiority of the leaders of the Hebrews in religious ideas over the related Semitic tribes, or the neighboring peoples of other races.

From our long habit of regarding inspiration as an act solely of God, and not accompanied by any receptivity or motion of the human will on the part of those who are thus elevated, we do not sufficiently render justice to the Jews' great services in human history. We feel the obligations of modern progress, for instance, to the Roman ideas of law and to the Greek ideas of beauty. We recognize the immense indebtedness of the world to the elevated conceptions of Plato and Socrates. But when we consider what Abraham or Moses has done for the advance of mankind, how few are ready to render them the gratitude they deserve. They seem mere instruments in the hands of an all-wise Providence. It was God that worked in them, not they themselves. But a closer study of their history and of their surroundings will show that they were men of like passions with ourselves. They struggled with endless temptations, and many nearest to them yielded; but their victory has blessed all succeeding generations.

Abraham, according to the tradition, sitting almost under the shadow of the famed temple of the Moon-god at Ur, and surrounded by a thousand solicitations to Akkadian magic, is yet able to hold his mind open to the inspiration of the One God, and in this faith to leave country and kindred, and break even from his father's religion.[1] Though his kindred still cling to the worship of many gods, he is immovable in his belief. He may be said to have founded the purest monotheism of history. When one considers the transmitted effects of his life, and later of the leadership of Moses, it may truly be said that these early Jews are the greatest benefactors of mankind in ancient history. Amid tribes of far greater wealth and higher refinement given over to superstition, these remarkable leaders preserved themselves and a few of their people from the contamination of polytheism, and handed down the faith in a pure religion. No equal services had ever been rendered before to human progress. The Jews of modern days ought to be forever honored for such progenitors; and a race which could produce such men deserves the lasting respect of mankind.

The objections of Kuenen and others, that the Jews were not monotheistic till the time of the Prophets, and then only among a select class, do not seem sound. This great inspiration or belief was transmitted from age to age

[1] Genesis xii. 1–3.

among a limited number of Hebrews, and thus preserved for the modern world. That great numbers were false to it is true. In like manner, multitudes among every Christian people are untrue to Christianity; and yet its great truths and inspirations are transmitted from one century to another. Moreover the early Jewish belief in many gods does not exclude the belief in one Supreme God, even as a modern Christian may believe in many evil spirits of greater or less power, and yet have no doubt of a Supreme Spirit. Even the belief in a God especially favoring a given people is consistent with a faith in his universal government. Many a modern Englishman believes that God has a special charge of the queen and the British kingdom, and yet has no doubt he is the God of the whole earth.

Jahveh was indeed the God of the Hebrews, but many knew him as "Lord of all nations."

The Unknown God was thus revealed, as appears in these Akkadian psalms, thousands of years ago to a poetic and inventive people in the valley of the Euphrates, probably related to the Hebrews. Under this inspiration they uttered words which "cannot die," which descended among the poets and singers of the Jews to later ages, and through them still move the world. It is not improbable that in future ages all other poetry of Greek or Latin or English poets and dramatists will be like echoes preserved in the phonograph of forgotten melodies, while the utterances and songs of ancient Akkadians and Hebrews will still be preserved fresh in the hearts of common people, and will be the chosen expression of man's highest aspirations and purest prayers.

Both races draw in part their great ideas of monotheism from an ancient tradition of creation, which with the Akkadians became so intertwined with polytheism as to degrade their whole conception of the universe, and finally to unfit the people for leading human progress. No human faith or morality can be enduring unless it rests on a belief in one God of righteousness.

Note. — The entire rejection by a certain school of critics of the historical existence of the Jewish patriarchs and of Abraham, seems not justifiable by any sound rule of criticism. It must be remembered that destructive writers like Seinecke, Wellhausen, Kuenen, Tiele, Stade, and numerous others, have no sources of knowledge superior to those of Ewald, Stanley, Hommel,[1] and like scholars, and their inferences are drawn from facts in the possession of all students. The profound and indelible impression made by the personality of Abraham on the traditions of three religions, the Jewish, Mohammedan, and Christian, would alone be an argument for his historical reality. Then the narrative of the "Book of Origins" (Genesis) has an archaic and simple character which belongs to ancient traditions. The story of Abraham's life is interspersed with allusions to forgotten and unknown peoples, and to antique customs and childlike faiths, which are a characteristic of remote ages and their annals. Furthermore, the cuneiform investigations confirm the truth of their "local coloring," and of the probability of their historical reality. The names of cities and peoples which occur accidentally in the Genesis narrative

[1] Father Hommel, a very impartial and somewhat rationalistic writer, declares in his Semitische Völker, p. 131, his entire disagreement with Stade and his school, as to the historical existence of Abraham and the general truth of the ancient Jewish history.

are often found in Akkadian inscriptions, and allusions to historical events in the Jewish annals can be filled out from the cuneiform tablets of Babylonia. The date for Abraham (about 2000 B. C.) which is assumed by some cuneiform scholars such as Budge,[1] Sayce,[2] and others, is an inference from a statement in the cuneiform records of an Elamite invasion of Chaldea, and of a king supposed to be the brother of the Chedorlaomer mentioned in Genesis (xiv. 1–9).

It may truly be said that no single fact brought forth by the cuneiform tablets, which cover the history of thousands of years in Babylonia and Chaldea, tells against the historical accuracy of the Book of Origins, and many incidentally confirm it. The silence of these records of mighty races and ambitious conquerors in regard to a small tribe of emigrants who left the luxurious cities and populous plains of their kinsfolk for conscience' sake, is what might be expected. Even a great moral personality like Abraham might be utterly unknown to Akkadian and Assyrian scribes and court historians, especially as he had rejected the faith of his people.

The Ur-Chasdim (Ur of the Chaldees), home of Abraham, is believed by many scholars to be Mugheir, west of the Euphrates, on the border of the desert, a former seaport, and distinguished by its famed temple to the Moon-god.

Even if the composition of the Pentateuch should be more and more made probable as occurring in later ages, and by several authors, it would not materially change the historical probability of the events described. Were Moses the compiler, he must have used the traditions or written documents current among his people. The emigration of Abraham and his family from Mesopotamia, in order to maintain a pure religion, is a fact, like the departure of the Puritans from England in the seventeenth century for similar objects, which would probably be stamped indelibly on the memories and traditions of the emigrating race. Even if all records perished, a true and sufficient history would survive in the oral narrative transmitted. But Abraham left a people who possessed an important literature, and some of his followers may have understood the art of writing or stamping on clay tablets.

[1] Babylonian Life, p. 43.
[2] Ancient Monuments, p. 49. Meyer: Geschichte des Alterthums, p. 161.

The use of signet rings[1] implies writing. At all events, the vast fund of Eastern traditions in regard to this great character gives assurance of a striking historical personality behind them; and the tradition in the Book of Origins seems at once the most simple and most probable.

The lack of all allusion to Abraham in Assyrian cuneiform tablets is no proof of his being an unhistorical character. If the Puritans had not been the forefathers of a powerful nation, how little should we have heard of them in English histories. Their departure would have been a mere ripple on the surface of affairs in the British Empire of the seventeenth century. And the emigration of Abraham and a few hundred persons was probably only one of many such movements by small Semitic tribes from the great Semitic-Assyrian Empire " beyond the River" to Canaan and Egypt.

[1] Genesis xxxviii. 18.

CHAPTER IV.

THE GREEK MYSTERIES.

Ceres hath made the Athenians two gifts of the greatest value, — corn, which brought us out of brutality, and the Mysteries, which those who share, have hopes sweeter than all the rest of existence. — ISOCRATES.

REMARKABLE associations existed among the classic peoples which at periods of their history had a certain resemblance to the churches of Christian times. These societies were secret, and members were admitted after rites of purification. The effects of initiation were supposed to be of the highest moral and spiritual kind; and to the members of the inner circles of these associations, truths were believed to be revealed of the most sublime nature. It is supposed that these truths were conveyed by signs and symbols, and therefore were not clear to common minds; so that the masses gathered one class of beliefs from the "Mysteries," and initiated quite another. The very name given by the Greeks to these initiations, Teletai,[1] is of the same root as that applied by the Epistles of Saint Paul to perfection of character, — the "finishings" or "completings" of the soul.

[1] Plutarch gives another rendering of this word "Teletai," as of the "last" and deepest speculations about the gods, wherein they are made the source of all good (Morals, iv. 432).

The full comprehension of these secret societies is rendered the more difficult in that, owing to the secret character of their rites and their nightly meetings, they ran very early into wild and unlicensed revels and indulgence. Furthermore the testimony about them seldom comes from their contemporaries, but from classic writers long after the time of their highest bloom. Yet this testimony comes from such varied writers and at such distant periods, and the most agreeing so nearly in the main features, that it must at least be received as representing the common opinion of the most cultivated races of antiquity, and no doubt conveyed essential truth.

The idea then of the Orphic and similar Mysteries among the Greeks seems to us to be the uniting of men and women for secret worship and for the hearing of certain great truths symbolically taught, which had been handed down by Egyptian priests and others among the initiated.

Though we know not exactly, it is altogether probable that these representations were like the Mystery-plays of the Middle Ages. The sceptical Greek or Roman was introduced into the grand dim-lighted hall, and there saw the gods of Hades, and the fearful punishments of the wicked, and the different sentences passed on the various classes of the vicious; or, again, was permitted a vision of the happy Elysian fields, where with the upper gods the dead were passing an eternal life of unbroken peace and joy. Then following these powerful dramatic scenes, were uttered by the priests, in mysterious voices as if from oracles, the great truths that had probably descended from Egypt,—the existence of one eternal God, Father and source of all; the immortality of the soul; the coming judgment; and the possible union of the human spirit with its divine origin. These and like truths, taught amid such scenes, made an enduring impression on the spectator, and he could say truthfully, as did Diodorus, that all life was sweeter and better after sharing in the Mysteries.

The continuity of religion carried down the beliefs in the unity of God, the immortality of the soul, and a coming moral judgment, from Egyptian thinkers through these secret associations to the early and later Greeks, and even to the time of the Roman Empire.

The ancient Greek hymns called the "Orphic Hymns" no doubt bore a part in this transmission of ancient Egyptian theology, and were probably recited in the celebration of the Mysteries. The Unknown God was acknowledged. Thus an ancient hymn sung in the Eleusinian Mysteries by the priest said, "Go on in the right way and contemplate the sole governor of the world. He is One, and of Himself alone, and to that One all things owe their being. He worketh through all, was never seen by mortal eyes, but doth himself see every one."[1]

[1] Eusebius: Prep. Evang., lib. xiii.

In the Orphic Hymns, the first principle in the universe is declared to be "the thrice Unknown Darkness;[1] but Zeus is the All-parent, the Principle and End of all."[2]

> "All that is past and all that e'er shall be
> Occultly in fair connection lies,
> In Zeus, ruler of the skies."[3]

> "Thus Zeus within his breast all things concealed
> And into beauteous light from thence revealed.[4]
> Zeus is first, Zeus last, origin of all, king of all,
> One power, one ruler, one God!"[5]

Orphic Hymns.[6]

ZEUS.

O Zeus Kronios, sceptre-bearer, most high, mighty one, self-begotten, father of gods and men, begetter of all, beginning of all things, end of all things, earth-quaker, increaser, purifier, all-shaker, lightener and thunderer, creator Zeus, hear me; thou of many forms, grant me health without fault, and divine peace, and the glory of wealth without stain!

ZEUS.[7]

... Great glory to thee, O most high Kronides, giver of blessings, giver of shelter from harm; who can sing the deeds of Zeus? Hail to thee, Father, hail again, and give us perfectness and plenty! Without virtue, wealth knoweth not how to increase a man, nor without abundance, virtue. But give us both virtue and plenty!

---

[1] σκότος ἀγνῶστον τρίς.   [2] Taylor, p. 46.
[3] Ibid., p. 47.   [4] Ibid.; ἀρχη πάντων, πάντων τε τελευτή.
[5] Taylor: Eleusinian Mysteries.
[6] Quoted by Sturz., ed. Cleanthes. I am under obligations to Prof. J. G. Croswell for these translations.
[7] Callimachus.

Hymn.[1]

... Having looked upon the divine vision, meditate steadfastly thereon, directing the whole gaze of thy mind's eye upon it. Step forward boldly upon the path, and behold the sole king of all the universe!

One is he, self-begotten, from him are all things sprung, and in them all he moves. No mortal hath seen him, but he surely seeth all men. He giveth evil after good to mortals, horrid war and tearful grief. There is no other one beside the great King; himself I do not see; a cloud is round about him. In all mortal eyes there are only mortal pupils, too weak to see Zeus, reigning over all things. He, sitting on his golden throne, rests on the brazen sky, and the earth hath he put under his feet. His right hand he stretcheth to the ends of the ocean, the high hills tremble round about, and the rivers, and the deeps of the hoary and dark blue sea.

Socrates, just before his death, is represented as saying:

"Well then, so prepared, the soul departs into that invisible region which is of its own nature, — the region of the divine, the immortal; and then its lot is to be happy, in a state in which it is freed from fears and wild desires, and the other evils of humanity, and spends the rest of its existence with the gods, as those are taught to expect who are initiated in the Mysteries. . . . We may well believe, therefore, that they who instituted the Mysteries were not mere triflers, but that there was in truth a hidden meaning in that old figure, wherein they said that he who went uninitiated and unconsecrated to the world below should wallow in mire, but that he who had been purified by initiation should dwell with the gods."[2]

[1] Quoted by Justin Martyr, Clemens of Alexandria, Eusebius, and Cyril.

[2] Phædo, p. 68.

Pindar is quoted by Saint Clemens as saying of the Eleusinian Mysteries, —

"Blessed is he who having seen those common concerns in the under-world, knoweth both the end of life and its divine origin from Zeus."[1]

Cicero, copying Isocrates, says beautifully in the Laws:

"There is nothing better than those Mysteries by which we are cultivated and softened from a wild, half-savage mode of life into a spirit of humanity; and not only receive with joy a mode of living, but even of living with a better hope."[2]

Many classic writers speak of this better hope (*spes melior*) which was sought in the Mysteries.

Aristotle admits that the great efficiency of these secret associations was in their giving certain moral and religious impressions, and creating certain states of mind, — a description which would accord well with the theory that they taught religious truths dramatically.

The classic writer who has spoken most of the Mysteries is unhappily not one to inspire the most confidence, — Apuleius, an author who has written on the most obscene and the most elevated themes. He describes the initiated as passing through a rite resembling baptism, and receiving precepts from the priest better than all words.[3] They went forth almost convinced of a future life, and that terrible punishments awaited the wicked there,

---

[1] Clemens: Stromata, lib. iii.
[2] De Legibus, ii. 14; *cum spe meliore vivendi.*
[3] Metamorphosis, xi. 23: *meliora voce.*

and sweet peace and happiness the good and pious. He says: —

"I approached the limits of death, and touched the very threshold of the dark kingdom of Proserpine. I passed through all the elemental forces of nature, and was permitted to return to life again. At midnight I saw the sun shine with unclouded brilliancy. I came near to the mighty gods of heaven and earth. I saw them face to face."[1]

This certainly looks like the impression made by a religious drama.

Initiation seemed a kind of voluntary death and resurrection. The believers died to their old past and rose to a new life; a new sun shone upon them, and they were filled with divine influences.[2] Apuleius addressed an Egyptian goddess revealed in these Mysteries in the most impassioned words, which were evidently borrowed from the Egyptian litanies we have quoted in a preceding chapter.

Even Jews admitted the good influence of these rites, for Josephus says that the Mysteries taught that God contains all things, and is a Being every way perfect and happy, is self-existent and sole cause of all existence, beginning, middle, and end of all things.[3] He argues that the same revelation was made to the Jews in their holy writings as by the Mysteries. Eusebius also, using the

[1] Metamorphosis.
[2] Apul., xi. 21-24; *sole novo læti, plenique deorum.*
[3] Con. Ap., ii. 22.

same words as were employed in regard to initiation in these secret rites, urges that the Jews had the special honor of being "initiated" in the knowledge of God the Creator, and of true piety towards him.

Clemens says that the Egyptians were not wont to reveal the Mysteries indiscriminately to all, nor expose their truths concerning their gods to the profane, but to those only who were to succeed to administration in the State, and to such of the priests as were most approved by their education, learning, and quality.[1]

It was a common assertion by classical writers that the great truths taught in these secret associations, such as the unity of God, the immortality of the soul, and a future moral judgment, came forth from Chaldea and Egypt. The doctrine of metempsychosis also seems to have been spread through the teachings of these societies. "The gods," says Diodorus, "assured through the Mysteries an eternal life, of which the constant occupation should be sweet worship."[2] Of the Samothracian rites he says: "Under these all the initiated are held as righteous; they find their sins atoned for. . . . They say that the initiated are more pious, more just, and every way better than they were before."[3] These secret religious societies were the ancient church of the non-Christian Greek races, and there seems to have been baptism or purification as a condition

[1] Stromata, v. 566.   [2] Quoted by Döllinger, p. 176.
[3] Did. Sec., v. 549.

of membership. Even the satirists allude to their influence. Aristophanes represents two things as securing his countrymen a better reception in the under-world, — initiation in the Mysteries, and kindness to strangers and citizens.[1]

Of all classic writers, Plutarch speaks the most feelingly of these rites, and of the faith which had come down from Egypt. "Isis," he says, "communicated her doctrine to those who by their perseverance in a life sober, temperate, and separate from the pleasures of the senses, the passions of the flesh, aspire to a participation in the Divine nature; to those who exercise themselves constantly in the temples in severe practices, vigorous abstinences, the end of which is the knowledge of the first and sovereign Being, which the soul alone can conceive, and which the goddess invites man to look for in herself as in the sanctuary where she resides. Isis is wisdom, the brightness of the eternal light, the mirror without stains of the divine majesty, and image of its goodness."[2]

Or again: "All our life is only a sequence of errors, painful efforts, long courses by tortuous roads, and without issue. At the moment of quitting it, fears, terrors, tremblings, mortal sweats come to oppress us; but as soon as we are gone out of it, we pass into delicious fields where one breathes the purest air, hears musical harmonies and sacred discourses; in fine, where one is struck by celestial visions. There man, become perfect by his new initiation,

[1] Ran., p. 451. [2] De Isis, pp. 1, 2.

restored to liberty, truly master of himself, celebrates, crowned with myrtle, the most august Mysteries, converses with souls just and pure, and sees with contempt the impure troops of profane and non-initiated, always plunging and struggling in the mire of darkness."[1]

"The initiated are three times happy, in that when they penetrate to Hades, to them alone is given life; for others there is only suffering."[2] It was admitted generally that the Mysteries revealed the true end of life and prepared men thus for death. "To die," says Plutarch, "is to be initiated in great mysteries. . . . As for what you hear others say who persuade the vulgar that the soul when once freed from the body suffers no inconvenience or evil, nor is sensible at all, I know that you are better grounded in the doctrines handed down to us from our ancestors, as also in the sacred mysteries of Bacchus, than to believe such stories; for the religious symbols are well known to us who are of this fraternity."[3] In the Mysteries it is taught that the universe is not without mind, or reason, or a pilot.[4]

The poets often speak of the high morality and purity required in these associations; that the initiated were the only happy, both here and hereafter, and that initiation began a new life. Both metempsychosis and a future life were taught under these sacred rites. The Christian

[1] Fragt. de Imm. Stob. Serm., c. 274.
[2] Plut.: Soph. Fragm.
[3] Plutarch: Consol. ad Uxorem, p. 393.
[4] ἀνόον καὶ ἀλόγον καὶ ἀκυβέρνητον. Isis et Osiris.

writers even agree with this view; thus Porphyry compares the state of mind of the initiated during the Mysteries to that of the blessed.[1]

It was believed that Plato, guided by the mystic ceremonies, testified to the different allotments of the purified and impure souls in Hades, their several conditions, and the three-forked path which led from the peculiar places where they were, and that this was all according to traditional institutions, every part of which was full of a symbolical representation, as is a drama.[2] Theon states also in his description of the Mysteries that the end of all these rites is "friendship and interior communion with God."[3]

And again, in the words of Plato: "I must not omit to mention a tradition which is firmly believed by many, and has been recommended from those learned in the Mysteries; they say that crime will be punished in the world below, and also that when the perpetrators return to this world they will suffer for what they did by a compensation of Nature, and end their lives in like manner by the hands of another."[4]

It is but just to say that he also speaks of the Mysteries at times with a deep contempt: "They produce a host of books, written by Musæus and Orpheus, who were children of the moon, and the Muses, by which they perform their ritual, and persuade not only individuals but whole

---

[1] Ap. Stob. Eclog. Phys.
[2] Proclus- (Plato), p 374
[3] Mathematica, quoted by Taylor, p. 47.
[4] Laws, ix. 670.

cities that expiations and atonements for sin may be made the sacrifices and amusements which fill a vacant hour, and are equally at the service of the living and the dead; the latter sort they call Mysteries, and they redeem us from the pains of Hades, but if we neglect them no mortal knows what awaits us."[1]

It is possible, of course, that these various writers of different ages may have mistaken somewhat the true object of the classic Mysteries. It is true that the doctrines which they were supposed to teach did not spread widely among the members of these secret societies. The belief in the unity of God, in a future life, and a coming judgment, did not apparently reach any great number of thinkers in the Greek and Roman communities. The origin of all things was still "the thrice Unknown Darkness." These doctrines were probably taught by symbols and dramas, and were comprehended by only a few wise spirits. They certainly did not affect to any wide degree the morality or religion of the people. The Mysteries themselves also degenerated, and were often the covers to hidden license and wild orgies. Still, the thread of continuity which connects human beliefs no doubt bound together the early monotheism of Egypt and its belief in a moral judgment to mankind with the elevated religion, some of whose doctrines were represented by Socrates, Plato, Plutarch, and some among the great Stoics.

[1] Republic, ii. 364.

CHAPTER V.

ZEUS AS SPIRITUAL GOD.

O Zeus, whate'er he be,
If that name please him well,
By that on him I call.
Weighing all other names, I fail to guess
Aught else but Zeus, if I would cast aside
Clearly in every deed
From off my soul this weight of care.

AGAMEMNON, v. 158.

AMONG the ancient Greeks there appears in their religious belief a grand and solemn figure not unlike the Jahveh of the Jews. "Zeus is the beginning of all things, the conductor of all,"[1] says an ancient hymn; the "Leader of nature," in the words of an early Stoic;[2] the "God who made heaven and earth," says another; "No one is free but Zeus;"[3] "He existeth by himself;"[4] "O Zeus, Father Zeus," says another, "thou governest the heavens, thou watchest the guilty and unjust actions of men, thou dost punish the monsters of the world."[5] Solon, at the beginning of his laws, invokes Zeus as the

---

[1] Ζεῦ πάντων ἀρχή (Terpander, quoted by Clemens: Stromata. vi.).
[2] Cleanthes.   [3] Æschylus: Prometheus, 50.
[4] Æschylus: Suppliants, v. 600.   [5] Archilochus: Fragm. xviii.

God of justice; he is the source of life and death;[1] he has remedies for all human ills;[2] he is the God of the suppliants, the very mild,[3] merciful God. "Raise thy eyes to Zeus," says the poet; "from the heights of the heavens he observeth the unfortunate who receive no succor; the God of suppliants is angry when the cries of the unfortunate are not heard."[4] The word "God" is used by the poets as a synonym for Zeus. "God governeth all things according to his will," says Pindar. "Good fortune is God's gift to mortals." Zeus is the king of kings; he is the God of cities and republics; he inspires the deliberations of assemblies; he is the protector of good faith in transactions; he is the god of hospitality, a friend to strangers, good and helpful, the deity of homes and of firesides, the god of friendship, the avenger of murder and adultery, the protector especially of the married woman. Like Jahveh he is the god of armies and the protector of liberty.[5] He was "stronger than time and age and all-flowing nature," says an ancient writer.[6] "He fills the world and is above it," writes Æschines. "Zeus is the God of gods," says Plato. Terpander sings of Zeus as "the head of all things, the beginning of all." "Zeus was, and is, and is to be," said the ancient Dodonian

---

[1] ζωῆς καὶ θανάτου πείρατα νέμων (Ap. Stob.).
[2] πάντων φάρμακα ἔχει.   [3] Μειλίχιος.
[4] Æschylus: Suppliants. 387.
[5] Ἐλευθέριος.
[6] κρείττων αἰῶνος (Maximus Tyrius, 3).

inscription,[1] — words evidently derived from the celebrated Egyptian inscription. Even with Homer and Hesiod, despite their corrupt mythology, Zeus is often the all-seeing, all-knowing, all-wise, omnipotent, governing the universe; the just one, and Father of men and gods. He sendeth war and peace, health and sickness, hunger and plenty; kings hold from Zeus law and sceptre, honor and majesty. He is the god of oaths and justice; he punishes unjust judgments, perjury, and all sins; he is the friend of the poor and the stranger, the father of music and song. He presides over property, and becomes the divinity of landmarks. He is the highest;[2] like Indra, the god of thunder, the king of kings,[3] the shepherd of peoples. "There is but one god, greatest among men and gods, and not like mortals in form or mind."[4]

Hesiod compares the eye of Zeus to "thrice ten thousand immortals watching over the ways of mortal men."[5] The duty of man is to avoid the smooth road to evil,[6] to choose the straight path of good, which, rough at first, becomes easy to those who work in it.[7] We are to deal with all men after the rule of righteousness which cometh from Zeus.[8] Justice and Truth shall in the end prevail[9] over pride and violence. They who do evil to others do

---

[1] Pausanias.
[2] ὕψιστος.
[3] Βασιλεὺς βασιλέων.
[4] Xenophanes (Clemens).
[5] Hesiod: Works and Days, 252.
[6] Ibid., 288.
[7] Ibid.
[8] Ibid., 35.
[9] Ibid.; δίκη δ' ὑπὲρ ὕβριος ἴσχει

it to themselves.[1] The eye of Zeus[2] having seen all things and observed all things, also regards these things, if he so pleaseth; nor does it escape him of what nature is the justice which the city encloseth.

This great conception of Zeus belongs to a certain stage of Greek thought, but is no doubt soon mingled with a low mythology. Aristotle says that with the ancient poets the highest and ruling Power, the original Being, was not, as in so many mythologies, the Night or Chaos, or Heaven or Water, but Zeus.[3]

Saint Paul quotes from Aratus what is said of Zeus as if spoken of the Unknown God.[4]

"Let us begin with Zeus, whom we men will never leave unnamed; and all streets are full of Zeus, and all the market-places, and men; and the sea too is full, and the ports; and we everywhere stand in need of Zeus, for we are his offspring (τοῦ γὰρ καὶ γένος ἐσμέν).

No grander thought ever penetrated the Greek imagination than this of the great Father of gods and men. Phidias was able to embody this lofty conception in a statue of such nobleness and sweetness, such majesty and benignancy, that the Greeks felt its moral power as they did of no other work of Greek art. Repeated testimony shows that the aspect of it was to the worshipper like a sudden glimpse of ineffable beauty, and of majesty beyond

[1] Hesiod: Works and Days, 263.   [2] Ibid., 265.
[3] Metem.
[4] Phænom., 1-5; Stobæus: Eclogæ Physicæ, i. 7; Acts xvii.

all other imagination of man. Even Christian testimony confirmed this. Dio Chrysostom says that a man could forget all the pangs and sorrows of human life, who could stand in the presence of that sublime image.

Unfortunately the modern world has only a few imperfect representations of it on ancient coins. The face of the Olympian Zeus of Phidias bears a striking resemblance to the traditional profiles of Christ. The later Greek poets and dramatists preserve this high conception of Zeus, and often regard this name as only a means of indicating the unnamable moral power and Being who presides over all. He is the θεὸς ἄγνωστος (Unknown God). Says Sophocles: —

"Thy power, O Zeus, what proud ordinance of men can repress, — that power which sleep never overtaketh, nor the divine unwearying progress of the months? Through undying time thou dwellest in the brightness of Olympus; thy laws are all-pervading; they have been, and shall be forever."[1]

Electra, when she denies herself for the sake of her dead father, is pictured as pious toward Zeus.[2]

"O Zeus! if thou art rightly named, let it not be hidden from thee and thy everlasting will, that men are disregarding oracles, and that religion is passing away."[3]

The poet appeals to Zeus as the highest power, whether "that be the right name or not."[4]

[1] Antigone, 605; Abbott's translation.
[2] Electra, 1095; Ζηνὸς εὐσεβείᾳ.
[3] Œdipus Tyrannus, 902.   [4] Agamemnon, 160.

"May it be mine, in every act and word of life, to preserve the piety and purity ordained by those high laws of which Olympus is the only sire, whose birth was in the sky above, and nothing human gave them being. In them is a divine power which groweth not old."[1]

Here the heaven and the sky god, or Zeus, are identical. Œdipus appeals to the pure holiness of the gods.[2] They are beyond the reach of human pollution. Their vengeance may linger or come quickly, or the sins of the fathers may be visited on the children, but it will surely come. The gods love the good, and will punish the evil. No one is wise whose wisdom is not from above.

In Æschylus, Zeus is all-causing, all-sufficing, all-mighty, all-seeing, all-accomplishing, Lord of lords, most holy of holies.[3] "In thy hands is the balance; what can mortals accomplish without thee? What without Zeus can befall any man? Justice is the child of Zeus. He leadeth mortals to wisdom, in that he ordained that to suffer is to learn."[4]

"And from high towering hopes he hurleth down
To utter doom the heir of mortal birth;
Yet sets he in array
No forces violent.
All that God works is effortless and calm,

---

[1] Œdipus Tyrannus, 863.   [2] Ibid., 830; ὦ θεῶν ἁγνὸν σέβας.
[3] Suppliants, 524: μακάρων μακάρτατε.
[4] Agamemnon, 175.

> Seated on loftiest throne,
> Thence, though we know not how,
> He works his perfect will." [1]

> "Look thou on him who looks on all from heaven,
> Guardian of suffering men
> Who, worn with toil, unto their neighbors come
> As suppliants, and receive not justice due.
> For these the wrath of Zeus, —
> Zeus, the true suppliant's god,
> Abides, by wail of sufferer unappeased." [2]

> "Zeus the great god of kindred in these things
> Watches over both of us
> Holding an equal scale, and fitly giving
> To the base, evil, to the righteous, blessing;
> Why, when these things are set
> In even balance, fear'st thou to do right?" [3]

> "For not a subject hastening at the beck
> Of strength above his own,
> Reigns he subordinate to mightier powers;
> Nor does he pay this homage from below,
> While one sits throned in majesty above,
> Act is for him as speech
> To hasten what his teeming mind resolves." [4]

> "But since as sharer in the throne of Zeus compassion dwells,
> Regarding all our deeds." [5]

> "If still there dwells beside the throne of Zeus
> The eternal right that rests on oldest laws." [6]

---

[1] Æschylus: Suppliants, 90. [2] Ibid., 375.
[3] Ibid., 395. [4] Ibid., 588.
[5] Œdipus at Colonus, 266. [6] Ibid., 1381.

The poets even offer the comfort of a future life. Antigone, near death, says: "When I come there, such is the hope I cherish, I shall find love with my father, love with my mother, and love with thee my brother!"[1] It will be a life far longer than the lower life. In that life are no mistakes. Justice dwelleth with the gods below.[2]

According to Sophocles, the laws of righteousness are established in heaven, and in them God is great and cannot grow old. With Euripides, if the gods do aught that is wrong, then are they not gods at all.[3] Says Æschylus:

"There [in the unseen], as men relate, a second Zeus
Judges men's evil deeds, and to the dead
Assigns the last great penalties."[4]

"Though 'neath the earth he flee, he is not freed;
For the blood-stained shall find upon his head
Another after me,
Destroyer foul and dread."[5]

"Zeus, who leadeth man in wisdom's way,
And fixeth fast the law,
Wisdom by pain to gain."[6]

In the Bacchæ, Euripides says: "O foolish pride, which pretends to be wiser than the sages and ancient laws! Ought it to cost our feebleness to avow the force of a

[1] Antigone, 887.   [2] Ibid., 451.
[3] Εἰ θεοί τι δρῶσιν αἰσχρὸν
οὐκ εἰσὶν θεοί. — Frag. Bell., xix. 589.
[4] Suppliants, 227.   [5] Eumenides, v. 118.
[6] Agamemnon, v. 170.

Superior Being, whatever be its nature, and to recognize a holy law anterior to all time."[1] "Who knows," asks this poet, "but death be life and life death?"[2] "God," says Aristotle, "who is happy and blessed, not through any external from himself, but himself through himself.[3] One power, that which reaches through all things, arranged the entire sea, and earth and ether, and sun and moon, and the whole heaven, . . . compelling the most obstinate natures in it to harmonize, and from these things devising safety for the whole. . . . These things, too, we ought to think in regard to God, who in might is most strong, in beauty most fair, in life most immortal, in virtue most excellent, because being imperceptible by mortal natures he is perceived by his works themselves."[4]

"And we say that God is a Being everlasting and perfectly good, so that life and duration, continuous and endless, belong to God; for this is God."[5] "But this virtue is without a name, because there is no such thing as the virtue of God; for God is better than virtue."[6]

"Zeus was the first, and the last was Zeus, with bolt of which lightning Zeus was the head, Zeus the middle; from Zeus all things are created."[7]

"A kind of original and ancestral belief, then, have all men, that of God and by God all things have been composed for us,

---

[1] Bacchæ, 887. [2] Plato: Gorgias, 104; Τὸ κατθαν-ῖν δὲ ζῆν.
[3] De Rep., vii. 1. [4] De Mundo, v. 6.
[5] De Mundo, p. 397.
[6] Mag. Moral, p. 1200. Prof. R. M. Smith's translation.
[7] De Mundo, pp. 400, 401.

and that no nature alone is sufficient in itself, if deprived of the safety that comes from him."¹

"And in brief, what a pilot is in a ship, a driver in a chariot, a leader in a chorus, law in a State, a commander in a camp, this is God in the universe, except that to those ruling is wearisome and full of effort and full of care, but to him it is without worry, without toil, and free from all bodily weakness. For, seated unmoved, he moves all things, and turns them where he wills and as he wills, in different shapes and natures."²

The religion which had come down by secret channels to the Greeks, or which sprang from their intuitions, brought with it its own stimulus to morality. Euripides makes the just man, "him who is born for his neighbors."³

The Athenians held in theory to the Golden Rule. Isocrates says: "Do not to others what you would not suffer from them, and be towards others what you would wish I should be towards you."⁴ An ancient Greek hero, Bonzyges, is made by Hesychius to say, "Do to others what you would should be done to you."⁵ Euripides pictures Macaria, daughter of Hercules, as saying, "If I saved my days at the expense of those of my brothers, should I be the happier?"⁶ A certain person (Boas) is represented as delivering young girls from slavery, and sending them back to their parents, to whom, instead of demanding ransom, he sent presents. Religion was felt

¹ De Mundo. p. 397.   ² Ibid., p. 400.
³ Herac.   ⁴ Oratio ad Nicoclem, c. 61.
⁵ Maury.   ⁶ Herac v. 528.

to be the foundation of the highest morality. "Whatever good you do, refer it to the gods," said an ancient writer.[1] There is a morality, says Menander, founded on the nature of man, independent of all speculative opinion, anterior to all conviction; but more, there are in virtuous souls intellectual faculties which one calls reason, — a reflection of the divine nature of God himself.[2]

It was often repeated that God was the soul of the good. Simonides had said, "God alone is good, and it is impossible for a man not to be a sinner."[3] "Men loved of the gods are the most virtuous."[4] Even Homer, with all his lower mythology, pictures the blessed gods as "loving not impious actions, but they honor justice and the pious works of men."[5] "On him ruling justly and mildly God looketh favorably,"[6] says the great tragic dramatist. "He that honoreth his parents is cherished by the gods in life and after death."[7]

God abaseth the proud and raiseth the humble; and even in the Pythian games the victor is exhorted to remember that God is the author of his glory.[8] The state of mind most often encouraged by poet and moralist is humble moderation ($\sigma\omega\phi\rho o\sigma\acute{u}\nu\eta$) towards gods and men, as one suited to a being exposed to so many

[1] Diogenes Laertius.
[2] Quoted by Saint Justin.
[3] Plato: Protagoras, p. 84.
[4] Ibid., p. 87.
[5] Odyssey, xiv. 80.
[6] Æschylus.
[7] Euripides: Fragments, p. 182.
[8] Pindar: Pyth., v. 23.

chances and perils, and dependent on the upper powers. Faith is frequently taught. "Finish your sacrifice to God," says Menander, "with faith, being just and adorned with purity of soul as with a brilliant garment. If you hear the thunder do not fly, since your conscience makes you no reproach, for God seeth[1] you and holdeth himself near you." The greatest sacrifice to God is to be pious.[2] Isocrates says: "Remain inviolably attached to the religion of your fathers. Remember that the homage of a just and virtuous soul honors the immortals more than the pomp of outward worship and a multitude of victims. It is by justice, rather than by sacrifices, that one obtains what one asks."[3] "Honor first the immortals by faithfulness to your oaths more than by the multitude of victims."[4]

"Worship is due the gods," says Aristotle, "because they are the source of the greatest benefits we have received, and we owe them intelligence as well as life."[5]

"Good thoughts are the greatest gift of God,"[6] says the poet. Pindar declares that those who imagine they can conceal any of their actions from divinity are mistaken.[7]

---

[1] ὁ γὰρ θεὸς βλέπει σε, quoted by Eusebius: Prep. Ev., xiii. 131.
[2] Menander.
[3] Isocrates ad Nicoclem, c. 20.   [4] Isocrates ad Dem , p. 23.
[5] Ethics, viii. 12.
[6] . . . τὸ μὴ κάκιον φρονεῖν θεοῦ μέγιστον δῶρον (Agamemnon).
[7] Olymp.

Pythagoras declares the best thing to be to follow God and become like him.[1] Aristotle says: "It is an old word of our fathers that from God and through God all things stand."[2]

The idea of resignation under God's decree is everywhere found, and the deeper thought that Zeus sends trials for discipline. The gods below give two blessings for one evil. What Zeus sendeth, one must bear.[3]

On Mount Menale was a temple dedicated to the "Good God." Of this inscription the historian says: "If to the gods men owe all the goods they enjoy, and if Zeus be the King of gods, this must be his surname."[4]

Prayer.—In a later age, the great Roman moralist could say of prayers that all men are agreed to look upon crops and fields and all kinds of material goods as blessings of the gods; but none considers virtue as a gift of God. "Jupiter is called the Best and Greatest, not because he has made us just, temperate, and wise, but because he has made us healthy and well-supplied, and enriches us with all earthly blessings."[5] But in the earlier ages men had a higher faith. Homer and Pythagoras held wisdom and virtue as gifts of the gods, and to be obtained by their help; and so with Pindar and others. Socrates asked God for inner moral purity and

---

[1] Olymp., i. 491.
[2] De Mundo, p. 6; πάτριος λόγος.
[3] Odyssey, vi. 189.
[4] Pausanias, viii. 36.
[5] Natura Deorum, iii. 36.

beauty. "One ought not to wish for children," he says, "in one's prayers, nor riches, nor power, nor long life. One must simply ask for wisdom and what is good for us; once we are penetrated with these sentiments, nothing more salutary and purifying to our feebleness than to invoke God in all important interests of our life, and at the beginning of all our labors." Sacrifices were generally offered for material goods.

An ancient Greek writer defines prayer as "a fortifying process with God; a testimony that the soul renders of its virtue in thanking him who has inspired us with it; an encouragement which virtue gives itself in asking of God goods which by his favor it finds and draws into itself."[1]

The conception of Zeus, expressed by these writers, was, as the Apostle Paul clearly saw, an idea of the Unknown God. It was mingled with a childish mythology, and obscured by low and sensual ideas and imaginations; but in some points it reflected back the divine inspiration.

Jove as Spiritual God.

A like inspiration in regard to the Unknown God visited also the Latin race, though with them it was more quickly overcome by polytheistic beliefs and the influences of the myth-making fancy. There was an age

[1] Denis: Histoire des idées morales. p. 247.

when the God of the Latins was worshipped as Jupiter, the "Best and Greatest" (*optimus maximusque*) of beings, — the Father of gods and men, the all-powerful, the King of all kings, the progenitor and producer of all, the God of gods, the One and all.[1] The poets make him address other gods as his limbs, appointed by him to certain functions.[2]

Varro speaks of a "Spirit governing the universe"[3] by his own action and reason. Ennius says, "Look at that sublime vault of heaven which all call Jove!"[4] — in this making manifest that to some the highest god was still the Heaven. But from the Heaven-god came life and all things. The other gods were explained by Varro as only personifications of the forces of Nature.

The ancient inscriptions[5] show that Jupiter was regarded as the Highest and Most Excellent Being, the Ruler of divine and human things, the arbiter of the fates, the God of gods, "who art alone powerful." One temple showed the moral idea attached to divinity by its

---

[1] Omnipotens, rerum rex ipse Deusque. Progenitor, genetrixque, Deorum Deus, Unus et omnes (Quintus Valerius. Aug.: Civ. Dei, vii. 9).

[2] Cœlicolæ mea membra, dei quos nostra potestas officia divisa facit.

[3] Anima mundum gubernans.

[4] Aspice hoc sublime candens quem invocant omnes Jovem.

[5] 3 Orelli, 1267. Jovi summo, excellentissimo; divinarum, humanarum rerum rectori, fatorum arbitro, Deo deorum qui solus potes!

inscription, "Enter good! go forth better!"[1] In a later age Pliny says that frail mortality, mindful of its weakness and sufferings, had divided up the original godhead into parts, so that each human being might have what he most needed.[2]

Saint Augustine quotes a letter from a heathen of his day, who says: "Under different names we adore the only Divinity whose eternal power animates all the elements of the world."[3]

This spiritual worship of a grand deity — Jove, the Best and Greatest — degenerated, however, into fear and superstition towards innumerable spirits and gods, until the Unknown God of the universe was almost forgotten, and religion was nearly severed from morality. Its final degradation seems indicated in an ancient inscription of praise on the tomb of a priest, — "He gave to his disciples kisses, pleasures, and fun."[4]

When this and others similar could be written over the grave of the servant of a god, the empire was near its final moral dissolution. The stern and august worship of Zeus and Jupiter had come to a pitiful end.

[1] Bonus intra, melior exi! (Renier: Inscription de l'Algérie, No. 1657).
[2] Quest. Nat., ii. 7. Fragilis et laboriosa mortalitas.
[3] Augustine: Epistles, p. 16.
[4] Orelli, No. 6042. Basia, voluptates, jocum alumnis suis dedit.

CHAPTER VI.

THE RELIGION OF SOCRATES AND PLATO.

It is the clear view of truth, the possession of eternal beauty, the contemplation of absolute good, which makes up the life of the just and happy. — PLATO.

THE idea of the Unknown God had thus descended through Greek tradition from ancient Egyptian and Chaldean sources. The Orphic hymns had voiced it almost in the words of the old Egyptian oracles. The Mysteries had expressed it, and had perhaps added to it the Egyptian dogmas of the immortality of the soul, of a future moral judgment, and of the retribution which comes in the changing abode of the soul through ages in animals or men.

But there was little belief among the Greeks in the love of this mysterious unknown Being for men, or the sentiment of love for him. A stern and pitiless destiny governed gods and men. Zeus, as well as his creatures, was under an implacable fate. Love was not the key of the universe, but justice; and man only owed to his neighbor the obligations of justice. Universal sympathy was almost unknown. Under such religious conceptions the future life became vague and shadowy. In the oft-quoted words of the poet, one would rather be a poor hind in the abodes of men than a king in the dim realms of Hades. Mythology took possession of religion and degraded it to the lowest depths. The fancies about the gods lowered the moral ideas of daily life, and gradually the practical world lost hold of any faith which could purify passion, soften human selfishness, console sorrow or mitigate cruelty, or lighten up the valley of the shadow of death.

But the Divine Spirit ever struggles with the soul; and down through the channels of human belief had come to certain great thinkers of Greece the ancient inspirations, and these falling on good ground had borne fruit among the best and purest souls known outside of Christianity.

In briefly considering the faith of Socrates and Plato, we need not for the present purpose seek to distinguish the beliefs of each. It is not improbable that Plato made Socrates the mouthpiece of many of his own ideas and theories; but there is enough verisimilitude in the picture of the rugged moralist to get from it a true impression of the points of agreement and difference between the statements of the cunning dialectician and the poetic expounding of the ideal philosopher.

Socrates, it is evident, took a more intellectual view of religion than did his great disciple. With him virtue and knowledge were often the same. Yet knowledge here may often mean "seeing the truth," as distinguished from self-deceptions, and guiding the life by these realities instead of following sentiment and passion and self-interest. In the definition of the "philosopher" by Socrates, the modern reader could easily substitute "religion" for "philosophy," as in the following: —

"It is not generally recollected as it ought to be that those who truly apply themselves to philosophy [religion], are really studying how to die, and how to be ready for the state after death; but if this is really so, it is a most absurd proceeding, that men who have been all their lives studying this thing, when the thing comes that they have looked for and studied for, should be startled and grieved."[1]

Plato, on the other hand, took a broader view of virtue and religion. He made allowance for the power of habit and tradition as well as for knowledge and reasoning, and to him religion was life, an influence imbuing the whole character and governing both thoughts and actions. It was not so much knowledge as inspiration; it was a moral life coming from God himself.

The position of both these great thinkers in regard to Grecian mythology was peculiar. It was not unlike that of some rationalistic scholars at this day towards miracles and the supernaturalism of Christianity. The ancient myths seemed to them to cover and express great moral and spiritual truths. They were old and revered poetic revelations of the great facts of religion. The essential

[1] Phædo, p. 21.

in them was eternally true, the form was imaginary and temporary; yet these philosophers would not rudely overthrow even the form. It was ancient and therefore reverend; it was intertwined with morality and order and devoutness, and therefore should be carefully handled by the thinker. Moreover, these myths belonged to a realm where nothing was certain, and where strange combinations and stranger beings might coexist. The gods might be demons or spirits or unknown powers beneath the Omnipotent. They were existences about whom the wise would neither affirm nor deny. So the two philosophers recognized the popular mythology, and used it for these great moral purposes, only half believing it, and extracting from it the truths which are everlasting. Of one thing, however, they were certain. Whenever the myths represented the gods as acting contrary to the eternal principles of morality, then they did not hesitate to say they were false.

"And do you really believe," asks Socrates, "that the gods fought with one another, and had dire battles and quarrels and the like, as the poets say, and which we see represented in the works of great artists? The temples to the gods are full of them. ... Are all these tales of the gods true?"[1]

"Neither," says Plato, "if we mean our future guardians to regard the habit of quarrelling as dishonorable, should anything be said of the wars in heaven and of the plots and fightings of the gods against one another, which are quite untrue."[2]

[1] Euthyp., vi.   [2] Republic, ii. 378.

"At Athens there are tales preserved in writing which the virtue of your State, as I am informed, refuses to admit. They speak of the gods in prose as well as verse, and the oldest of them tell of the origin of the heavens and the world; and not far from the beginning of their story they proceed to narrate the birth of the gods, and how often they were born, and how they behaved to one another. Whether these stories have a good or bad influence I should not like to be severe on them, because they are ancient; but I must say that looking at them with reference to duties of children to their parents, I cannot praise them, or think that they are useful or at all true."[1]

"For if, my sweet Adeimantus, youth seriously believe in such misrepresentations of the gods, instead of laughing at them as they ought, hardly will any of them remember that he himself being but a man can be dishonored by similar actions; neither will he rebuke any inclination which may arise in his mind to say and do the like."[2]

It must be remembered also that Plato himself is not a dialectician or a systematic theologian. He is essentially a poet. We cannot tell always precisely what he means; and in a field of thought so remote and so difficult as that in which he labors, he seems often to attain higher and perhaps more real glimpses of truth than more systematic thinkers since.

Thus the Divine Being is to him the centre of all things, and a Person, and yet at times he is impersonal, the equivalent of Truth or Beauty or the Good; and again he often uses interchangeably the words "gods" and "God." It would seem, so grand is his conception

[1] Laws, x. 886.   [2] Republic, iii. 888.

of this unnamable and awful Power, that he expresses it in almost opposite terms of human thought. Plato is not a pantheist, but he once speaks of Zeus as the "Mind of the Universe."[1]

God to him is omnipotent, but He is controlled by the nature of matter and of the human will.

"Then God is perfectly simple and true both in deed and word; he changeth not; he deceiveth not, either by dream or waking vision, by sign or word."[2] "Few are the goods of human life, and many are the evils, and the good is to be attributed to God alone; of the evils, the cause is to be sought elsewhere, not in him."[3] "God is not the author of evil, but of good only."[4]

"All things are from God, and not from some spontaneous and unintelligent Cause."[5] "Now that which is created must of necessity be created by a Cause. But how can we find out the Father and Maker of all this universe?... If the world be indeed fair and the artificer good, then, as is plain, he must have looked to that which is external, ... for the world is the fairest of creatures, and he is the best of causes."[6] "Let us begin then by asking whether all this which they call the universe is left to the guidance of an irrational and random chance, or, on the contrary, as our fathers declared, is ordered and governed by a marvellous intelligence and wisdom."[7]

---

[1] There is in the universe a mighty Infinite and an adequate limit, as well as a Cause of no mean power, which orders and arranges years and seasons and months, and may be justly called Wisdom and Mind. And in the divine nature of Zeus would you not say there is the soul and mind of a king, and that the power of the Cause engenders this? (Phil. 30.)

[2] Republic, ii. 382.   [3] Ibid., 379.   [4] Ibid., 380.
[5] Sophistes, 765.   [6] Timæus, 28.
[7] Philebus, 78.

God cares for all.

"For surely no wise man thinks that when set at liberty he can take better care of himself than the gods take of him."[1] "The gods care about the small as well as the great; ... they are perfectly good, and the care of all things is most entirely natural to them."[2]

He is just and righteous.

"The good man finds in the Eternal God the model of that which he seeks, and he who would be happy and just ought to attach himself to him and force himself to imitate him."[3] "God is perfectly just, and nothing among men more resembles him than he who has arrived at the highest degree of justice."[4] "Knowledge of God is true wisdom and virtue, and ignorance of him is utter ignorance[5] and wickedness."

"God, as the old tradition declares, holding in his hand the beginning, middle, and end of all that is, moves according to his nature in a straight line towards the accomplishment of his end. Justice always follows him, and is the punisher of them who fall short of the divine law."[6]

He is truth.

"Can you imagine that God will be willing to be or to make a false representation of himself, whether in word or deed?"[7]

Of Him, according to Xenophon, Socrates says: —

"All divinities bestow blessings upon us without being visible. But the Supreme God, he who directs and sustains all the uni-

---

[1] Phædrus, 62. See also Timæus, 30, 44; Sophistes, 265; Philebus, 28; Laws, x. 709-899; Republic, x. 612, etc.

[2] Laws, x. 900.   [3] Phædrus, 64.
[4] Thætetus, 81, 176.   [5] Ibid, 85; $ἀμαθία$.
[6] Laws, xiv. 716.   [7] Republic, ii. 382.

verse, he in whom reunite all good, all beauty, who for our use maintains it all entire in a vigor and youth always new, who forces it to obey his orders quicker than thought, and without ever distracting himself, — this God is visibly occupied with great things, but we do not see him govern." [1]

"Socrates," says the same author, "engaged his disciples to do nothing impious, shameful, criminal, not only in presence of men, but in view of the gods, from whose regards one could not escape." [2]

Of the just man, Plato adds: —

"We must then believe of the just man, that whether he be assailed by poverty, or by sickness, or by any other seeming evil, it will all in the end turn out for good, either during his life or after his death. For he cannot be deserted by the gods who has earnestly striven to be a just man, and who by the cultivation of virtue has endeavored to become like God so far as man can." [3]

"God is the measure of all things in a sense far higher than any man, as they say, can ever hope to be; and he who would be dear to God, must as far as possible be like him, and such as he is." [4]

"And this is the conclusion, which is also the noblest and truest of all sayings, that for the good man to offer sacrifice to the gods, and hold converse with them by means of prayers and offerings and every kind of service, is the noblest and best of all things, and also the most conducive to a happy life." [5]

The future life, with both thinkers, enters into all their beliefs.

"And whenever," says Plato, "the soul receives more of good and evil from her own energy and the strong influence of others, — when she has communion with the Divine, she is carried into

[1] Xenophon: Memorabilia, ix. 3.   [2] Ibid., i. 4.
[3] Republic, x. 612.   [4] Laws, iv. 716.   [5] Ibid.

another and better place, which is also divine and perfect in holiness; and when she has communion with evil, then she also changes the place of her life (for that is the justice of the gods who inhabit heaven)."[1] "O youth or young man who fancy that you are neglected by the gods, know that if you become worse, you shall go to the worse souls, or if better to the better, and in every succession of life and death you will do and suffer what like may fitly suffer at the hands of like.

"This is a divine justice, which neither you nor any other unfortunate will ever glory in escaping, and which the ordaining powers have especially ordained. Take good heed of them, for a day will come when they will take heed of you. If you say I am small and will creep into the depths of the earth, or I am high and will fly up to heaven, you are not so small or so high but that you shall pay the fitting penalty, either in the world below or yet in some more savage place still, whither you shall be conveyed."[2]

Eternal Beauty. — "But what if man had eyes to see the true beauty (the Divine Beauty, I mean, pure and clear and unalloyed, not clogged with the pollutions of mortality and all the colors and vanities of human life), thither looking and holding converse with the true beauty, divine and simple! Do you not see that in that communion, only beholding beauty with the eye of the mind, he will be enabled to bring forth, not images of beauty, but realities (for he has hold, not of an image but of a reality), and bringing forth and nourishing true virtue to become a friend of God and be immortal, if a mortal man may?"[3]

"It is the clear view of truth, it is the possession of eternal beauty, it is the contemplation of absolute good which make up the life of the just and happy."

Immortality. — "If the soul be immortal, then does she stand in need of care, not only during this period which we call life, but for all time; and we may well consider that there is terrible danger

---

[1] Odyss., xix. 43. [2] Laws, x. 904. Jowett's trans.
[3] Symposium, 212.

in neglecting her. If death indeed were an escape from all things, then were it a great gain for the wicked, for it would be a release from the body, and from their own sin, and from the soul at the same time; but now as the soul proves to be immortal, there is no other escape from evils to come, nor any other safety, but in her attaining to the highest virtue and wisdom; for she goes to the world below possessed of nothing but whatever training or education she may have received, and this we are told becomes either the greatest help or the greatest hindrance to the dead at the very first instant of his journey thither." [1]

"And when she, the soul, has entered into the company of other souls, if she be found impure, or to have done impure deeds, whether stained with wanton murders, or with other crimes akin to these, which are the works of kindred souls, then do the other souls flee from her and avoid her, nor will any consent to be her companion or her guide; ... but the soul which has gone through life reasonably and purely, with the gods as companions and guides, comes to dwell in her fitting abode." [2]

"That man should be of good courage in regard to his soul, who in his lifetime has bidden farewell to all the pleasures and ornaments of the body as foreign to and likely rather to work evil against him, and who, having striven after knowledge, and adorned his soul with no foreign ornaments, but with those which alone befit her, — moderation and justice, and freedom and truth, — thus awaits his journey to the world below." [3]

"Well, then, the soul so prepared departs into that invisible region which is of its own nature, — the region of the Divine, the Immortal, the Wise; and then its lot is to be happy in a state in which it is freed from fears and wild desires, and the other evils of humanity, and spends the rest of its existence with the gods, as those are taught to expect who are initiated in the Mysteries." [4]

---

[1] Phædo, 107. Miss Mason's translation. [2] Ibid., 108.
[3] Ibid., 114. [4] Ibid., 68.

Socrates' last words best show his faith: —

"You, too, O judges, it behooves to be of good hope about death, and to believe that this at least is true, — that there can no evil befall a good man, whether he be alive or dead, nor are his affairs uncared for by the gods."[1]

The two great Greek thinkers, in their religious philosophy, struck on a conception of the universe which no Egyptian or Oriental philosophers (so far as we know) had ever grasped, and which rests on the same basis with the philosophy of the Christian. They found that the moral universe in its inner structure rests on the foundations of sympathy, love, justice, and truth. Or, in other words, that the nature of man is so constituted that his highest health and happiness are only to be reached in unselfishness and truth and justice. Whatever appearances may show, that man can alone be happy and sound who is true and good. He may be a rich and successful tyrant, or the great king himself; but if he is false and unjust and selfish, his soul is covered with wounds and sores and scars, and there is no health or happiness in him. The wicked man cannot by any possibility ever be truly happy or successful. The nature of man is made for goodness. But as human life is not constituted to show this true state of things, the future life reveals the soul as it is, without regard to circumstances or condition; and punishment, or

[1] Apology, 41.

probation, begins there the true recovery to health and a restoration to soundness.

From these premises Socrates is represented as drawing these foundation-principles, which equally belong to Christianity: (1) That it is better (or happier) to suffer wrong than to do wrong; (2) That it is better for the wrong-doer to suffer punishment than to escape punishment; (3) That it is better to be than to seem, and all false seemings are to be shunned.[1]

From this structure of the moral universe Plato infers that its Maker is of like nature; that he is the ideal of love and justice, of sympathy and purity and truth; that his happiness is also in beneficence and in truth. Man is made to be like him, and by loving eternal beauty in God to become as he is. He holds, as we have seen, that nothing can turn out evil to him that loves God. Death will only bring the soul nearer to its Creator. And as this world does not in its affairs and issues fully realize this plan and idea, the Divine Being has constituted punishments, purifications, and transmigrations to restore the health of the soul, or to satisfy justice. Man in this life may be led towards health and soundness by pain and penalty; but his highest recovery is brought about by union and likeness to the Divine Original.

The great Creator being such must be happy in making his creatures happier and better; and hence the great

[1] Gorgias.

hope of immortality, the *bellum somnium* (beautiful dream), as Seneca called it, but the assured conviction of Socrates and Plato, — a faith so firm in the former that his last words (often misunderstood) called upon his friend to offer a sacrifice of thanksgiving to the God of health and resurrection, as if to show that to him death was life, sickness health, and burial of the body a new arising to a higher vigor and fresh youth.

We review again the main points of the great argument. These philosophers no doubt reasoned, as did their disciples among the Stoics after them, that such a structure of the universe, wherein true happiness and moral health is always conditioned on goodness and truth and unselfish love, cannot be an effect of chance; for chance might equally well bring about selfishness and untruth and hate as the successful elements of human life. The facts belong to the foundation-structure of the human soul. It is made for purity and truth and benevolence. Its faculties are best and most vigorous when directed by these moral principles. It is most happy under them. "Harmony with the universe" depends on the degree according to which the mind is thus guided. The plain and irrefutable inference from it all is that this constitution of things is a result of intelligent plan, and that the Contriver must be like his work; he, too, must be reasoning, truthful, benevolent, and just.

The exceptions to the workings of this plan — human sin and suffering — Plato did not attempt fully to explain. They were never to be attributed to Zeus. They might arise from matter, from free will; or they might be a means to ultimate good. The philosophers of the past, more even than those of the present, felt how small a segment of an infinite circle they beheld. They soon touched the "threefold darkness."

Surely, to these great thinkers the Unknown God was revealed. The human mind cannot in some directions reach more profound views of truth. Perhaps from our want of use to them, these pre-Christian revelations touch us at times more than the revelations through the Apostles and Christian saints. The souls of these great seers seem often nearer to the Unnamable, the Divine, than do those who have lived in a brighter light. They saw through the mystery of the universe, and on occasions were bathed in an effulgence which came not from earth, or star, or any lesser light, but from God himself, in contemplating whom they were changed from glory to glory.

CHAPTER VII.

THE FAITH OF THE STOICS.

ἄγου δέ μ' ὦ Ζεῦ καὶ σύ γ' ἡ Πεπρωμένη,
ὅποι ποθ' ὑμῖν εἰμὶ διατεταγμένος,
ὡς ἕψομαι γ' ἄοκνος· ἢν δὲ μὴ θέλω
κακὸς γενόμενος, οὐδὲν ἧττον ἕψομαι.

> *Lead thou me on, O Zeus!*
> *And thou, O Destiny!*
> *Whithersoever thou ordainest*
> *Unflinching will I follow;*
> *But if from wicked heart*
> *I will it not,*
> *Still must I follow!*
>   CLEANTHES.

THESE ancient verses were for some eight hundred years the chosen expression of the faith of the Stoics.[1]

The devout man of the classic ages, tossing on the waves of life, felt himself in a current over which he had little control, but which was directed by a Power unseen, eternal, beneficent. He gazed into the mystery of the universe and the great void beyond life, and helpless, but not fearful, he trusted, as one swept on by an

---

[1] From Cleanthes (200 B.C.) to Simplicius, commentator on Epictetus in the sixth century.

invisible force, in this all-controlling Power and this infinite Goodness. "Not as I will, but as Thou wilt," was his prayer. Not for what is usually called "happiness" was his struggle, — for to him "virtue was its own reward," — but "to follow Zeus," to "imitate God," to do what he had ordered him, was the great end of existence. His faith, like that of Plato, rested on the most profound moral facts of life. The motto of his school for eight centuries was "to live in harmony with God and nature."[1] And by "nature" they did not mean the then present inherited tendencies of the human soul, for some of the Stoics have said that we all tend to sin, and all are stained with evil, and are weakened by a feeble will.[2] But they meant that the nature of man is made and constituted to get its highest happiness, and be in the most perfect health and soundness, from unselfishness, purity, and goodness. It is more miserable to injure than to be injured.[3] The utmost blessedness is to imitate God in being kind to the unthankful and the evil.[4] This is "nature," or the constitution of the "universe." There is no real happiness or moral health in selfish-

---

[1] ὁμολογουμένως τῇ φύσει ζῆν. Secundum rerum naturam vivere et Deorum exemplum sequi (Seneca: Benef.).

[2] Natura contumax et in contrarium nitens (Seneca: Clem., i. 24). Omnes peccavimus, etc.

[3] . . . Ex illius constitutione miserius est nocere quam laedi (Seneca: Ep, xcv.). Summum Bonum vir habitur optimæ mentis; sanitas et libertas animi, ipsa pretium, etc. (Nat. Quest.).

[4] Seneca: Benef., iv. 25.

ness or malice, or untruth, or lust, or passion. The nature of man and the universe is not made for evil. He is unhappy, crippled, sick, and weak, so far as he is under sin. No matter what his apparent success may be, what power, or place, or wealth he may have, if he is wicked he is miserable.

If the moral world is so constituted, it must be like its Creator. Zeus must be Truth and Order and Justice and Love itself, and his happiness must be in these. Human virtue, in its last and highest expression, must be the agreement of our reason with the Reason governing the universe.[1] One cannot find any other principle of justice than Zeus, or first and universal Nature.[2] One ought not to say with Orpheus that Justice sits on the right hand[3] of Zeus. He is himself Right and Justice. He is the most perfect of laws; the universal law is the reason of Zeus, who is Master of all, and from whom come all harmony and order. God is a living Being, eternal, rational, perfect, and intellectual in his happiness, unsusceptible to any kind of evil, having a foreknowledge of the world, and all that is in the world.[4] Zeus, says a Stoic authority, is the Soul, Mind, and Reason of the world; he is Law, Destiny, Providence, — a perfect, happy, all-knowing, beneficent Being.[5] Zeus,

---

[1] Chrysostom. Diogenes, vii. 1, 2. [2] Chrysostom.
[3] Ibid. [4] Diog. Laert., vii. 52.
[5] Stobæus: Floril.; μεγαλόφρων, φιλάνθρωπος.

says another (Aratus), quoted by Saint Paul, is he of whom streets and markets, sea and land, are full, whose "offspring is man," and who in regard to man has appointed signs in the heaven to regulate the year.

The first and last word of Stoicism is spiritual. The poetic mind of the Stoics felt as David did toward Jahveh, — that the highest work of man is to utter in fit words the praises of the greatest of Beings. Cleanthes may be said to have opened the history of this religion (about 200 B. C.) with one of the noblest hymns ever uttered by man.

Cleanthes' Hymn to Zeus.[1]

Hail to thee, most glorious of immortals, O thou of many names, Almighty Zeus, nature's first Cause, governing all things by law. It is the right of mortals to address thee, for we who live and creep upon the earth are all thy children, and to us only is given power of speech like unto thine. Therefore will I sing of thee, and praise thy power forever.

Thee doth all this Cosmos obey, rolling about our earth as thou dost guide it, and by thee willingly ruled. For thou dost hold subservient in thy unconquerable hands the two-forked, fiery, ever-living lightning. Under its stroke all things in nature shudder. . . . Thou dost fulfil that universal plan which goes through all things, shining in all the greater and the lesser lights. Naught is done without thee upon earth, O spirit, nor in the firmament above, nor in the sea, save what the wicked in their folly do. But thou knowest how to make transgression righteousness, confusion order, and things not lovely are lovely to thee, for thou dost shape to one end all things both good and bad, till one eternal law is brought to

---

[1] Translated by Prof. J. G. Croswell.

light from all. This purpose the wicked neglect, and flee, unhappy, who, though forever desiring possession of good, see not, and hearken not to the law of God, which, if they obeyed, they would lead the life that is best. But separated from all that is beautiful, they rush self-willed to this and that, some with jealous thirst for glory, some given to gain without limit, some to ease and the body's delight, all hastening to bring to pass the opposite of their purposes.

But, O Zeus, all-giver, dark-clouded, thunder-ruler, save man from this fatal ignorance, dispel it from the soul; and grant us to share that wisdom with which thou dost thyself guide all things. Thus honored by thee will we return honor to thee, praising thy deeds continually. There is no greater glory for men or gods than forever fittingly to sing hymns in praise of thy universal law.[1]

Epictetus, among the last of the saints of Stoicism (about 117 A.D.), often repeats that one of the highest employments of man is to sing the praises of God; and his commentator, Simplicius, in finishing his work on the Enchiridion, piously says: —

"I supplicate, O Lord, that thou wouldst wash away the dust (ὄχλην) of our spirit-eyes, that we may know well both God and man!"[2]

But evil does not come from the will of God. Zeus willed men to be good and wise and temperate, but their wills too are free.

Thus far all is the expression of pure faith in a Divine Being and a Divine Order. But there comes a time in the

---

[1] Stobæus: Eclogæ, i. 30; κύδιστ' ἀθανάτων ... Ζεῦ.
[2] Epictetus: Enchiridion, p. 526.

history of Stoicism when the confusion of Zeus with the universe served to introduce pantheism, and to weaken the religious sense of the Stoics. In the expressive words of Bossuet, "All was God except God himself;"[1] they felt the mystery of God as Tennyson has expressed in early verses: —

"The sun, the moon, the stars, the seas, the hills, the plains,
Are not these, O soul, the vision of him who reigns?

"Is not the vision he, tho' he be not that which he seems?
Dreams are true while they last, and do we not live in dreams?

"Earth, these solid stars, this weight of body and limb,
Are they not signs and symbol of thy division from him?

"Speak to him, then, for he hears, and spirit with spirit can meet:
Closer is he than breathing, and nearer than hands and feet.

"And the ear of man cannot hear, and the eye of man cannot see;
But if we could see and hear this vision, were it not he?"

But the grand conception of God as One returned to the later Stoics, to Seneca and Marcus Aurelius, and it reached its purest and highest form in Epictetus.

The popular view of Stoicism is taken from one stage of its progress. There came periods both in Greek and Roman history when to the wise man the times seemed "out of joint." The tyrants, or the cruel, selfish rulers of the world, were in power. Liberty was trampled under

[1] "Tout était Dieu excepté Dieu même."

foot. Ambition, greed for money and office, cruelty, lust, and corruption seemed universally to prevail. Religion had become priestcraft, idolatry, and superstition. Worst of all to the good man, the light of God's countenance had faded away. The evil powers of the universe guided it, and all was chance and drift. Zeus was only man's ideal projected on the black background of eternity, — the dream of a being whom the rapid current of chance and destiny was hurling on towards nothingness. All without was hopeless, all within black in thick darkness.

Then the Stoic, looking, as it were, into the face of Goodness and Truth, said to himself: "I have lived for them, I will die for them! The world's applause and rewards are nothing. The gods themselves are nothing. Life is a failure, and eternal life a dream; but I am in harmony with the universe. No pain or sorrow or wrong can touch me. I belong to the everlasting world of truth and purity and love. I have served them, and they, not the prizes they bring, are my reward. No heaven of mythology is worth the half they offer in themselves. If there be no Zeus, there is still the law of the universe; and I have found that to help others and be true to myself is the fabled life of the immortals. I wrap myself in peaceful thoughts, and make a departure with my own hand from a world of shadows to realities."

It often seems remarkable to the Christian student how deep an impression these stoical heroes make upon the mind, — often deeper than do the lives of devout believers. Perhaps it is the thorough disinterestedness of their position, and their utter faith in principles. The great majority of Stoic thinkers, however, have no atheistic position. The crown of Stoicism is its belief in a God, and the community of all men in their union with him. Even its morality sprang from this faith in a moral ruler of perfect goodness.

Prayer. — The followers of Zeno scarcely believed in temples, or in prayer for material objects. They spoke of places of worship with contempt. They seemed (along with the Christians) to be the atheists of that day. Seneca says: "No prayer is needed, except to ask for a good state of mind, for health of soul."[1] "God is within thee. It is absurd to fear the gods, for they are ever beneficent. The only worthy temple of God is the universe; he is not to be worshipped by temples, but by a pure heart; not by sacrifices, but by a good life."[2] The worship of that ignoble crowd of gods he pronounces to be from habit more than from real feeling.

Cicero, who was deeply influenced by the Stoics, says that the best worship is to venerate the gods with pure

[1] Bonam mentem, bonam valetudinem animi (Epistle, x.).
[2] Epistle, xcv. 47.

mind and word.[1] Marcus Aurelius, the imperial saint of Stoicism, says: "Pray not to save thy child, but that thou mayst not fear to lose him."[2] Epictetus, the former slave, but the great apostle of the faith, makes these expressions of utter trust: —

"Lastly, for all other pleasures substitute the consciousness that you are obeying God, and performing, not in word, but in deed, the duty of a wise and good man."

"Zeus hath been pleased to let me recognize this within myself, and himself to discern whether he hath in me one fit for a soldier and a citizen, and to employ me as a witness to other men concerning things uncontrollable by will. See that your fears were vain, your appetites vain. Seek not good from without; seek it within yourselves, or you will never find it. For this reason he now brings me hither, now sends me thither, sets me before mankind, poor, powerless, sick; banishes me to Gyaros, leads me to prison; not that he hates me, — Heaven forbid ! — for who hates the most faithful of his servants? Nor that he neglects me, for he neglects not one of the smallest things, but to exercise me, and make use of me as a witness to others. Appointed to such a service, do I still care where I am, or with whom, or what is said of me, instead of being wholly attentive to God, and to his orders and commands?"

"For I came when it seemed good to him, and again, when it seems good to him, I depart; and in life it was my business to praise God within myself, and to every auditor, and to the world."

The faith of the Stoics[3] is that all things are from God, and return to him; that there is a divine law, the will of

---

[1] Natura Deorum, ii. 28. [2] Meditations, ix. 40.
[3] Zeller.

God, and that all good acts are the fulfilment of this law; that citizenship of the world depends on this relation to God, and inward peace and independence of soul are fruits of this relation.

If such a belief is not a religion, it is difficult to imagine what is. We can understand why the great Christian Apostle quoted from the Stoics in his sermon on Mars Hill. This is the worship of the Unknown God. Its highest expression is the words of the ancient hymn, —

> "Lead thou me on, O Zeus!
> And thou, O Destiny!"

It had in some directions the true effect of a religion. It influenced practical life. Its double phrase, "Bear and forbear!" (*Abstine! Sustine!*)[1] reached all acts of daily life.

The universe is the City of Zeus, therefore all events belonging to it by nature must be borne.

"I have submitted to God my desire. He makes that I should have a fever, and I have it. . . . What he does not wish, I do not wish. He wishes that I die, and I am certain to die."[2]

"If what philosophers say of the kinship between God and men be true, what has any one to do, but, like Socrates, when he is asked what countryman he is, never to say that he is a citizen of Athens, or of Corinth, but of the universe?"[3] "Why may not such a one call himself a citizen of the universe; why not a son of God? And why shall he fear anything that happens among

---

[1] ἀπέχου! ἀνέχου!
[2] Arrian, iv. 1; Epictetus.
[3] Epictetus.

men? Shall kinship to Cæsar, or any other of the great at Rome, enable a man to live secure above contempt and void of all fear whatever; and shall not the having God for our maker, and father, and guardian, free us from griefs and alarms?"[1]

"Whatever must be suffered from the constitution of the universe, let it be borne with a great soul. To this oath we are bound, — to bear mortal ills, not to be disturbed by those which it is not in our power to avoid. In this kingdom we are born. To obey God is liberty."[2] "The relation to God is the source of every virtue. It is not possible for souls who have never been able to live in union with other souls to attain to that more perfect and happy union with God."[3] "The lover of God becomes by that fact a brother of all men. He is pleasant to his friends, and gentle to enemies."[4] "In doing good to others, he does good to himself. He learns that to bear is human."[5] "Where is the place for the highest good? you ask. The soul. But this can never receive God unless it be pure and holy."[6]

The father of Stoicism, Zeno, says: "All men are by nature equal, and virtue alone makes a difference."[7] The great poet of this faith, Lucan, asks if there be any habitation of God but virtue, and dreams of a time when all nations shall cast aside arms and love one another.[8] And his ideal is of one who believes himself born not for him-

---

[1] Epictetus.
[2] In regno nati sumus. Deo parere libertas est (Seneca).
[3] Simplicius: Comm., xlii.
[4] Amicis jucundus inimicis mitis (De Vit. Beat.).
[5] De Ira.
[6] Hic nisi purus ac sanctus, Deum non capit (Seneca: Epistles).
[7] Diog. Laert.
[8] Inque vicem gens omnis amet (Phars.).

self but for the whole world.[1] Cicero speaks of "a citizen of the whole world."[2]

From this Stoical principle of the brotherhood of man came forth the greatest influence of Stoicism, that upon the ideas of Roman jurists in international law. Cicero, who, though not a Stoic, felt these influences, speaks of "a love for the human race."[3]

Seneca alludes to a common law of the human race.[4] Florentinus speaks of a relation of nature which belongs to natural law, by which all men are equal.[5] Ulpian claims that by natural law all men are born free.[6]

These ideas have profoundly influenced modern political thought, and even practical institutions of government. They are the one great bequest of Stoicism to modern times, and they plainly sprang from its religion.[7] It is a mistake to suppose that Stoicism was always harsh and cruel. Zeno is quoted as saying that "the God who rules the city is Love." The followers of this philosophy were full of the idea that man belongs to all others, and that he is a stranger to none. No school ever taught the brotherhood of man more clearly. It dealt too with questions of

---

[1] Nic sibi sed toti genitum se credere mundo (Phars., ii. 38).
[2] Civis totius mundi (De Leg., ii. 23).
[3] Caritas generis humani (De Finibus).
[4] Commune jus generis humani (Epistles).
[5] Omnes homines æquales sunt.
[6] Jure naturali omnes liberi nascerentur.
[7] See Laferrière: Mem. de l'Acad., x.

casuistry from the highest point of view. Such questions as the moral right to sell a cargo of grain at famine prices, the owner knowing privately that a new supply is just outside the port, are discussed in a manner which would invigorate a Christian moralist.[1]

Stoicism had also the enthusiasm of a religion. It furnished not a few men who were willing to die for their principles. Epictetus says that the wise, the true Stoics, are true "deacons and martyrs,"[2] servants[3] of men and witnesses to truth.

[1] Antipater and Diog.; Cic., De Off.; etc.
[2] διάκονοι καὶ μάρτυρες (Diss., iii. 26).
[3] The word "deacon" is literally a *dust*-worker; "martyr" means witness.

CHAPTER VIII.

THE FAITH OF THE STOICS. — SENECA.

Ubicumque homo est, ibi beneficio locus est. . . . Homo sacra res homini.
SENECA: Epistles.

THERE comes a period in human history, after a long course of polytheism and idolatry, when the mind of man hungers for something in belief more solid and enduring, and the soul becomes open to the divine inspirations that are always acting. Then ideas are abroad which strongly resemble those we derive from Christianity. Men seem to get foretastes of divine revelations. The world is ready for a higher faith. At such a period as this, in the same century with Paul, there lived, mostly in Rome, a Spanish rhetorician and essayist of the keenest mental quality, Seneca, who, without perhaps feeling the current religious ideas deeply himself, yet possessed an unsurpassed ability in gathering them up and expressing them. He called himself a disciple of the "Stoa," but never himself could act on Stoical principles. His form of expression in conveying these great thoughts and hopes was such as few Latins were ever gifted with. Seneca's picture of Stoicism may be accepted as a truthful representation of what was in the minds of many men at that period.

Whether he ever came directly in contact with Christianity has been much discussed.[1] It is at least doubtful if he had ever read the sacred writings of our faith. But Paul must have preached to the lower retainers of the imperial court in Rome while he was one of its literary members. His elder brother, M. A. Novatus, called Gallio from his adopted father, had met Paul in the celebrated scene in Achaia, where the Roman had acted like a philosophical and broad-minded ruler, and refused to interfere with secular power in differences relating to religious ceremonies and metaphysical beliefs.[2] The air of Rome among the common classes must have been full of the phrases of the new religion. Slaves and scribes and soldiers, and the unfortunate and poor must have repeated one to another its words of consolation and spiritual life. A rhetorician like Seneca would naturally catch up these expressions and ideals and adapt them to his own theories and hopes; even as a religious writer now might make use of the terms of Spiritualism or Animal Magnetism, without necessarily believing in the truth of the theory.

---

[1] See the able discussions by Baur (Seneca und Paulus), and Dourif (Du Stoicisme et Christianisme, etc.); also Boissier (La Religion Romaine), ii. 48.
[2] Acts xviii. 12.

Certainly on one occasion, in a private letter, Seneca describes a mental change which had come over him, in words that might well have been used by a Christian in picturing his own conversion: —

"I have been not so much emended as transformed, — so sudden is the change.[1] . . . Thou askest me what progress I have made. I have just begun *to be a friend to myself.*"[2]

His use of such expressions as "carnal," as opposed to "spiritual," and *sacer intra nos spiritus* ("the Holy Spirit within us"), as a power "without which no man can be good," and "we all have sinned, some to a less degree, some worse,"[3] — this all shows certainly a familiarity with Scripture phrases and ideas not usual in classic writers.

To the modern Christian it is a matter for wonder and warning that so many great and noble natures of the classic period, having opportunity, never in the least grasped the truths of Christianity. They were men apparently looking for truth everywhere, and open to whatsoever things were noble and reverend and gracious. Yet this new faith was to them as Mormonism or Buddhism is to most Christians now.

That gloomy moralist, Tacitus, — the Carlyle of his

---

[1] Intellige, Lucili, non emendari me tantum sed transfigurari, . . . tam subitam mutationem (Epistles).

[2] Epistles.

[3] . . . Omnes peccavimus (De Clem.).

day, — ready to see the hidden meaning in the strangest customs of the barbarian Teutons, only alludes to the purest faith which had ever appeared on earth, in one of his condensed phrases of contempt, as an "execrable superstition." Epictetus, one of the most saintly beings who ever appeared in the world, speaks of the Christians dying as if purely from "habit." And the noble Marcus Aurelius scarcely alludes to them, except to their heroic deaths as from "obstinacy,"[1] while in public life he punished and persecuted them. Once, indeed, Epictetus speaks of the "Jews" (by whom he probably means the Christians) as if they were a model in life and conduct far above the lives of the Stoics.[2]

Seneca hardly mentions the Christians except with bitterness or contempt. If the wise and noble of the past can thus overlook the great truths revealed in their own times, how can we now be sure that we have seen in our day all the revelations of God?

·

The great doctrine of the Stoics, the belief in an all-controlling Creator, was deeply planted in Seneca's philosophy. He frequently speaks of God as the Governor

---

[1] Meditations, xi. 3.

[2] "We are Jews only in words, for our feelings do not agree with our discourse; and though we boast our science, we are very far from the use and practice of the things we talk" (Arrian: Epictetus).

of the Universe, the Builder and Governor of all things, the Ruler of the World.[1]

"The same whom we call Jove is the ruler and guardian of the universe, the Soul of the world; to him every name suits."[2] "Do you wish to call him Fate, you will not err, for he it is from whom all things are suspended, the Cause of causes. Do you wish to call him Providence, you will say rightly, for he it is by whose counsel this world is provided for. Or will you call him Nature, you will not be mistaken, for he it is from whom all things are born, by whose spirit we live. This God is within our thoughts, near to us.[3]" "Between him and good men there is friendship and union, virtue conciliating. Friendship, do I say; rather affinity (*necessitas*) and likeness.... A good man is his disciple and true offspring."[4]

There is for man and for God nothing higher than the good in itself; and absolute good is for both the highest object.

"As a true soldier will bear wounds, number his scars, and though transfixed with weapons, dying, will love him for whom he falls [his emperor], so the good man will have in mind the old precept, 'Follow God!'"[5]

But this Being is more than a Providence; he is a personal, moral Ruler. He does not keep a good man in delights; he tries him, and hardens him, and prepares him for himself.[6] "I obey not God, but agree with him.

---

[1] De Prov.; Epistles. Rector universi, Omnium Conditor, Arbiter Deus universi (De Vit. Beat.; Quest. Nat.).

[2] Ibid.; Cui nomen omne convenit.

[3] Prope est a te. Deus tecum est, intus est (Epistles).

[4] De Prov.   [5] De Vita Beata.

[6] This certainly has a Christian sound: Hos itaque Deus, quos probat, quos amat, indurat, recognoscit, exercet (De Prov.).

I follow from the heart, not because I must."[1] To the Stoic this faith brought the highest moral gifts.

"Mercy is the quality which brings man nearest to God"[2] "Standeth not he nearest the gods who showeth a godlike nature in his bearing, — blessing, beneficent and powerful, for the noblest ends?"[3] "Mercy is with God and man the quality which, not injures and destroys, but preserving and upholding, works, and is ever directed through love and goodness to this, — to let all these blessings come to human society on which its well-being and success depend?"[4]

This faith of the Stoics has the true effect of a religion, according to the Roman moralist. Seneca says: —

"Our task is to live according to nature, and to follow the example of the gods; they give everything without reward. If one imitates the gods, one must do good to the unthankful." "Better to do a benefit to the wicked, than withdraw on their account a hand from the good."[5] "The rain falleth on the fields of the wicked and ruthless; so should man's benefaction be."[6] "Thou must live for another, if thou wouldst live for thyself."[7] "There is no one under the name of a man who is not pleasing to me."[8] "Wherever is man, there is a place for benefaction. Man is a sacred thing to man."[9] "We must love all men, of all conditions, even enemies, to the last end of life. It belongs to a great soul to despise injuries. Revenge is an inhuman word."

[1] Epistles.
[2] De Clem.
[3] Ibid.
[4] Ibid.
[5] De Benefact.
[6] Ibid.
[7] Alteri vivere oportet. si vis tibi vivere (Epistles).
[8] Nemo non, hominis nomine, apud me gratiosus est (De Clem.).
[9] Ubicumque homo est, ibi beneficio locus est. . . . Homo sacra res homini (Epistles).

Seneca looks upon mankind as a body, in which individuals are limbs; he conceives a love embracing all humanity. In this view the slave is a man, and we are to treat the lowest as the highest. Cruel and bloody shows are, of course, utterly opposed to this philosophy. Upon these Seneca utters one of his finest epigrams: —

"Now let us back to the great city! Too long have we been without its applause and din. Now it is such a pleasure to taste again of human blood!"[1]

Yet it is to be borne in mind that the great rhetorician was false to his Stoical principles, both in regard to slavery and the cruel custom of exposition of children. Of Providence and the soul, our Roman Stoic discourses as becomes his school: —

"At the last, the wise man is bound to the same necessity as the gods. One irrevocable current carries both divine and human things."[2] "We, the dying, receive things that must die."[3] "There is something lofty, regal, unconquered, unwearied in the virtuous soul."[4] "Dost thou wish to profit the gods, be good; he has worshipped them sufficiently who has imitated them."[5] "The wise man knows he must bear his own burden."[6] "We must serve in a kind of campaign, where is no rest and no furlough."[7] "Restrain your desires, how often? As often as you shall sin."[8]

[1] De Tranq. Animi.   [2] De Prov.
[3] This condensed epigram, "Accepimus perituri, peritura." is also from his essay on Providence.
[4] De Vita Beata.   [5] Epistles.   [6] Ibid.
[7] Ibid.   [8] Ibid.

He tells Lucilius that then he is perfect when he fully understands that the most unfortunate are the fortunate.[1]

"He is not wise unless his mind is transformed. . . . He is great who never groaned at evils, never complained at his fate; . . . who turned the minds of all to himself, since he was ever gentle and humane; who had the perfect mind, above which is nothing but the mind of God."[2]

Death. — Death, and the region beyond death, was the unfailing topic for the Stoic's reflections in all ages. In earlier times his belief in a future life had not been always unshaken; but in the later period of the new Stoics this belief shone out brightly, though often beclouded.

Of death, Seneca says: "He will live badly who does not know how to die well."[3] The death-day, in his view, is the birthday of immortality (*eterni natalis*).

"The body is a brief lodging-house [*hospitium*] which the noble soul does not fear to lose. All earthly things are only the baggage which we did not bring into the world and cannot take with us."[4] "Something great and noble is the human soul. It admits no limits beyond what are common to it with God. It accepts no low fatherhood; . . . its country is space, it embraces the highest; . . . it hath no limits to its age; 'All years are mine.' When that day cometh which separateth the mingling of the divine and human, then will I leave the body behind where I have found it;

---

[1] . . . Felices infelicissimos (Epistles).
[2] Epistles.
[3] . . . Male vivet quisquis nesciet bene mori (De Tranq. Animi).
[4] Epistles.

I will give myself back to the gods. . . . Another origin awaits us, another state of things. Therefore look forward undauntedly to death."

Beyond is the *quies eterna*, — a great and eternal peace. In Seneca's "Consolation to Marcus"[1] he says the dead are free from all care and sorrow, and are happy in that glorious society of blessed spirits (*felices animas*). Death to this philosopher is the great day of judgment. This thought of a future life permits nothing sordid or low or criminal to sink into the soul. Death interrupts but does not destroy life.[2] The hour of death is not for the soul the last thing, but only for the body;[3] and his soul is never more divine than when conscious that man is born for this, — to leave life. Most clearly does it show its higher origin when it holds its present seat as too narrow, and does not fear to leave it. For whither it will go, he shows who remembers whence it came.[4] "I am greater, and born to greater things, than that I could be a slave to the body, which I consider as nothing but a chain laid about my freedom." In his "Consolation to Polybia,"[5] he writes: —

"Thou art mistaken. To thy brother the light has not set; a more trustworthy thing became his portion; hither goes all our common road; he has not left us, he has gone before. The dead is not really gone, only the image is lost; he himself is eternally in

---

[1] Epistles.
[2] Ibid.
[3] Ibid.
[4] Ibid.
[5] Cons. ad Polybiam.

a better lot, freed from strange burdens, and entirely belonging to himself.[1] Death is only a passage to a better body. It is not power and name, but goodness, which lifts to heaven; souls must wait for purification before they rise to heaven. Finally a great and eternal peace (*pax magna et eterna*) receives him. He is freed from all pain and envy and trouble. No shadow will darken that brilliancy. Then wilt thou say thou hast lived in darkness, when thou shalt see the whole light. How will divine Light seem to thee when thou seest it in its own place.[2] We have then reason to congratulate ourselves, when our spirit, delivered from darkness, not merely sees a glimmer of distant brightness, but the full day, etc.[3] ... There friends shall meet, and the departed teach us heavenly things.[4] ... The wise man, unshaken by calamities and untouched by passion, calm amid tempests, is like God himself."[5] "God is the source of all good, but it is the possession of true good which makes true happiness."[6] "Virtue makes a man worthy to come into union with God."[7]

Sin. — Seneca often repeats that no one is without sin.[8] "How much is demanded of us by piety, the love of man, generosity, justice, and truth, all of which stands not in tables of the law. If we think of this, if we are more reasonable against those who fail, more forgiving to those who insult us, might we not cease to be angry with ourselves and most of all with the gods?" The path to goodness is through faults and errors; he speaks of "the struggle of the flesh and the spirit," and of the chains and darkness of the soul in which we are in-

---

[1] Consolatio ad Marcum.
[2] Epistles.
[3] Epistles.
[4] Consolatio ad Marcum.
[5] Epistles.
[6] Ibid.
[7] Consortium Dei (Quest. Nat.).
[8] De Ira.

volved.[1] Sin is the universal insanity (*insania communis*). We are all lost, and reserved for death.[2] The first step is knowledge of our sin,[3] but we cannot be healed by ourselves. Some one must lend a hand, some one educate.[4] "Choose some good man whom thou admirest: hold this model ever before thy eyes; make conscience thy guide and mentor; each night examine thy actions and thought for the day."[5]

These great thoughts and principles, which Seneca has treated with the consummate skill of a practised rhetorician, became the guiding thoughts and motives of some of the still later Stoics. We shall give more fully in the succeeding chapters the thoughts and maxims of the lame Phrygian slave Epictetus, and of the Emperor Marcus Aurelius. These express certainly some of the highest principles of life and conduct ever reached by the human intellect. They are full of trust, faith, resignation, and the spirit of the utmost self-sacrifice. The belief in God seems profound and controlling, and the desire for goodness, truth, and purity, the strongest possible. They form with the thoughts and writings of the earlier Stoics a complete and pure religious faith.

[1] Consolatio ad Marcum.
[2] Quest. Nat.
[3] Epistles.
[4] Epistles.
[5] De Ira.

CHAPTER IX.

STOICAL WRITINGS. — EPICTETUS.[1]

(ABOUT 117 A.D.)

Stoical Independence.

"It is in your power to prevent my continuing a senator; but while I am one, I must go." — "Well, then, at least be silent there." — "Do not ask my opinion and I will be silent." — "But I must ask it." — "And I must speak what appears to me to be right." — "But if you do, I will put you to death." — "When did I ever tell you that I was immortal? You will do your part, and I mine; it is yours to kill and mine to die intrepid; yours to banish, mine to depart untroubled" (p. 10).

I shall never be Milo, and yet I do not neglect my body; nor Crœsus, and yet I do not neglect my property; nor should we omit any effort from a despair of arriving at the highest (p. 12).

A Son of God.

If a person could be persuaded of this principle as he ought, that we are all originally descended from God, and that he is the father of men and gods, I conceive he never would think of himself meanly or ignobly. Suppose Cæsar were to adopt you, there would be no bearing your haughty looks; and will you not feel ennobled on knowing yourself to be the son of God? (p. 12.)

---

[1] These translations are from Higginson's excellent revision of Mrs. Carter's version.

Now if virtue promises happiness, prosperity, and peace, then progress in virtue is certainly progress in each of these. For to whatever point the perfection of anything absolutely brings us, progress is always an approach towards it (p. 13).

God as Master.

"Are we not of kindred to God, and did we not come from him? Suffer us to go back thither from whence we came; suffer us at length to be delivered from these fetters that bind and weigh us down. Here thieves and robbers, courts and tyrants, claim power over us through the body and its possessions. Suffer us to show them that they have no power." And in this case it would be my part to answer: "My friends, wait for God till he shall give the signal, and dismiss you from this service; then return to him" (p. 30).

Why, if you have it, slave, you will have it; if not, you will go out of life. The door is open, why do you lament? What room remains for tears; what occasion for flattery? Why should any one person envy another? Why should he be impressed with awe by those who have great possessions, or are placed in high rank, especially if they are powerful and passionate? For what will they do to us? The things which they can do, we do not regard; the things about which we are concerned they cannot reach (p. 31).

Suicide.

"You are ridiculous in thinking that if your general had placed me in any post I ought to maintain and defend it, and choose to die a thousand times rather than desert it; but that if God hath assigned me any station or method of life, I ought to desert that for you" (p. 31).

I wrote for him in a submissive style; but after reading my letter he returned it to me, and said, "I wanted your assistance, not your pity; for no evil hath befallen me" (p. 32).

I cannot be hid from thee in any of my motions. . . . A wise and good man, after examining these things, submits his mind to him who administers the whole, as good citizens do to the laws of the commonwealth. He, then, who comes to be instructed, ought to come with this aim: How may I in everything follow the gods? How may I acquiesce in the divine administration, and how may I be free? (p. 40.)

God as Father.

O slavish man! will you not bear with your own brother, who has God for his Father, as being a son from the same stock, and of the same high descent? (p. 44.)

And cannot he who made and moves the sun, a small part of himself, if compared with the whole, — cannot he perceive all things? (p. 46.)

So that, when you have shut your doors, and darkened your room, remember never to say that you are alone, for you are not alone; but God is within, and your genius is within; and what need have they of light to see what you are doing? . . . Never distrust, nor accuse, nor murmur at any of the things appointed by him; nor shrink from doing or enduring that which is inevitable (p. 47).

Praise to God.

For if we had any understanding, ought we not, both in public and in private, incessantly to sing and praise the Deity and rehearse his benefits? Ought we not, whether we dig or plough or eat, to sing this hymn to God. . . . For what else can I do, a lame old man, but sing hymns to God? Were I a nightingale, I would act the part of a nightingale; were I a swan, the part of a swan. But since I am a reasonable creature, it is my duty to praise God. This is my business. I do it. Nor will I ever desert this post, so long as it is permitted me; and I call on you to join in the same song (p. 50).

Survival of the Best.

But show me that he who has the worse principles can get the advantage over him who has the better. You never will show it, nor anything like it; for the law of Nature and of God is this, — let the better always prevail over the worse (p. 85).

If you were a statue of Phidias, as Zeus or Minerva, you would remember both yourself and the artist. . . . And are you now careless how you appear, when you are the workmanship of Zeus himself? (p. 115.)

How, then, is this to be effected? Be willing to approve yourself to yourself; be willing to appear beautiful in the sight of God; be desirous to converse in purity with your own pure mind and with God (p. 155).

Union with God.

Let any of you show me a human soul desiring to be in unity with God; not to accuse either God or man; not to be disappointed of its desire, nor incur its aversion; not to be angry, not to be envious, not to be jealous; in a word, desiring from a man to become a god; and in this poor mortal body aiming to have fellowship with Zeus. Show him to me; but you cannot.

Who is there whom bright and agreeable children do not attract to play, and creep, and prattle with? But who was ever taken with an inclination to divert himself or bray with an ass? for be the creature ever so little, it is still a little ass (p. 185).

The Stoic's Wealth.

Your father deprives you of your money; but he does not hurt you. He will possess more land than you; as much more as he pleases, but will he possess more honor, more fidelity, more affection? Who can deprive you of this possession? Not even Zeus; for he did not will it so, since he has put this good into my own power, and given it me, like his own, uncompelled, unrestrained, and unhindered (p. 201).

Self-Examination.

"Ere every action of the former day
  Strictly thou dost, and righteously survey.
  What have I done? In what have I transgressed?
  What good or ill has this day's life expressed?
  Where have I failed in what I ought to do?
  If evil were thy deeds, repent and mourn;
  If good, rejoice."

We should retain these verses so as to apply them to our use, not merely to say them by rote, as we do with verses in honor of Apollo (p. 219).

This, too, you should be prepared to say with regard to a father. It is not lawful for me to affront you, father, even if a worse than you had come, for all are from paternal Zeus. And so of a brother, for all are from kindred Zeus; and thus we shall find Zeus to be the superintendent of all the other relations (p. 222).

Whenever you lay anything to the charge of Providence, do but reflect, and you will find that it has happened agreeably to reason (p. 234).

God's Will.

Consider carefully, know yourself, consult the Divinity, attempt nothing without God; for if he counsels you, be assured that it is his will, whether that you should become eminent, or that you should suffer many a blow (p. 250).

Shall we never wean ourselves, and remember what we have heard from the philosophers, — unless we have heard them as juggling enchanters, — that the universe is one great city, and the substance one of which it is formed; that there must necessarily be a certain rotation of things; that some must give way to others, some be dissolved, and others rise in their stead; some remain in the same situation, and others be moved; but that all is full of beloved ones, first of the gods and then of men, by nature endeared to each other? (p. 266.)

Zeus as Father.

For he had not merely heard it as matter of talk, that Zeus was the father of mankind, but he esteemed and called him his own Father, and performed all that he did with a view to him (p. 267).

You must observe the duty of a soldier, and perform everything at the nod of your general, and even, if possible, divine what he would have done. For there is no comparison between the above-mentioned general and this whom you now obey, either in power or excellence of character (p. 270).

As became a minister of Zeus, at once caring for men and obedient to God. Hence the whole earth, not any particular place, was his country (p. 275).

Hence a wise and good man, mindful who he is and whence he came, and by whom he was produced, is attentive only how he may fill his post regularly and dutifully before God. . . . Whatever post or rank thou shalt assign me, like Socrates, I will die a thousand times rather than desert it (p. 279).

God the Creator.

For whence had I these things when I came into the world? My father gave them to me. And who gave them to him? And who made the sun? Who the fruits? Who the seasons? Who their connection and relations with each other? And after you have received all, and even your very self from another, are you angry with the giver? And do you complain if he takes anything away from you? Who are you, and for what purpose did you come? Was it not he who brought you here? Was it not he who showed you the light? Hath not he given you companions? Hath not he given you senses? Hath not he given you reason? And as whom did he bring you here? Was it not as a mortal?

Was it not as one to live with a little portion of flesh upon earth, and to see his administration? To behold the spectacle with him, and partake of the festival for a short time? After having beheld the spectacle and the solemnity, then, as long as it is permitted you, will you not depart, when he leads you out, adoring and thankful for what you have heard and seen? (p. 305.)

But how should we have been of use to any? For where must they have dwelt? If we were useful alive, should we not be of still more use to mankind by dying when we ought and as we ought? And now the remembrance of the death of Socrates is not less, but even more useful to the world than that of the things which he did and said when alive (p. 315).

The Friend of God.

But I do not applaud where it is unbecoming. I will pay no undeserved honor, for I am free, and the friend of God, so as to obey him willingly; but I must not value anything else, neither body, nor possessions, nor fame, — in short, nothing. For it is not his will that I should value them. For if this had been his pleasure he would have placed in them my good, which now he hath not done; therefore I cannot transgress his commands. Seek in all things your own highest good (p. 319).

And is it possible that any one should be thus disposed towards these things from madness, and the Galileans[1] from mere habit? (p. 340.)

Piety.

If death overtakes me in such a situation, it is enough for me if I can stretch out my hands to God and say: "The opportunities which I have received from thee of comprehending and obeying thy administration I have not neglected. As far as in me lay, I have not dishonored thee. See how I have used my perceptions; how my convictions. Have I at any time found fault with thee?

[1] Christians.

Have I been discontented at thy dispensations, or wished them otherwise? Have I transgressed the relations of life? I thank thee that thou hast brought me into being. I am satisfied with the time that I have enjoyed the things which thou hast given me. Receive them back again, and distribute them as thou wilt; for they were all thine, and thou gavest them to me" (p. 356).

God alone Master.

No one therefore is my master, either to procure me any good or to involve me in any evil; but I alone have the disposal of myself with regard to these things. Since these then are secured to me, what need have I to be troubled about externals? What tyrant is formidable? What disease? What poverty? What offence? "I have not pleased such a one?" Is he my concern then? Is he my conscience? "No." Why then do I trouble myself any further about him? "But he is thought to be of some consequence." Let him look to that, and they who think him so. But I have One whom I must please, to whom I must submit, whom I must obey, — God, and those who surround him (p. 366).

Freedom of the Stoic.

For my part, I have examined the whole. No one has authority over me. God hath made me free; I know his commands. After this no one can enslave me. I have a proper vindicator of my freedom, proper judges. Are you the master of my body? But what is that to me? Of my little estate? But what is that to me? Of banishment and chains? Why, all these again, and my whole body, I give up to you; make a trial of your power whenever you please, and you will find how far it extends (p. 342).

Because, if I am not admitted, I would not wish to go in, but would much rather that things should be as they are; for I esteem what God wills to be better than what I will. To him I yield myself as a servant and follower (p. 342).

CHAPTER X.

STOICAL WRITINGS. — MARCUS AURELIUS.[1]
(ABOUT 175 A.D.)

Right Living.

SINCE it is possible that thou mayest depart from life this very moment, regulate every act and thought accordingly (book ii. § 11).

Harmony with Nature.

But this consists in keeping the daemon within a man free from violence and unharmed, superior to pains and pleasures, doing nothing without a purpose, nor yet falsely and with hypocrisy, not feeling the need of another man's doing or not doing anything; and besides, accepting all that happens, and all that is allotted, as coming from thence, wherever it is, from whence he himself came; and, finally, waiting for death with a cheerful mind, as being nothing else than a dissolution of the elements of which every living being is compounded. But if there is no harm to the elements themselves in each continually changing into another, why should a man have any apprehension about the change and dissolution of all the elements? For it is according to nature, and nothing is evil which is according to nature (book ii. § 17).

The power of making use of ourselves, and filling up the measure of our duty, and clearly separating all appearances, and con-

---

[1] These translations are from George Long's excellent version of the Meditations of Marcus Aurelius, in Bohn's Classical Library.

sidering whether a man should now depart from life, and whatever else of the kind absolutely requires a disciplined reason, — all this is already extinguished. We must make haste, then, not only because we are daily nearer to death, but also because the conception of things and the understanding of them cease first (book iii. § 1).

Manhood.

And further, let the deity which is in thee be the guardian of a living being, manly and of ripe age, and engaged in matters political, and a Roman, and a ruler, who has taken his post like a man waiting for the signal which summons him from life, and ready to go, having need neither of oath nor of any man's testimony. Be cheerful also, and seek not external help nor the tranquillity which others give. A man then must stand erect, not be kept erect by others (book iii. § 5).

Political Ideals.

And from him [Severus] I received the idea of a polity in which there is the same law for all, a polity administered with regard to equal rights and equal freedom of speech, and the idea of a kingly government which respects most of all the freedom of the governed (book i. § 14).

The Quick-passing Opportunity.

Remember how long thou hast been putting off these things, and how often thou hast received an opportunity from the gods, and yet dost not use it. Thou must now at last perceive of what universe thou art a part, and of what administrator of the universe thy existence is an efflux, and that a limit of time is fixed for thee, which if thou dost not use for clearing away the clouds from thy mind, it will go and thou wilt go, and it will never return (book ii. § 4).

Readiness for Death.

Every moment think steadily as a Roman and a man to do what thou hast in hand with perfect and simple dignity, and feeling of affection, and freedom, and justice, and to give thyself relief from all other thoughts; and thou wilt give thyself relief if thou doest every act of thy life as if it were the last, laying aside all carelessness and passionate aversion from the commands of reason, and all hypocrisy, and self-love, and discontent with the portion which has been given to thee. Thou seest how few the things are, the which if a man lays hold of, he is able to live a life which flows in quiet, and is like the existence of the gods; for the gods on their part will require nothing more from him who observes these things (book ii. § 5).

Charity of Opinion.

It is natural that these things should be done by such persons, it is a matter of necessity; and if a man will not have it so, he will not allow the fig-tree to have juice. But by all means bear this in mind, that within a very short time both thou and he will be dead; and soon not even your names will be left behind (book iv. § 6).

Do not act as if thou wert going to live ten thousand years. Death hangs over thee. While thou livest, while it is in thy power, be good (book iv. § 17).

The City of Zeus.

Everything harmonizes with me which is harmonious to thee, O universe! Nothing for me is too early nor too late, which is in due time for thee. Everything is fruit to me, which thy seasons bring, O Nature! From thee are all things, in thee are all things, to thee all things return. The poet says, Dear city of Cecrops; and wilt thou not say, Dear city of Zeus? (book iv. § 23.)

The Day of Death.

If any god told thee that thou shalt die to-morrow, or certainly on the day after to-morrow, thou wouldst not care much whether it was on the third day or on the morrow, unless thou wast in the highest degree mean-spirited; for how small is the difference. So think it no great thing to die after as many years as thou canst name rather than to-morrow (book iv. § 47).

Simple Prayer.

A prayer of the Athenians: Rain, rain, O dear Zeus, down on the ploughed fields of the Athenians and on the plains. In truth we ought not to pray at all, or we ought to pray in this simple and noble fashion (book v. § 7).

And so accept everything which happens, even if it seem disagreeable, because it leads to this, to the health of the universe and to the prosperity and felicity of Zeus (book v. § 8).

Contentment.

Live with the gods. And he does live with the gods who constantly shows to them that his own soul is satisfied with that which is assigned to him, and that it does all that the daemon wishes, which Zeus hath given to every man for his guardian and guide, a portion of himself. And this is every man's understanding and reason (book v. § 27).

Transitoriness of Life.

Soon, very soon, thou wilt be ashes, or a skeleton, and either a name, or not even a name; but name is sound and echo. And the things which are much valued in life are empty and rotten and trifling, and [like] little dogs biting one another, and little children quarrelling, laughing, and then straightway weeping.

The Stoic's View of the Universe.

Look round at the courses of the stars, as if thou wert going along with them; and constantly consider the changes of the elements into one another, for such thoughts purge away the filth of the terrene life (book vii. § 47).

The art of life is more like the wrestler's art than the dancer's, in respect of this, that it should stand ready and firm to meet onsets which are sudden and unexpected (book vii. § 61).

Self-questioning.

On the occasion of every act, ask thyself, How is this with respect to me? Shall I repent of it? A little time and I am dead, and all is gone. What more do I seek, if what I am now doing is the work of an intelligent living being, and a social being, and one who is under the same law with God? (book viii. § 2.)

[Consider] that men will do the same things nevertheless, even though thou shouldst burst (book viii. § 4).

In the next place, having fixed thy eyes steadily on thy business, look at it, and at the same time remembering that it is thy duty to be a good man, and what man's nature demands, do that without turning aside; and speak as it seems to thee most just, only let it be with a good disposition and with modesty and without hypocrisy (book viii. § 5).

Thou hast not leisure [or ability] to read. But thou hast leisure [or ability] to check arrogance; thou hast leisure to be superior to pleasure and pain; thou hast leisure to be superior to love of fame, and not to be vexed at stupid and ungrateful people, nay, even to care for them (book viii. § 8).

Thou sufferest this justly; for thou choosest rather to become good to-morrow than to be good to-day (book viii. § 22).

Am I doing anything? I do it with reference to the good of mankind. Does anything happen to me? I receive it and refer it to the gods, and the source of all things, from which all that happens is derived (book viii. § 23).

The Happy Death.

It would be a man's happiest lot to depart from mankind without having had any taste of lying and hypocrisy and luxury and pride (book ix. § 2).

The Stoic's Prayer.

Either the gods have no power or they have power. If, then, they have no power, why dost thou pray to them? But if they have power, why dost thou not pray for them to give thee the faculty of not fearing any of the things which thou fearest, or of not desiring any of the things which thou desirest, or not being pained at anything, rather than pray that any of these things should not happen or happen? (book ix. § 40.)

When thou art offended with any man's shameless conduct, immediately ask thyself, Is it possible, then, that shameless men should not be in the world? (book ix. § 42.)

For at the same time that thou dost remind thyself that it is impossible that such kind of men should not exist, thou wilt become more kindly disposed towards every one individually (book ix. § 42).

Harmony with Nature.

So also as man is formed by nature to acts of benevolence, when he has done anything benevolent, or in any other way conducive to the common interest, he has acted conformably to his constitution, and he gets what is his own (book ix. § 42).

If a man is mistaken, instruct him kindly and show him his error. But if thou art not able, blame thyself, or blame not even thyself (book ix. § 4).

Destiny.

Whatever may happen to thee, it was prepared for thee from all eternity; and the implication of causes was from eternity spinning the thread of thy being, and of that which is incident to it (book x. § 5).

To her who gives and takes back all, to Nature, the man who is instructed and modest says, Give what thou wilt; take back what thou wilt. And he says this not proudly, but obediently, and well pleased with her (book x. § 14).

According to Nature.

Let men see, let them know a real man who lives according to nature. If they cannot endure him, let them kill him. For that is better than to live thus [as men do] (book x. § 15).

No longer talk at all about the kind of man that a good man ought to be, but be such (book x. § 16).

Readiness for Death.

What a soul that is which is ready, if at any moment it must be separated from the body, and ready either to be extinguished or dispersed or continue to exist; but so that this readiness comes from a man's own judgment, not from mere obstinacy, as with the Christians, but considerately and with dignity, and in a way to persuade another, without tragic show (book xi. § 3).

Have I done something for the general interest? Well then I have had my reward. Let this always be present to thy mind and never stop [doing such good] (book xi. § 4).

> "Me and my children if the gods neglect,'
> This hath its reason too" (book xi. § 6).

Self-Respect.

Suppose any man shall despise me. Let him look to that himself. But I will look to this, that I be not discovered doing or saying anything deserving of contempt. Shall any man hate me? Let him look to it. But I will be mild and benevolent towards every man, and ready to show even him his mistake, not reproachfully, nor yet as making a display of my endurance, but nobly and honestly, like the great Phocion, unless, indeed, he only assumed it. For the interior [parts] ought to be such, and a man ought to be seen by the gods neither dissatisfied with anything nor complaining. For what evil is it to thee, if thou art now doing what is agreeable to thy own nature, and art satisfied with that which at this moment is suitable to the nature of the universe, since thou art a human being placed at thy post in order that what is for the common advantage may be done in some way? (book xi. § 13.)

A Man Worthy of the Universe.

If, then, whatever the time may be when thou shalt be near to thy departure, neglecting everything else thou shalt respect only thy ruling faculty and the divinity within thee; and if thou shalt be afraid not because thou must some time cease to live, but if thou shalt fear never to have begun to live according to nature, — then thou wilt be a man worthy of the universe which has produced thee, and thou wilt cease to be a stranger in thy native land, and to wonder at things which happen daily as if they were something unexpected, and to be dependent on this or that (book xii. § 1).

God.

God sees the minds [ruling principles] of all men bared of the material vesture and impurities. For with his intellectual part alone he touches the intelligence only which has flowed and been derived from himself into these bodies (book xii. § 2).

Future Life.

How can it be that the gods, after having arranged all things well and benevolently for mankind, have overlooked this alone, that some men, and very good men, and men who, as we may say, have had most communion with the divinity, and through pious acts and religious observances have been most intimate with the divinity, when they have once died should never exist again, but should be completely extinguished? (book xii. § 5.)

All the Gift of God.

And thou hast forgotten this too, that every man's intelligence is a god, and is an efflux of the deity; and forgotten this, that nothing is a man's own, but that his child and his body and his very soul came from the deity; forgotten this, that everything is opinion; and, lastly, thou hast forgotten that every man lives the present time only, and loses only this (book xii. § 26).

Thus, then, with respect to the gods, from what I constantly experience of their power, from this I comprehend that they exist, and I venerate them (book xii. § 28).

Eternity.

How small a part of the boundless and unfathomable time is assigned to every man, for it is very soon swallowed up in the eternal! And how small a part of the whole substance; and how small a part of the universal soul; and on what a small clod of the whole earth thou creepest! Reflecting on all this, consider nothing to be great, except to act as thy nature leads thee, and to endure that which the common nature brings (book xii. § 32).

Life a Drama.

"But I have not finished the five acts; only three of them." — "Thou sayest well: but in life the three acts are the whole drama; for what shall be a complete drama is determined by him who was once the cause of its composition, and now of its dissolution; but thou art the cause of neither. Leave the stage then satisfied, for he also who releases thee is satisfied" (book xii. 36).

After reading these and similar elevated expressions of Stoical thoughts, the question constantly comes up, Why was not this faith more controlling and more successful? Why was its influence confined to a few noble spirits, and why, even with the leaders of the faith, did it not save them from strange inconsistencies and errors?

One great defect of their system was continually felt by the more religious Stoics,— the want of a personal model for the virtues they inculcated. Seneca, as we have seen, laments this, as do others; and to all, pure Theism was somewhat bare and cold. Marcus Aurelius appeals to the life of Epictetus, and the latter recalls Socrates and his death. Seneca cites noble examples; but in all the history of Stoicism there were scarcely any examples faultless and inspiring, and the best — that of Epictetus — was presented near the close of the history of this system. There was no single life, or personality, except his, in the eight hundred years of the history of Stoicism, which could be considered even a partial revelation of the Divine Spirit. There was nothing about which the affection and veneration of the masses could cling.

The prevalence of pantheism at one period of its existence of course weakened its influence over the mind of the Greek and Roman peoples. Then there were certain great moral defects in the lives of its leaders which lessened its power. The defence and practice of suicide by some of the Stoics (though Epictetus is here an exception), the indifference of some to cruelty and slavery and sensuality, the excuses made by others for the exposition of children and unnatural crime,[1] and above all the severe and hard tone of some of its teachings, unfitted it for the more humane and mild habit of mind which was creeping over the Roman Empire. Its religion was not definite enough for the masses. It did not bring God sufficiently near to man. He was too much a distant Ruler, or a cold Fate, or a mere moral drift of the universe. Man in all ages craves an incarnation of Divinity, and relationship of affection, and close union through a human manifestation.

Stoicism formed great heroes and noble thinkers; it did not stimulate the sweet and gentle benefactors of every-day life. It was a grand protest against a world in which the honest man was almost ashamed to live. It did not create a new world of righteousness. It could not endure the City of the Emperor, and was not able to build an ideal City of God. The lack of profound faith in immortality prevented its being a message of hope and consolation to the sorrowing and oppressed. It is true some of its leaders, like Seneca, discourse as Christian saints might do of the blessed life beyond death; but these pictures were rather dreams of poetic rhetoricians than convictions of believers. The true Stoic went forth into the

---

[1] For instances of these errors see Diog. Laer., 33, 131; Sext. Pyrrh., iii. 201, i. 160; Plut., l. c., 21, 1.

great darkness trusting in the immortality of virtue, not of the individual soul. Except in one direction, which we have mentioned, Stoicism did not leave any profound influence on society. It is doubtful if the masses knew anything about it. The leaders themselves were often priggish, inconsistent, only superficially noble, and sometimes full of inflated pride. They were never in touch with common people. But on the Roman lawyers the Stoical theories and ideals had an abiding influence and power. They colored the whole system of Roman International Law, and through that have reached all modern States, and have affected political progress for eighteen centuries.

The Stoical principle of the Brotherhood of man prepared the way for the Christian idea of the Fatherhood of God and the fraternity of all races and classes. "For the Christ just coming, the way was thus made ready," said an early Christian apologist.[1] In fact, it is not improbable that the great Roman jurists felt in the moral atmosphere of the age, even as Seneca did, the Christian truths of the unity of all men, and their equality before one great Father, — truths which were circulating among the masses of the Roman Empire.

Saint Augustine admits that the reading a semi-Stoical work by Cicero first aroused his mind and turned

[1] Christo, jam tum venienti crede, parata via est (Prud. con. Symm., ii. 620).

him toward Christianity;[1] though he says, poetically, that it is one thing to see from some woody hill-top the country of peace, and quite another to keep the path leading thither.[2]

The world was ripe for a higher faith than Stoicism, which was soon to appear. Yet the moralist will ever be grateful for this great and heroic school of thought. It is something that there have been men who could look upon sickness and pain and sorrow, and death itself, as only passing ills to a soul resting in its harmony with the universe and the infinite Creator; who believed and acted on the conviction that the only real evil was baseness and selfishness, and all other misfortunes were but flitting shadows; who could say with life-long sincerity, —

> "For virtue alone, of human things,
> Takes her reward not from the hand of others, —
> Virtue herself rewards the toils of Virtue;"

some of whom regarded death as the middle point of a long life,[3] and others plunged into nothingness with unshaken peace because Zeus and Destiny willed it.

The Christian can only regard these souls with reverence, because they rose so much above human meanness, and were so steadfast with so little light to guide them.

---

[1] Surgere cœperam ut ad te redirem (Conf., iv. 4).

[2] Aliud est de silvestri cacumine videre patriam pacis . . . et aliud tenere viam illuc ducentem (Conf., vii. 21).

[3] Longæ vitæ . . . Mors media est (Lucan, i. 457).

All mankind are "debtors to the Greeks and Romans," in that they produced men who "knew how to die;" who looked upon death as nothing, compared with dishonor and wickedness; and who, under the tyranny of governments, and amid the universal corruption of society, could show what the human soul may be when sustained by God, and union with his universe.

It should in no way lessen our esteem for the power of Christianity that it naturally filled the gaps which Stoicism left in the popular mind of the Roman Empire, and did what that system could not do. It offered a perfect model for all succeeding ages, faultless and inspiring. It taught the brotherhood of man in fuller and broader measure than even Seneca or Epictetus ever dreamed of. It not only trained men to live, but taught them to die with glad trust. No Stoical sufferer ever faced death, not only with the courage, but with the joy and elation which made the Christians a proverb for their obstinacy and fearlessness. It undermined slavery, and broke up the cruel habits of the populace as Stoicism had never done. It reached the masses as this philosophy could not; and the great oppressed and suffering multitude of the world felt themselves in a new brotherhood of sympathy, and with new hopes and comforts. The rhetorical consolations of Seneca and the vague hopes of Aurelius became the assured faith and confidence of tens of thousands of common men and women. Like the belief of the best of the Stoics, this new morality and benevolence and hope rested on love for a common Father, unlike the Stoical Deity in his manifestation in the life and death of One called the "Son of God."

It was this last fact, especially, which has carried this religion on with increasing power to the present day, while Stoicism is now only a study for the curious and a field of investigation for the scholar.

CHAPTER XI.

REVIEW.

Follow you the star that lights a desert pathway, yours or mine,
Forward till you see the highest Human Nature is divine.

. . . .

Follow Light and do the Right, for man can half control his doom,
Till you find the deathless Angel seated in the vacant tomb.

TENNYSON.

AS we follow down in our thoughts the remarkable facts detailed in the preceding chapters, we see a continuous revelation of great truths granted to various races and peoples, and transmitted by them to their descendants. The idea of the Unknown God as the original uncreated Power of the Universe, the source of all life, and the centre of moral forces as well as material, is there. His everlasting power and divinity are seen through "the things that are made." He is not always "Father," but he is beneficent and just; and the hope of union with him and of likeness to him is the inspiration of the soul. This of course is not the primeval faith, but a growth from a conception of Heaven as god, and then of the Heaven-God. Far behind this come lower conceptions of a divine Being or beings. But throughout all ages and among peoples of a comparatively low state of progress were inspirations of an intelligent Power above and behind all things. Why such races grasped this sublime idea and were imbued and impelled by it cannot be explained. It did not come from their material progress or their intellectual advancement. The Hebrews, who showed this inspiration more than any other people, were far inferior to the Egyptians or the Greeks in civilization or intellectual power. Even another branch of the Semitic race, the Phœnicians, who were especially idolatrous and sensual, were in advance of the Jews in the arts and sciences. In fact, the latter tribe, while their leaders were acting under the highest inspirations of Jahveh, the Self-existent, were in an almost barbarous condition, as many archaic customs show. It would seem that certain tribes, like certain individuals, were peculiarly open to the higher religious ideas, and received them and lived on them in a manner not to be expected from their progress in other directions.

Besides the ideas of the unity and self-existence of God, we find the conception of this Being as an all-wise Power of Righteousness, and the source of all things good and beautiful; he had not left himself without a witness. The human mind, receiving the intuition of an intelligent Being at the head of the universe, conceives him as unlimited in all things, and especially as perfect in the highest human qualities. He becomes the essence of righteousness and purity, and the type of all-embracing sympathy. He is the highest impersonation of the love and justice of man;

he embodies the ideals of humanity. According to the moral ideal of Divinity in a given people will be the power and permanence of their faith. The full realizing of a perfect divinity, connected by bonds of sympathy with man, involves the duty of each person to conform to his will, and the hope of likeness to him. Then naturally follow from the goodness and justice of such a Being the belief in a future life to set right the inequalities of this, and the hope of happiness in more perfect union with and likeness to him. Hence come the ideas of a future existence, of a resurrection, of a judgment-day, and rewards and punishments in the future. These we have found passing down with more or less distinctness through the history of the different races we have briefly examined.

There come forth also among various races a hope and belief of a human manifestation of the divine, of one who has, though of the gods, taken on himself the form of man, borne sins and sorrows, and sought everywhere to remove the evils of humanity. Sometimes it is a tradition of one who is past, sometimes a hope of one who is to come. If he has been in the world, his life has been full of blessings to mankind. He has perhaps been removed by a violent death, and now in the unseen life watches over his followers and becomes their Judge and eternal Friend. Or if he is to come, he will remove the fear of death, and will do away with human suffering and sin. Whether these beliefs are premonitions of certain great facts to appear in the world's history, or whether they represent the necessary mode in which the mind of man embodies its hopes and moral beliefs, is difficult to decide. They form at least an important part of the religious beliefs of certain races.

The question here naturally arises, Why did these various intuitions and revelations among the races whose beliefs we have sketched, die out? Why has not the religion of the Egyptians or Babylonians or Greeks been enduring in the world's history? Why is it that the faith of a humble and despised tribe like the Hebrews still rules in its higher and later form the civilized world, while Osiris and Istar and Zeus remain only as portions of forgotten mythology or as the characters of immortal poems, and the faith which once embraced them is known only in ancient inscriptions?

It is impossible, of course, to answer such questions exactly. We know too little of the facts in each case. The Egyptian religion lasted longer than Christianity has yet endured. It no doubt fed the hopes and aspirations of countless human beings for several thousand years; but it ran doubtless into pantheism and then into polytheism and worship of animals, which unfitted it for human progress. Its great truths were too much esoteric and confined to a learned class to be able to reach the masses. The fact too that these truths were conveyed in difficult symbols not known to strangers would contract the range of such a faith. Moreover, the nation during the purest ages of this religion was under a powerful priesthood and an absolute monarchy. Both these human conditions would tend to corrupt divine inspirations. It is possible that the beautiful myth of Osiris had no historical foundation, or with some basis in fact was soon converted into a sun-myth. At all events, there was not sufficient reality in the story to feed mankind after ages had passed. The belief in Osiris lacked the simplicity, humility, and depth of Christianity. It did not contain the wonderful humanity and sympathy of the teachings of Galilee; it did not reveal God as a Father. All that we know certainly is that this ancient faith fell into the grossest polytheism and idolatry, and that its great truths passed down through other channels in human history and enriched mankind in far-away places and later ages.

We have seen how the Egyptian revelation probably affected the mind of Moses and a few of the Jews. Through the Mysteries and the ancient Greek faith it passed down to the Greeks and Romans. Plato and Socrates and Plutarch show traces of its influence. It can hardly be doubted that through the Alexandrians it colored the expressions and forms of thought of the Apostle John, and so has mingled with Christianity itself.

Akkadian Faith. — Of the Akkadian beliefs we know too little to affirm or deny anything positive in regard to them. The translation of the cuneiform is yet too uncertain, and the results too limited, to enable us to analyze with confidence these ancient faiths of the peoples on the Euphrates.

There are seemingly two distinct strata of population, — the ancient Akkadian races, and the Assyrian people of Semitic origin, who perhaps mingled with these tribes. The older peoples are filled with superstition and devoted to magical incantations and the worship of elemental powers. They and the Semitic Assyrians have evidently drawn many of their legends and beliefs from the same source as the Jews; but the tablets and cylinders which contain the cuneiform inscriptions, from which all our information is drawn in regard to both, have so mingled the two classes of language and the two stages of thought that it is impossible clearly to separate them. It is not improbable that the two mental conditions and the two modes of expression went on side by side for many ages. One may have been the learned and official language, and the other the popular. The multitudinous charms and incantations and beliefs in the evil powers of Nature may have expressed the religion of the lowest classes, while at the same time the lofty psalms and prayers and spiritual petitions may have arisen from the few devout and faithful.

The religious ideas commingle strangely. The penitential psalm ends in a magical incantation, and the superstitious invocation to elemental demons rises into adoration of the One Infinite Spirit. No doubt the future scholar, tracing the religious progress of Europe during the past fifteen hundred years, will find side by side the superstitions of heathendom and the elevated conceptions of Christianity. Such contradictory ideas seem capable of existing side by side in the popular mind during many centuries.

Wherever the Hebrews were, there must have been the grand ideas they contributed to human history. Their inspiration was a belief in a personal spiritual God of righteousness, who governed the world by the laws of truth, justice, and mercy. The chasm between this faith and the low, sensual mythology and polytheism of the tribes on the Euphrates was in many instances worldwide. It is true that numbers of the Jews wandered from this belief. Even the father of Abraham was an idolater. Yet ever in the line of descent appeared some new man or woman inspired with the grandest thought that can enter the human breast,— the belief in the One, infinite, all-knowing, all-loving. Abraham himself, one of the greatest figures on the stage of history, received this inspiration. He rose above the elemental worship of the Akkadians around him; he would not, with his Semitic brethren, "behold the sun when it shined, or the moon walking in brightness,"[1] and permit his "heart to be secretly enticed," and his "mouth to kiss his hand," for

[1] Job xxxi. 26-28.

that "were an iniquity to be punished," and he would have "denied the God that is above." All the pantheon of Assyrian gods were to him but as evil spirits, or subordinate powers under the infinite Jahveh. So he left kindred and country to hold forth? these ideas to the world.[1]

The Akkadian races seem to have been touched with the same inspirations which reached the Hebrews as to a righteous God, and sins against his will and law. The psalms we have quoted show the same profound feeling of spiritual purity and impurity, and the same sense of a God of rightness, as do the psalms of the Jews. They must have come from the same Semitic source. How this spiritual life faded away, we know not. Many of the races in that part of Asia fell early into sensuality and gross polytheism. Their religions seemed to contain little that was permanent and spiritual. Sensualism devoured them. Those races were visited by the angels of truth and purity (as these Akkadian psalms show), but they received them not.

It is probable that the belief in one God was not sufficiently distinct and powerful to penetrate deeply even the leaders of the Akkadian people. Their peculiar faith in certain gods did indeed reach the classic peoples. But their monotheism and deep spiritual intuitions probably alone survived in Abraham and his people, who were

[1] Acts vii. 3.

allied to the conquering nation of Babylonia. Yet with the "Father of the Faithful" there must have been individual inspirations and revelations which separated him from his superstitious kindred, and finally drove him out "beyond the river" to found the highest religion known to man.

One cause of the passing away of many ancient faiths, as contrasted with the endurance of the Jewish, we believe to be the inferiority of form of their sacred writings as compared with our sacred Scriptures. Many of the holy writings of the past, like the Egyptian, Chaldean, and others, were in a mysterious or learned language. It was one unknown to the masses, or only employed by scholars, or difficult for strangers to learn. Then the rhetorical form of nearly all these litanies and records and psalms is singularly defective. Even the Akkadian is mixed with an immense proportion of chaff. The Egyptian is equally faulty, and at times apparently compounded with rubbish. The Iranian or Zoroastrian religious literature (as we shall note), though unsurpassed in its elevated and pure religious tone, is immensely inferior to the Bible in its simple, poetic, vigorous style. The laws of the highest expression seemed to be unknown to these ancient races. And yet a half-nomadic, and later a very plain agricultural tribe, like the Hebrews, without learning or culture, is found uttering words which mankind cannot let die,— which, after three thousand years of advancing civilization, is still the highest and purest expression of its hopes and fears and moral aspirations. No doubt the spiritual inspiration of the Jews touched their faculties of imagination and expression, and the lofty truths with which they were imbued ennobled their language and simplified their thought.

No utterance of religious emotion has ever equalled that of the Psalms and of David!! No words of seer and popular teacher have ever been so grand and inspiring as those attributed to Isaiah. And dramatic poetry contains nothing more sublime, eloquent, and elevating than the ancient dialogues of the Book of Job.

It is no doubt difficult to make some of the psalms attributed to David harmonize with what the Bible relates of his life. Still, ancient popular traditions as to the authorship of poems and sacred songs are to be treated with great respect by the historical scholar. Moreover, in a wild, semi-barbarous tribe like the Jews there will always be found great inconsistencies in individual characters. The profound conviction of Jahveh as a God of righteousness, and an intense feeling of sin as an offence against him, might well be united with wild passions and barbarous bursts of anger and hate. The one influence might for a time overcome the other, and the poetic nature express each ruling feeling in appropriate language. Many of the moulds of expression in the psalms, whether of David or others, had been transmitted probably from the ancient Akkadians. They were the fitting words which the intense believers in Jahveh as a God of righteousness had in all ages of the Semitic race used in prayer and hymn.

Greek Mysteries. — These ancient secret associations, it is quite evident, taught some of the great truths which their members had received from Egyptian priests. There is clearly implied in the accounts we receive of their doctrines, the ancient belief of the priests on the Nile in an original and self-existent Creator, in a continued life after death, and a future moral judgment. But it is doubtful if these truths were held by any but the leaders of these societies, or if they ever influenced in any profound degree the masses of the members. Roman and Greek habits and practices were certainly very little affected by them. As we have before said, these truths were probably taught symbolically or dramatically, so that the ignorant and thoughtless did not grasp them, and they were not illustrated by any historical life or by any real or supposed divine manifestation. They were simply strange and grand beliefs taught to the multitude under mysterious forms and poetic symbols. The secret character, too, of these ante-Christian churches tended gradually to abuses, and they at last ended in orgies of lust and meetings for the most sensual indulgence. Even Plato finally could only speak of them with contempt.

The Greek Faith in Zeus. — It may not perhaps be distinctly enough remembered, amid the beautiful expressions we have culled from early Greek poets and dramatists and thinkers as to the spiritual Zeus, or God, that this faith went on side by side with a very different conception. A low mythology and high spiritual religion seem to be capable of coexisting in the human mind, as has been abundantly shown in the history of the Christian Church. The Zeus of the Pelasgians and early Greeks, of the Orphic Hymns and of Cleanthes, is no more different from the Zeus of Homer and Hesiod, than are the Christ and God of Paul and John from those of the legends of the Christian Church of the seventh century.

Under the influence of the myth-making fancy, the majestic figure of the spiritual Zeus sitting on the clouds of heaven changed into that of a dissolute and unresting ruler engaged in the most base transactions and sensual amours. Even by the same poet he is pictured as the cloud-compelling spirit of the air, and as the rake and petty tyrant of a celestial household. It was plainly the myth-making fancy which degraded the lofty ideals of ancient Greek faith. Perhaps there was nowhere in Greek annals so plain a historic manifestation of the Infinite Spirit as to control the wild imagination of the Greeks; or perhaps the sensual tendencies of the race overpowered the spiritual aspirations, and the transmitted inspirations of ancient thinkers and saints. Clearly, the Greek faith in Zeus could not elevate the race above its passions and selfishness, and so at last failed to promote its moral progress.

The Religion of Plato and Socrates. — The ideals of these great thinkers contained some of the grandest truths revealed to the human mind. There was certainly enough in them to inspire life and ennoble death. But they lacked a historical background; and though both Plato and Socrates used the ancient myths for moral lessons, it was with but a half belief in their reality. The current and popular mythology was repugnant to both. Socrates expressed the hope that somewhere, even among the barbarians, some one would arise who could charm away the fear of death from the soul of man, and so bring "immortality to light." It is of course possible that he had heard of the Jewish or Persian hopes of a Redeemer. He felt the need of such a divine manifestation. Plato, too, longed for a nearer revelation of God. Spiritually he had received the most profound conception of God; and philosophically he sustained these ideas by the most ingenious course of reasoning. Yet his God was far away, and did not enough control the selfishness of the soul. It was not sufficiently a God of love and sympathy. The consequence was, with these great thinkers, that their theories of human society, and to a certain degree their practice, was not in the highest direction of purity and unselfishness. There was a stain of sensuality in their most beautiful ideals.

The highest dreams of Plato of the Divine Beauty were united with theories of such unnatural human relations and such degrading fancies that they are utterly incomprehensible to the modern reader.[1] Compared with the purity of the Zoroastrian faith these ideas seem, at one point of view, sensuality itself. But in all these matters custom and habit have a singular and almost absolute power on the human mind.

The God of Socrates and Plato was too cold and stern to be the God of the multitude; and their morals lacked the highest elements, — even unselfish love and childlike purity. Their noble views and elevated philosophy entered into the Christian history, and deeply affected mankind through prominent Christian thinkers; but as a separate system of faith and practice it has ceased profoundly to influence human progress.

We have sufficiently shown why the sublime faith of the Stoics, though continuing for some eight hundred years, at last failed to satisfy the human mind. The truths on which they lived are still the support of pious souls in hours of pain and despondence. Even now, the devout Christian in his utmost trial has no philosophical truth more comforting and strengthening than that the structure of the moral universe makes for righteousness; that to be in harmony with it and the Divine mind which inspires it

[1] See the Symposium.

is his highest attainment; that the most complete health and sanity of the soul is in truth and disinterested love; and that the Maker and Contriver of such a universe must be of like nature. But in addition to these philosophic truths is granted to the Christian a revelation of the Divine Being which forever strengthens him in his efforts "to live in harmony with the universe and its Creator," and should save him from the errors and follies of the Stoics.

CHAPTER XII.

ZOROASTRIANISM.

What reward thou hast given to those of the same law as thyself, O Lord, All-knowing, that give thou to us! May we attain to that; namely, union with thy purity for all eternity! — ZEND-AVESTA, Yaçna xi.

THE early Iranian, the forefather of the Mede and the Persian, looked at the problems of the universe from a point of view somewhat different from anything among early peoples we have thus far contemplated. He saw clearly the two sides of the world: the bright morning, the cheerful sun and the light, and, on the other hand, the clouds, gloomy mist, storm, and dark night which swallowed these up; the green meadows, bright flowers, rose-tinged mountains, rich leafy valleys and groves and fields, and, on the other side, the waste swamp, the desert, the stern crag and desolate rock, and dark, storm-beaten heights. He felt the genial rays of the sun, and the biting, resistless frost. He noted the graceful and useful animals of creation, the birds, the kine, the deer, the horse, and the beaver, and, on the other hand, the serpents, the parasites, poisonous insects, vermin, hideous crawling creatures, and wild, savage beasts of nature. He found many existences, as it were, half formed and imperfectly planned, whose lives seemed only made for misery. Ravin and relentless struggle seemed to him the law of nature beneath man. In the world of humanity he found sweetness and unselfishness, and love and truth and heroism, on one side, and again on the other, greed and selfishness, and hate and deceit and baseness. Health and sickness were offset to one another everywhere, plenty and poverty, happiness and misery, cheerfulness and sorrow. And the greatest contrast of all checkered the universe with alternate bands of gleaming light and the blackest night, — the profound and tremendous facts of holiness and sin, of moral good and moral evil, of pure beings and malignant beings; and beyond this life he believed the like contrast to endure while time should last, — of Paradise and Hell.

The ancient Iranian believed in the Ahura Mazda, or Ormazd, the "Lord All-knowing." He was the creator of *asha*,[1] or righteousness, and he could not create evil. He was the pure one, and could not make impurity; he loved beauty and order and happiness. It was not in him to create things ugly and hateful, and disordered and malignant. He was Mazda, the spirit of all knowledge, and could not call into being creatures that were half-formed, and useless in their end and object; he was the essence of *asha*, or righteousness, and could not, of necessity,

---

[1] Asha. — purity, moral order, the universe of righteousness (Darmesteter).

make sin or sinful beings. He, as the Healer,[1] Protector, Lover of all, did not create sickness and sorrow and pain. The Lord of Life could not bring death into the world; and the Best Spirit of all could not be the Father of the wicked spirits. The Heaven-God, dwelling resplendent in infinite luminous space, could not bring forth Hell, the place of darkness and the shadow of death.

The ancient Iranian, reasoning thus, struck upon the conception, rare in the annals of human thought, but most natural, of two contending Powers in the universe. But as day precedes the night, or the clear sky the storm, so the Good Power was before the Evil Power, and would be after him. The two principles, Ahura Mazda, or Ormazd, and Angra Mainyou, or Ahriman, or Satan, contend for the universe. All nature and eternity divide themselves between these two masters. To the Good belong light and beauty, all trees and flowers and growths that are sweet and useful, all animals beloved of man, all health and harmony, all purity and order and virtue, all things that make for peace and goodness, all the glory and happiness of the world. To him, the flowing waters and fleecy clouds and cheerful sunlight and rich harvests. To Ormazd also the stars (as opposed to the uncertain and malignant planets), the sun, the spirits of the just and pure, the gods of virtue and piety, and eternal life in the regions of the blessed.

[1] See different Yashts.

To Ahriman, or Satan, belong the night and darkness, the frost and storm, hail and snow, the desert and marsh, the poisonous creatures, vermin, noxious serpents and insects, the wild beasts of the desert. His are the plague and sickness,[1] want and poverty, wounds and deformities, wasting and death among men. Dear to him are lies and lusts and sins; his are calumnies and slander and doubt. He controls all the *devas*, or demons, of pestilence and deceit and passion and crime that afflict humanity. His are the hostile planets, and the awful abode of darkness and woe beyond life. The power of Ahriman is especially in the lie; his *Drugs* are spirits of deceit, while of Ormazd it is said, " He is Truth."[2] Yima, the fallen spirit who sometimes seems the original Ahriman, falls through a lie, and " his glory [the truth] was seen leaving him in the likeness of a beautiful bird."[3]

It is true that the division of nature between the two Powers is somewhat confused by the influences of mythology, so that the most sacred animal to Ormazd, whose death brings immeasurable punishments on the murderer, is a water-dog, or beaver, while two creatures given to Ahriman are the innocent frog and the industrious ant. But, in general, the separations are according to the relations of each part to light and darkness, purity and

---

[1] The 99.999 diseases, say the sacred writings, which afflict humanity, are from Ahriman, and the deformed are, even as the vicious, excluded from the holy sacrifices.

[2] Yasht.   [3] Yasht.

impurity, good and evil. The contrast between these two mighty spirits goes on through all space and time.

Ahura Mazda has created good, or righteousness, and all beings who maintain and develop righteousness. On the other hand, Ahriman has made all those who would destroy the works of righteousness. The final end of the life of the world is to bring about the expulsion of evil, and the eternal reign of life and good.[1] The man who aids this is the man of righteousness; he who opposes it is a demon, or enemy of righteousness. If the good man is a priest, his weapon is prayer; if a warrior, he draws his sword against the infidels alone; if a laborer, his great weapon is the plentiful harvest. Whoever cultivates grain, cultivates the law of the Lord Omniscient, and enriches it with what is equal to a hundred sacrifices. The demons shriek when good crops spring from the ground, for they know that men cannot practise piety without food. The pious man is he who gives clothing to the naked, and who founds virtuous families. To increase the world of righteousness is the supreme end of human life.

The good man is called the "increaser;" and the final Saviour of the world, who shall make eternal the life and reign of good, is especially the Increaser.[2]

The great inspiration of Mazdæism for the world is its exaltation of truth. Humanity is not inculcated towards

[1] Darmesteter: Ormazd and Ahriman.   [2] Coshyos.

the infidel; but even to the infidel truth must ever be observed, for Ahura Mazda is the Light, and light is Truth. By truth man resembles the Lord All-knowing; the lie is demoniac, even when uttered for a good end. "The man of truth shall be more resplendent than the sun; the man of a lie goeth straightway to the Demon whence he cometh." Ahriman is the god of lies, and is manifested as a serpent, the creature of deceit, whom on the "day of immortality" the Saviour is to destroy.

Ormazd being Truth itself is never deceived; he seeth all things; he observeth without dream, without intoxication.[1] He cannot be deceived, is infallible. He is like unto the light in his body and the truth in his soul.

The Iranian felt himself in an inexorable logical dilemma in regard to this pure and perfect Being. If he was perfectly good he could not originate evil; if he was all-powerful he could not permit its existence. The conclusion which the old Persian reached was that the power of Ormazd was limited. Accordingly in the Avesta there are appeals from the Lord Omniscient to powerful (*fravashi*) spirits,[2] on whose aid he depends in the work of creation and administration. At times he seems but one of the seven Blessed Immortals (*Amesha spentas*) who govern the universe. He was in boundless time before Ahriman, and he continues after the disappearance of the Evil Spirit; but according to certain traditions the

[1] Vend., xix. 68.   [2] See Yaçna xliii., and others.

struggle between them is long, and various in success, there being first a period when Ahriman is conquered, then an age of evil when the light of Ormazd is obscured, and then an age of final victory for the truth.

As with so many races, the original conception of the Iranian God was of a Heaven-God, a Zeus, a Father in Heaven, a Being glorious, bright, pure, seen from afar, his body like unto light itself, the purest of all bodies; the sun his eye, the lightning his creation, who weareth the heavens as a star-decked garment, and who dwelleth in the boundless light-space.[1] Even in the time of Herodotus the Persians called the whole vault of heaven Zeus, or the Supreme God. Gradually the unity of this Being formed itself in the minds of the ancient Iranians, and was settled in the fifth century before Christ. No doubt Herodotus heard from the ancient Magi the same prayers and liturgies sung as those we shall quote from, and as the Medes and Persians had heard for ages before in old Persian, and had preserved in their Zend-Avesta, or "Commentary on the Law."[2] At that period the Ahura Mazda, or Lord All-knowing, had become the father and creator of the world and of light, the giver of life and father of gods, and of the tree of eternal life, and of the

---

[1] Vend., v. 59.

[2] Zend-Avesta, p. 30, Darmesteter. *Zend* is Commentary; *Avesta* (âbastâ, old Persian), Law. The texts were written originally in Media, and were promulgated circ. 325-330 A.D.

six undying holy spirits, who seem then only abstract conceptions of good qualities.

The inscriptions of Darius (circ. 521 B.C.) show a faith in a moral Governor and Creator. "Let man," says one, "go on according to the doctrine of the Lord Omniscient. He is thy deliverer. Leave not the straight way; sin not; keep thyself from violence."[1] It is he (Ormazd) who hath made this earth and heaven and all men; gods are created by him.[2] Man is in his hand; to his will kings owe their crown. It is he who hath made Darius and Xerxes. Ormazd brings me succor; by the grace of Ahura Mazda (Ormazd) I conquer.[3]

The final conclusion of the struggle between the two spirits is thus given in the Gathas, or Psalms of the Avesta: —

"When at the end, *asha* [righteousness] shall have cast down Satan [Drug]; when in the day of immortality shall have been made that final separation between mortals and demons which hath been lyingly denied by infidels, then will mount upwards towards thee a mighty hymn of praise and adoration, O Lord!"[4]

The teachings of truth and honesty in the Zoroastrian faith, and based upon religion, left a profound impression upon the Persian character, as all ancient historians agree. The follower of Zoroaster was pre-eminent for truthfulness.

[1] Duncker: Ges. d. Alter., ii. 344.
[2] Ins. of Elvend. Darmesteter.
[3] Persian Inscription. Darmesteter. Ormazd is the Parsee form of the name, as is also Ahriman of that of the Evil Spirit.
[4] Yasht 47, 1.

And without doubt the Mazdean conception of purity, or righteousness, as the moral foundation of the universe, and the essence of God himself, did leave a permanent stamp upon the world. It seems one of the divine inspirations. The doctrines of Satan, the adversary of the Highest, and of demons, of bodily resurrection with a final judgment of souls, in all probability entered the Jewish mind from these sources, and meeting similar beliefs, were incorporated with them in the Jewish history. They may all rest on divine inspirations, partially understood, which were granted to many races; or they may be the necessary modes of view which the human mind takes of great moral truths, and logical inferences from these views. They seem some of the most remarkable mental inheritances of the race.

The conception of a duality of powers in the world is a most natural one, and has very powerful supports in the apparent structure of the universe. Still, it could not satisfy the heart or intellect of mankind, and soon ended in gross superstitions. At the very time of the highest bloom of the Mazdean dogma the Jews held firmly to the belief in a God who had created all things and all beings, who had no equal, and no adversary other than he permitted.

The same difference in form is found between the sacred writings of the Jews and of the Persians which we have noted between the Jews and the Chaldees, and which no doubt has affected their power upon different generations of men. The Iranian revelations are filled with crudities and repetitions, and only occasionally convey truths with that simplicity and directness which cause them never to be forgotten. The sublime poetry of the Hebrew writings seems absent from those of the ancient Persians, though the moral conception is often quite as high. The Avesta reads like a collection of childish sayings about themes too grand for the writers; and even so beautiful an allegory as that of the maiden representing conscience in a future life (which we give later) is marred by infantile repetitions. The soul of the Hebrew seems to have been more open to divine inspirations, and thus his intellect reported them with more perfect simplicity and in a higher ideal form. The form in which human thought is conveyed certainly has much to do with the permanence of its influence.

Moreover, anything approaching the idea of two gods in the universe leads immediately to gross superstitions and a wild mythology. The unity and grandeur of a pure religion are lost. The ideal object of the soul's worship passes away. No doubt the teachings in regard to purity and truth in this faith left an impress on the Iranian race which lasted long; but the religion as a power died at length completely away, and only holds sway now over a few thousands of human beings.[1]

[1] The Parsees in India.

The Sacred Zoroastrian Teachings.

Charity. — "The law of the Lord will not deliver thee unto pain. Thou art entreated for charity by the whole living world, and she is ever standing at thy door in the person of thy brethren in the faith; beggars ever stand at the door of the stranger begging for bread. Ever will that bread [refused] be burning coals on thy head."[1]

"He, O Zoroaster, who tilling the earth would not piously and kindly give to one of the faithful, he shall fall down into the darkness of the Earth-Spirit, down into the world of woe, the dismal realm, down into the house of hell."[2]

Conscience after Death. — "At the end of the third night [after death], when the dawn appeareth, it seemeth to the soul of the faithful one as if it were conveyed amid plants and scents; it seemeth as if a wind were blowing from the regions of the south, a sweet-scented wind, sweeter scented than any other wind in the world. . . . Now it seemeth to him as if there were advancing towards him in that wind the form of a maiden, fair, bright, white-armed, strong, tall-formed, high-standing, noble, of a glorious race, as fair as the fairest things in the world. And as the soul of the faithful one spake unto her, saying, 'What maiden art thou, who art the fairest maid I have ever looked upon?' she answered him, 'O thou youth of good thoughts, good words, works, and religion, I am thine own conscience! Every one did love thee for that greatness, goodness, fairness, sweetness, victorious strength, and freedom from sorrow in which I appear to thee. When thou sawest a man making derision [of holy things], and doing works of idolatry, or rejecting the poor, and shutting the door to the poor, then thou didst sit, singing psalms and worshipping the son of the Lord, and with alms rejoicing the faithful from near and from far. I was lovely and thou madest me still more lovely. I was

---

[1] Vistasp. Yasht: Darmesteter, p. 338.
[2] Vend. Farg., iii. 15.

fair and thou madest me still more desirable . . . through that good speech, thought, and deed of thine. And so henceforth men worship me for having long had converse with the Lord Omniscient. . . . The first step that the soul of the faithful man made did place him in the Paradise of Good Thoughts; the second in the Paradise of Good Words; the third in the Paradise of Good Deeds; and the fourth in the Paradise of Endless Light.' . . .

"One of the faithful ones who had departed before him asked him, 'How didst thou depart this life, thou holy one . . . from the decaying world into the undecaying one? How long did thy felicity last?' And the Lord All-knowing said; 'Ask him not what thou askest him, who hath just trod the dreary path, full of fear and distress, where the body and soul part from one another. Let him eat of the food set before him, of the cream of the spring. This is the food for the youth of good thoughts, words, and deeds after he hath departed life.'"[1]

A corresponding picture is presented of the wicked meeting his bad conscience in the future life.

The Creator. — Zoroaster asks of Ahura Mazda :[2] "Who is the Father of the universe? Who hath made their path for the sun and the stars? Who causeth the moon to wax and wane? Who hath founded the earth, and the stars not floating [fixed]? Who hath given their course to the winds and clouds? Who, O wise one, is the creator of good thoughts? What skilful designer hath made the light and darkness; who the dream and the awakening? By whom go forth the morning, the noon, and the night? . . . These are what I ask of thee, Lord Omniscient, Creator of all things."

"O thou who maintainest forever the Law of Asha [righteousness] and the good thoughts, thou Lord All-knowing, teach me of

---

[1] Yasht xxii. [2] Yaçna xliii.

thy intelligence and thy lips, that I may say it in thy name, how the world begins!"[1]

Union with God. — "What reward thou hast given to those of the same law as thyself, O Lord Omniscient, that give also to us for this world and the next. May we attain to that; namely, union with thy purity for all eternity.[2] Let the pure men, O Lord, who desire after purity, warriors as well as husbandmen, be long rejoiced! . . . So may relationship, worship, and friendship be! That we may lift up ourselves to be thine, O Lord All-knowing, as pure and truthful, with sacrifice and offering."[3]

God. — "The garment which the Lord putteth on is like unto a robe inlaid with stars of a heavenly substance. . . . By me the earth liveth, which beareth material beings; by me the sun, moon, and stars; it is I who have organized the seed; it is I who have traced their veins in every kind of plants; I who have breathed into plants and other beings a fire which does not consume them; I who have created the new-born. . . . I who have given to the waters feet to run; I who have made the clouds that bear water to the world, and make fall the rain where it pleaseth."[4]

The Saviour. — The Avesta speaks darkly of one born of Zoroaster who shall crush the serpent, destroy Ahriman, and bring back the eternal reign of good, of life and light.[5] He shall be called Coshyos, or the Increaser, while the Evil Spirit ever contracts and narrows all things. He shall "reanimate the world, free it from old age and death, from corruption and pollution, and shall make it eternally living, eternally increasing, master of itself; then shall

---

[1] Yasht xxv. 11.
[2] Yaçna xi; Spiegel: Zend-Avesta, p. 99.
[3] Spiegel: Zend-Avesta, p. 99. [4] Yasht xiii. 2, 3.
[5] Yasht xix., lxxxix.

the dead rise again, immortality shall come, and the world receive its life through its prayers, — the world which through the law of purity shall be saved from death, — and Satan (Drug) shall disappear."

Prayer. — "Teach thou me, Lord Omniscient, from out thyself; from heaven through thy word, whereby the world first arose." [1]

To the Sun. — " He who offereth up a sacrifice unto the undying, shining, swift-horsed Sun to withstand darkness, to withstand the demons born of darkness, to withstand robbers and bandits, and Death that creepeth in unseen, offereth it to the Lord Omniscient." [2]

To a Star. — " We sacrifice unto the bright and glorious star that washeth away all things of fear, whom the Lord Omniscient hath established as the Lord and overseer of all stars, in the same day as he hath established Zoroaster among men, whom neither Satan nor demons nor sorcerers can deliver unto death, nor all the demons together prevail unto his ruin." [3]

" He who reciteth the ashem-vohû (the praise of holiness) in the fulness of faith, with a devoted heart, praiseth me, the Lord Omniscient; he praiseth the waters, the earth, the cattle, the plants; he praiseth all good things made by the Lord. . . . For the recital of that word of truth, O Zoroaster, increaseth strength and victory in one's soul, and piety." [4]

Zoroaster asked of the All-knowing, "What is the one recital of the praise of holiness that is worth all that is between the earth and the heavens, and this earth and that luminous space, and all the good things made by Mazda, that are the offspring of the good principle in greatness, goodness, and fairness?" And he answered, "It is that

[1] Yaçna xxviii.
[2] Korsh. Yasht, p. 86.
[3] Tir Yasht, p. 105.
[4] Yasht, Farg., p. 311.

one, O holy Zoroaster, that a man uttereth when he would renounce evil thoughts, evil words, and evil deeds."[1]

Purity. — "Thus, O holy Zoroaster, does the law of the Lord take away all the evil thoughts, words, and deeds of a pure man, even as the strong, swift wind clears the sky."[2]

"Grant that the pure may rule, the impure not rule! May the pure rule as they will, may the godless not rule as they will. I, who am Zoroaster, bless the wide extent and brightness of the whole creation of purity."[3]

"Purity is for man next to life the greatest good, — that purity gained by the law of the Lord, to him who cleanseth his own self with good thoughts, words, and works."[4]

"Who," asked Zoroaster of the Lord Omniscient, "who grieveth thee with the sorest grief, who paineth thee with the sorest pain?" The Lord answered: "It is Gapi [incarnation of female lust], O Zoroaster, who seeketh out the faithful and unfaithful, the worshippers of the Lord and those of Satan, the wicked and the righteous. Her look dryeth up a large part of the mighty floods that run from the mountains; her look withereth most of the growing plants and the grass wherewith the earth is clad; and her touch destroyeth in the faithful the most of his good thoughts, words, and works, — his strength, his fiend-killing power, his holiness. Verily I say unto thee, O Zoroaster, such creatures ought to be killed more than gliding snakes, howling wolves, or the wild she-wolf that falleth upon the fold."[5]

---

[1] Spiegel: Zend-Avesta, p. 313.
[2] Farg., III.
[3] Spiegel, p. 50.
[4] Farg., v. 21.
[5] Ibid., xviii.

"He who knoweth purity, knoweth the Lord; to such he is father, brother, friend."[1]

Zoroaster. — The great prophet of the Iranians is represented in the Avesta as the first of the Faithful, and the vanquisher of Satan by the mystic arm of prayer and worship.[2] He alone of men was born smiling; prodigies were related of his infancy, and he was fed by mountain sheep.[3] His personality is shrouded in mystery. When he lived, or where he was born, is uncertain, and many have doubted his existence. He apparently labored in the region of Bactria, and previous to the fourteenth century before Christ. The legends relate that when he appeared on the earth all Nature trembled with joy; the trees moved their leaves, and rivers rose in cheerful waves. The grotto where his infancy was passed was frequently lighted with fire from heaven.[4] His teachings are mainly given in supposed conversations with Ahura Mazda, or the Lord Omniscient, which have been handed down from immemorial time.

It is certainly remarkable that the purest religion of antiquity (excepting the Jewish) should have almost perished from the earth.

[1] Yaçna xliv.
[2] Yasht 13.
[3] Yasht 8, 29.
[4] Avesta, Harlez, 1875.

CHAPTER XIII.

HINDUISM.

Even those who worship idols,
Worship me, the God.
BHAGAVAD-GÎTA.

Let us meditate on the excellent glory of the divine Life-Giver; may He enlighten our understanding.
Prayer, from Rig Veda, most used in India.

THE ancient Hindu, as he sought to penetrate the mysteries of the universe, followed a path similar to that of most ancient races. He felt with reverence the august powers of Nature around him, and worshipped them. The storm, the thunder, the light, and the heavenly canopy were his gods. In time these became intelligent beings to him, and later the manifestations of the One Infinite Being. The grand inspiration telling of the One Boundless Existence, the Source and Cause of all, early visited the Hindu mind; but it was accompanied with peculiarities of belief and sentiment which have diminished its spiritual power in the world. The Hindu intellect was weighed down by the problems of existence. Questions which the European mind holds as incapable of being settled, and leaves in the limbo of insoluble propositions, the Oriental attempted to solve. The mysterious facts of suffering and inherited sin and evil he referred back to former and unknown conditions of existence. The wrong and pain of the present life were the fruit of a past life, and would be the seed of a future. Birth and ever-recurring re-birth were the stupendous evils of existence, and would be for all coming æons.

Then, to the Oriental, personality is not what it is to the Western mind. Under the tremendous forces and appearances of Nature in his climate the individual sinks away to nothingness. The grand and almost unnamable Power behind phenomena becomes everything. The man springs from him, the soul lives in him, and is to be absorbed at last in his nature. The happiness of eternity is to sink away in that fathomless sea of Love, and to know self no more. Absorption in Deity and freedom from re-birth is to the Hindu everlasting life. More than this, as all things exist in God, he is all, and nothing really lives but God. Man, the universe, moral good and evil, are only parts of that infinite existence.

The result of all this is a confusion of belief and feeling in the Hindu mind which has left most disastrous effects on its history. There is first the worship of deified nature-powers, sometimes as separate gods and sometimes as God, as expressed in the Vedic hymns from the fifteenth to the tenth century before Christ.

Then there is the spiritual pantheism of Brahmanism, wherein all the forces of Nature are included in one Being or Spirit. Then come all sorts of degenerate practices and beliefs derived from these previous faiths, or no-faiths. There is monotheism at one time, at another polytheism, at still another pantheism, wherein all creation is animated by One Spirit, and personal responsibility is gone, and this Spirit (Brahma) without personality or individuality. The questions of Brahmanism, says Williams, are, How to break the chain of repeated births; how to shake off personality; how to live with God in the same sphere, near God and like God.[1]

There is continually in the Vedas a craving, or feeling, for One God. It is sometimes said, "There is one God under many names."[2] "Cut is the knot of man's heart," says an ancient poem, "solaced are all his doubts, ended are all his works, when he has beheld the Supreme Being."

These ancient hymns often teach an omnipresent and omniscient Cause of all existence, the Creator of the universe. He is sole, secondless, without parts, entire, eternal, infinite, unchanging, the Soul of all things, who is Truth, Wisdom, Intelligence, Blessedness itself. Souls emanate from him as sparks from the fire; they proceed from him and return to him. The human soul, ruling the body, is not born, and does not die; it is a portion of the divine substance, and as such immortal and blessed. It suffers from its organs; but divested of them and returned

---

[1] Williams: History of Religious Thought in India.
[2] Rig Veda, i. 164, 86; viii. 58, 2.

to the Supreme, it is at rest and happy. It is not free and independent, but it is made to act by the Supreme in one life as it prepared to act in a former; thus it is punished here for deeds in a previous existence. But Brahma, in the Hindu theology, is not the author of evil.[1] The soul subject to future transmigrations visits other worlds to receive recompense for its works or suffer penalty for misdeeds. Sinners fall to various regions of punishment.[2] The good, liberated from the body and the world, ascend to the court of Brahma, or, if perfect, reunite with the Divine Essence. Different degrees of deliverance are obtained by sacrifice, or by religious exercises and meditations on God; but the highest is only won by perfect knowledge of God. The Rig Veda[3] often speaks of him as all-seeing, as Father, Generator, Disposer, who knoweth all worlds and giveth all the gods their names, and beyond all comparison of mortals.

Hymn.[4]

What god shall we adore with sacrifice?
Him let us praise, the golden child that rose
In the beginning, who was born the Lord, —
The one sole lord of all that is, — who made
The earth, and formed the sky, who giveth life,
Who giveth strength, whose bidding gods revere;
Whose hiding-place is immortality,
Whose shadow, death; who by his might is king
Of all the breathing, sleeping, waking world;

---

[1] Williams.   [2] Ibid.   [3] Rig Veda, 81, 82.
[4] I Mandala, Rig Veda, Ind. Wisd., p. 23.   Williams's translation.

Who governs men and beasts; whose majesty
These snowy hills, this ocean with its rivers
Declare; of whom these spreading regions form
The arms; by whom the firmament is strong,
Earth firmly planted, and the highest heavens
Supported, and the clouds that fill the air
Distributed and measured out; to whom
Both earth and heaven, established by his will,
Look up with trembling mind; in whom revealed
The rising sun shines forth above the world.
Where'er, let loose in space, the mighty waters
Have gone, depositing a fruitful seed
And generating fire, there he arose,
Who is the breath and life of all the gods,
Whose mighty glance looks round the vast expanse
Of watery vapor, — source of energy,
Cause of the sacrifice, the only God
Above the gods. May he not injure us, —
He, the creator of the earth, the righteous
Creator of the sky, creator too
Of oceans bright and far-extending waters!

Vedic Morals. — The ancient Vedic religion contained a deep sense of sin. The worshipper often grieves over his simplicity and ignorance, and prays the god to replace his weakness by divine knowledge. Sin is to him like the non-payment of a debt to the upper powers. A divine pity is conceived by the singer, and the sinner is imagined as a bird on its nest, imploring pardon for its offspring, and wishing in its fright to dash itself against the bosom of its God.[1] "If we have committed a fault, men as we are."[2]

[1] Rig Veda, ii. 29-5-6. [2] Ibid., iv. 12.

"It was not my will; the gods judge by the intention." "Thou dost not enjoy the sacrifice of the untrue, even when he is at thy gate."[1] Penitence is expressed even for the sin of gambling. Compassion holds the highest place among virtues. "He who giveth alms goeth to the highest heaven, goeth to the gods."

There came a period in Hindu thought when the longing for absorption in the Infinite One was not to be at rest from the storms of life in the bosom of infinite peace, or to be free from its pollution in the union with perfect purity, but rather to exist in utter inaction with a Being who is motionless and purposeless. The true worshipper does not seek to follow his will in the tangled web of human life, but with him to be free from all emotion and action, to escape desire and change, and pain and sin and re-birth. He seeks not his own happiness in the happiness of others, but utter peace in an eternal calm which no storm shall ever break. The purpose, to a certain extent, is selfish, and yet not entirely so; for it is a dream of a calm where the individual is in harmony with all others, and with Brahma; but the Infinite Spirit himself is peaceful in a boundless indifference, and the worshipper aims to be like him. Still, this state of feeling and these ideals will often be mingled with the purest and loftiest aspirations of self-devoting religion, — with conceptions of a God who lives in eternal beneficence, and with desires to sacrifice

[1] Rig Veda, viii. 11.

all here and hereafter for human happiness. About such a confused matter as Hindu religion one must not dogmatize too severely.

VARUNA.

The oldest picture of the Unknown God is as Varuna, or οὐρανός (Heaven). This ancient god is represented in the Hindu hymns as having meted out and fashioned and upheld heaven and earth; he dwells in all worlds as sovereign ruler; he made the golden and revolving sun to shine in the firmament; the wind is his breath; he has opened boundless paths for the sun, and has hollowed out channels for rivers, which flow by his command, pouring their waters into the ocean and never filling it. His laws are fixed and unassailable. They rest upon him unshaken, as upon a mountain. Through his laws the moon walketh in darkness, and the stars in the night-sky vanish at dawn. Neither birds flying in air nor flowing rivers can attain knowledge of his power or wrath; his angels behold both worlds; he knoweth the flight of birds in the sky, the path of ships on the ocean, the course of the far-travelling wind, and beholdeth all secret things that have been or shall be done. No creature can even wink without him; he witnesseth men's truths and falsehoods; he instructeth the saints (Rishi) in mysteries. But his secrets are not to be revealed to the foolish.[1] It is noteworthy that he is

---

[1] Muir's Sanskrit Text, v. 62, 63.

especially the God of righteousness, to whom the conscience of the sinner appeals.

Hymn to Varuna.

1. We break thy laws from day to day, men that we are, O Varuna.
2. Do not deliver us unto death, nor to the blow of the furious, nor to the anger of the spiteful.
3. To profit thee, O Varuna, we bind thy spirit with songs, as the charioteer the weary steed. . . .
7. He, Varuna, who knoweth the place of the birds that fly through the sky, who on the waters knoweth the ships . . .
8. He the upholder of order . . .
9. He who knoweth the track of the wind, the wide, the bright, the mighty, and knoweth those who dwell on high . . .
10. He, the wise, sitteth there to govern.
11. From thence perceiving all wondrous things, he seeth what hath been and what will be done. . . .
16. Fearing him, the far-seeing, my thoughts move onward like kine to their pastures.
19. Oh, hear this my prayer, Varuna. Be gracious now ! Longing for help, I have called upon thee.
20. Thou, O wise god, art Lord of all heaven and earth ; listen on thy way.[1]

Another Hymn.

1. Let me not, O King Varuna, go to the house of earth. Be gracious, O mighty God, be gracious !
2. I go along, O Thunderer, quivering like an inflated skin. Be gracious !
3. O bright and mighty God, I have transgressed through want of power. Be gracious !
4. Thirst hath overtaken the worshipper when standing in the midst of waters. Be gracious !

[1] Müller: Hist. Sanskrit Lit., p. 535.

5. Whatever offence this be that we mortals commit against the people of the sky, in whatever way we have broken thy law by thoughtlessness, be gracious, O mighty God, be gracious! I have gone, O self-sustaining Varuna, to thy vast and spacious house with a thousand gates.

6. He who was thy friend, thy intimate, thy best beloved, hath committed offences against thee. Let not us who are guilty reap the offence of our sin! Do thou, O wise God, grant protection to him who prayeth to thee![1]

Varuna — "The great one who ruleth over these worlds beholdeth as if he were close at hand. When one thinketh he is doing aught by stealth, the gods know it all. They perceive every one who walks, or glides along secretly, or withdraws into his house. Whatever two persons sitting together devise, Varuna the king, a third, knoweth it. This earth belongeth to Varuna, and that vast sky. He who should flee far from beyond the sky would not there escape from Varuna the king. His angels descending from heaven traverse this world. The thousand-eyed Varuna looketh across the whole earth. The winking of men's eyes are all numbered by him. He handleth all these as a gamester throweth his dice."[2]

He can cure every sickness, and drive away evil and sin; he is entreated to spare suppliants who daily transgress his law, and is gracious even to him who hath committed sin. He is the wise guardian of immortality, and the hope is held out that he, reigning in blessedness, shall be beheld in the next world by the righteous.[3]

Another Psalm to Varuna.

1. Wise and mighty are the works of him who burst asunder the wide firmament! He lifted on high the bright and glorious heaven; he stretched out apart the starry sky and the earth.

---

[1] Rig Veda, vii. 88, 89. [2] Athar. Veda, xvi. 4.
[3] Muir: Sanskrit Text, p. 165.

2. Do I say this in my own soul, How can I get under Varuna? Will he accept my offering without displeasure? When shall I with a quiet mind see him propitiated?

3. I ask, O Varuna, wishing to know this my sin. I go to ask the wise, the sages; all tell me the same. Varuna it is who is angry with me.

4. Was it an old sin, O Varuna, for which thou wishest to destroy thy friend, who always praiseth thee? Tell me, O Lord, and I will quickly turn to thee with praise, free from sin.

5. Absolve us from the sins of our fathers, and from those which we have committed with our own bodies.

6. It was not our own doing,[1] O Varuna; it was necessity, an intoxicating draught, passion, vice, thoughtlessness. The old is never to mislead the young; even sleep bringeth sin. . . .

7. Protect us, O gods, with your blessing.

"What injustice we have done to bosom friend,
  To loving comrade, to brother,
  In our own house or in stranger's,
  All this sin, O Varuna, forgive!

"If we have cheated in play, like false players,
  If we have erred, ignorant or knowing, —
  Whatever hath ensnared us, all this free us from,
Great Varuna, and again may we be clear before thee."[2]

Monotheism. — The hymns in the Rig Veda rise occasionally into pure monotheism. "That which is one," says one hymn, "sages name it in various ways." They call it Agni, Jama, and other names.[3] The wise poets represent by their words "him who is one, with beautiful

[1] Rig Veda, vii. 86; Sanskrit Lit., p. 535.
[2] Rig Veda, 85 (Grassman).
[3] Rig Veda, i. 164.

wings, in many ways."[1] "In the beginning there arose the golden germ; he was the one born lord of all; he established the earth and this sky. . . There is one eternal thinker, thinking of non-eternal thoughts; he, though one, fulfilleth the desires of many. The wise who perceive him within their spirit, to them belong eternal life, eternal peace."[2] "Even those who worship idols worship me [the god]," says, at a later period, the great Hindu poem.[3]

An Upanishad (a commentary of the later Brahmans) says, "There is only one Being who existeth." Three gods, Fire, Wind, and Sun, were together in the OM, or Supreme Soul; they call it Indra, Agni, Varuna, and various names.[4]

> "O god of gods, thou art to me
> Father, mother, kinsmen, friends.
> I, knowledge, riches find in thee;
> All good thy being comprehends."[5]

> "Thou lord of the universe, the only refuge
> Of living beings, the alleviator
> Of pain, the benefactor of mankind,
> Show me thy favor, and deliver me
> From evil. O creator of the world,
> Maker of all that hath been and will be,

---

[1] Rig Veda, x. 114. Compare the conception of the Greek poet of Zeus: πολλῶν ὀνομάτων μορφὴ μία.
[2] M. Müller: What India Thinks, p. 248.
[3] Bhagavad-Gîta.
[4] Rig Veda, i. 164; x. 114-115; Colebrooke, ii. 110.
[5] Translation by Muir.

> Of all that moves and is immovable,
> Worthy of praise, I come to thee, my refuge,
> Renouncing all attachment to the world,
> Longing for fulness of felicity, —
> Extinction of myself, absorption into thee."[1]

"The higher Brahmanism of the wise," says an Upanishad, "is the Right and the True. Through truth the wind bloweth, the sun shineth. Truth is the support of speech. By it is the universe upheld. It is the highest of all."[2] "Falsehood is encompassed by truth. It harmeth not him who knoweth this. The eternal world is that in which is no crookedness, no delusion, no lie."[3]

In the following is the conception of a moral order and a Creator: —

Cosmogony.

> From the enkindled fire-glow
> Sprang truth and right;
> From this sprang dark, dark night,
> From it the sea, the billows.
>
> And from the sea, the billows,
> Was produced the year's course,
> Dividing day and night; it rules
> All that the eye reaches.
>
> And in its order the Creator
> Formed the sun and the moon,
> The heaven and then the earth,
> The air arch and the ether space.[4]

---

[1] Vishnu Purâna, v. 23. [2] Weber, II, 80.
[3] Pr. Up., i. 16. Compare Egyptian ascriptions to Truth in Chapter I. of this volume.
[4] Rig Veda, x. 190.

These ancient hymns have given us the Hindu's ideas of death and heaven, and they are followed by later pictures in the great poems of a less antique period. These attempts to penetrate the great Darkness are most touching. The Unknown God has apparently revealed to this reverent and thoughtful race some glimpses of the eternal Light. The conception of Jama as the first-born of the dead, and the leader of all mortals through the dark valley, is peculiarly poetic.

The Hindu Heaven. — "In heaven, where our virtuous friends enjoy blessedness, having left behind the infirmities of their flesh, free from lameness or distortion of their limbs, they re-behold our parents and our children."[1]

"Place me in that imperishable and unchanging world where perpetual light and glory are found. Make me immortal in the realm where King Jama dwelleth, where the sanctuary of the sky exists and the great waters flow. Make me immortal in the third heaven, or the third sky, where action is unrestrained and the regions are luminous. Make me immortal in the world where are joys and delights for evermore."[2]

In the picture of the high stage of heavenly blessedness contained in the Mahâ-bhârata[3] there is no promise of any sensual gratification. The kind of persons who enter the heavenly world are those who have performed austerities or have offered great sacrifices, — the truthful, the ortho-

[1] Atharva Veda, iii. 28.   [2] Rig Veda, ix. 13.
[3] This poem, it must be remembered, is of a much later date than the Vedas.

dox, the righteous, the self-restrained, the meek, the liberal, the brave. The celestial abodes are shining glorious, and filled with all delights. There hunger, thirst, weariness, cold, heat, fear, are unknown; there is nothing disgusting or disagreeable, there is no sorrow or lamentation, no decay, no labor, no envy, no jealousy, no delusion. There the blessed are clothed with glorious bodies which are produced by their works, and not generated by any father or mother. The blessed there do not subsist on oblations, nor do they feed upon ambrosia. They have celestial, and not coarse, material bodies. The eternal gods, who dwell in these highest places, do not desire pleasure; they do not change with the revolution of æons; how then can they be subject to decay or death? They experience neither joy nor pleasure, neither happiness nor suffering, neither love nor hatred. This high estate beyond the reach of those who seek after pleasure is desired even by the gods. This celestial felicity is within the reach of mortal man, the fruit of his good deeds. The only drawback to the heavenly state is this: as the fruit of work done on earth is enjoyed in heaven, while no other new works are performed there, this enjoyment must come to an end, for this world is the place for works, and the other is the place for reward. The only life free from all defects is the pure, eternal light above the abode of Brahma. Thither none can proceed who are devoted to objects of sense, or who are the slaves of dishonesty, avarice, anger, delusion, or malice; but only the unselfish, the humble, those indifferent to pain and pleasure, those whose senses are under restraint, and those who practise contemplation, and fix their minds on the Deity. The final blessedness is supreme, eternal perfection, in the nature of Nirvâna, or perfect peace.[1]

The Bhagavad-Gîta,[2] a poem as late as the first century, says: —

"There is an invisible, eternal existence beyond the visible, which does not perish when all things else perish, even when the Great Day of Brahma's created life passes into night, and all that exists returneth to God whence it came. They who obtain this never return. . . . They proceed to that imperishable place which is illumined by neither the sun nor the moon; to that primeval Spirit whence the stream of life forever flows."[3]

"Whoever believeth me in all things, and all in me, I do not vanish from him, nor does he vanish from me; for in me he liveth."[4]

"Bright as the sun, beyond darkness, is he to the soul that remembereth him in meditation at the hour of death, — him the most ancient of the wise, the ruler, the sustainer of all."[5] "They who know me in my being, my power, and my manifested life, in the power of death, know me indeed."[6]

"They who devoutly worship me are in me and I in them."[7] "Rest thy mind in me, fix thy understanding on me, and thou shalt hereafter dwell in me."[8] "O Indra, we sages have been in

---

[1] Muir's Sanskrit Text, v. 326. [2] Bhagavad-Gîta, viii.
[3] Ibid., xv. Brahma's "Great Day" is 2,160,000,000 years.
[4] Bhagavad-Gîta, vi. [5] Ibid., vii.
[6] Ibid., viii. [7] Ibid., ix. 29.
[8] Ibid., xii. 8.

thee."[1] "This worshipper, O Agni, hath been in thee; O son of strength, he hath no other kindred."[2] "We, O gods, are in you as if fighting in coats of mail."[3] "Krishna is the light of lights; far from darkness is his name."[4] "But if I were not ever busy in work unwearied ... these worlds would perish if I did not work my work."[5]

"They are dead in me."[6] "I, Krishna, am he who am the highest way. I am the way, the beginning, and the end."[7] "I am the generator and destroyer of the entire universe; than me is nothing higher.... All existences abide in me, but I do not abide in them."[8] "Arjuna saith, 'Thou, Krishna, art the supreme Brahma, the highest essence, the eternal, divine One, unborn, all-pervading.'"[9] "Those who, fixing their minds on me with the completest faith, worship me with constant devotion, are esteemed by me the most devoted."[10]

The ancient Hindu worshipper poured forth his prayer for the beloved one dying, even as we do. There is the same agony and impassioned cry. There is hope, indeed, but not assured faith. It is "triple darkness" beyond, and little light shines.

Prayer for the Dying. — "Reverence death, the ender.... May this man remain here, united with his spirit in the domain of the sun, in the world of deathlessness. The divine beings have raised him up to health. Here is thy spirit, here thy breath, here thy life, here thy soul. He rescued thee from the bonds of destruction by divine utterance. Rise up! Hence, O man, casting

---

[1] Rig Veda, ii. 11–12.
[2] Ibid., x. 142.
[3] Ibid., viii. 47, 48.
[4] Bhagavad-Gîta, xiii. 17.
[5] Bhagavad-Gîta, iii. 23, 24.
[6] Ibid., x. 9.
[7] Ibid., vii. 18, ix. 18.
[8] Ibid., vii. 6.
[9] Ibid., x. 12.
[10] Ibid., xii. 2.

off the fetters of death; do not sink downward; do not depart from this world, from the sight of the fire-god and the sun! May the wind blow for thee, may the waters shower immortality on thee, may the sun shine healingly upon thy body, may death pity thee! Do not die! Thou must ascend, O man, and not descend. I give thee life and mind; let not thy soul go away thither; let it not disappear; do not wander away from the living; do not follow the fathers! May all the gods preserve thee! . . . Do not follow this path; it is terrible. I speak of that by which thou hast hitherto not gone. This, O man, is darkness; do not enter it. Beyond thou hast fear; on this side thou hast security."[1]

The following burial invocation belongs to the highest poetry of mankind.

Burial Prayer.[2]

To those unreached by penance,
Who have raised penance to the height of heaven,
Who have perfected great works of penance, —
To all these go hence!

To those who have fought in many a battle,
Have given up their lives, heroes bold!
Whose sacrifices reward mankind a thousand-fold, —
To all these, go hence!

To the ancients who have kept the **Right**,
Who have practised **Right** and increased **Right**,
O Jama! to the host of pious fathers, —
To all these, go hence!

[1] Muir's Sanskrit text, v. 444; Atharva Veda, viii. 1.
[2] Rig Veda, x. 154 (Grassman).

To the singers rich in wisdom,
They who are guardians of the sun,
Jama! to the host of pious poets, —
To all the pious, go hence!

"Give thyself to the motherly soil, the wide-embracing, gracious earth! A maiden tender as wool is she to the pious. Let her guard thee from destruction. Open thyself, O earth! Be accessible to the dead! As a mother covereth her son with a garment, so cover him, O ground!"[1]

Jama.

To Jama, mighty king, be gifts and homage paid;
He was the first man that died, the first to brave
Death's rapid rushing stream, the first to point the road
To heaven, and welcome others to that bright abode.
No pall can rob us of the home thus won by thee.
O king, we come; the born who have died must tread the path
That thou hast trod, — the path by which each race of men,
Souls of the dead, depart; fear not to take the road,
The ancient road by which thy ancestors have gone.
Ascend to meet the god, to meet thy happy fathers
Who dwell in bliss with him; fear not to pass the guards,
The four-eyed brindled dogs that watch for the departed.
Return unto thy home; also thy sin and shame
Leave there behind on earth; assume a shining form,
Thy ancient shape, refined, and from all ancient taint set free.[2]

Jama, the Leader to Death. — "Him who hath opened the way which leadeth from depth to height, him, Jama the king, celebrated Jama, hath first found a place for us, a home which no one can take from us, whither our forefathers have departed and all the living go. . . . The first-born of death, the first arrival in

---

[1] Rig Veda, x. 22.
[2] Translated by Williams, Hist. of Relig. Thought in India, p. 16.

the kingdom of the departed, — the natural head of the long procession who follow him, — Jama, the Prince of the holy, celebrate!"[1]

The prayer most used in India, from the Rig Veda, might be uttered by all Christians: "Let us meditate on the excellent glory of the Divine Life-giver; may He enlighten our understandings!"

The Upanishads, or later commentaries on the Vedas, give us many glimpses of divine inspirations, though mingled with gross errors.

God. — "Being in this world, we may know the Supreme Spirit. If there be ignorance of him, then complete death ensues."[2] "If a tree be cut down it springs up anew from the root. From what root does mortal man grow again when mown down by death? The root is Brahma, who is knowledge and bliss."[3] "The knowledge of these works, the Vedas, is a mere name, . . . and highest of all stands life; . . . this life ought to be approached with faith and reverence, and viewed as an immensity which abides in its own glory. That immensity extends from above and below, from behind and before, from the south and from the north. It is the soul of the universe, it is God himself. The man who is conscious of this divinity incurs neither disease nor pain nor death. . . . Know him, the Spirit, to be one alone; give up all words contrary to this. He is the bridge of immortality."[4]

The Supreme Being. — "That the Supreme Being is omniscient followeth from the fact that he is the source of the Vedas. As from that being every soul is evolved, so to that being does every soul return. . . . He, the Supreme Being, consisteth of joy. . . .

---

[1] Rig Veda, x. 1, 14. [2] Upanishad, Indian Wisdom, p. 39.
[3] Ibid., iii. 9, 28. [4] Ibid., vii. 1–4.

He, the one God, is the light. He is the life and breath of life. He is the life with which Indra identified himself when he said: 'I am the life, consisting of perfect knowledge; worship me, as the life immortal.'"[1]

The Lord of Righteousness. — "For the establishment of righteousness am I born from time to time. I am dearer to the wise than all possessions, and he is dear to me. In him are all beings, and by him was this universe spread out. Deluded men despised me when I had taken human form. In all the Vedas I am to be known."[2] "Whatever the state of mind of a man at the moment when he leaves the body, to that does he always go, being made to conform to that."[3]

True Goodness.

"Conquer a man who never gives by gifts;
Subdue untruthful men by truthfulness;
Vanquish an angry man by gentleness,
And overcome the evil man by goodness."[4]

"Triple restraint of thought and word and deed,
Strictness of silence, coil of netted hair,
Close-shaven head, garments of skin or bark,
Keeping of fasts, ablutions, maintenance
Of sacrificial fires, a hermit's life,
Emaciation, — these are all in vain
Unless the inward soul be free from stain."[5]

"To injure none by thought or word or deed,
To give to others and be kind to all,

---

[1] Indian Wisdom, p. 113. San Kara.
[2] Bhagavad-Gita, Indian Wisdom, p. 149.
[3] Ibid., viii. 6.
[4] Mahâ-bhârata, iii. 13253.
[5] Ibid., iii. 13245. This idea is frequently expressed in Buddhistic writings.

> This is the constant duty of the good.
> High-minded men delight in doing good,
> Without a thought of their own interest ;
> When they confer a benefit on others,
> They reckon not on favors in return." [1]

> "Two persons will hereafter be exalted
> Above the heavens, — the man with boundless power
> Who yet forbears to use it indiscreetly,
> And he who is not rich and yet can give." [2]

> "Bear raving words with patience ; never meet
> An angry man with anger, nor return
> Reviling for reviling ; smite not him
> Who smites thee. Let thy speech and acts be gentle." [3]

The following thoughts from the celebrated Hindu poem, Bhagavad-Gîta, are so strikingly spiritual that many have believed them borrowed from or influenced by Christianity itself, as they might possibly be, this poem being as late as from the first to the third century after Christ.

The Saviour. — "On the other hand, who worship me, committing to me all their actions, regarding me as the supreme end, and meditating on me, nothing else knowing, for them with hearts entered into me, I become, O son of Pritha, without delay the rescuer from the ocean of death-bearing, wandering existence. Fix thy thoughts upon me alone ; in me let thy faith dwell, and thou shalt hereafter abide in me without doubt." [4] "Those who worship thy immortality-bearing law, as declared, full of faith,

---

[1] Mahâ-bhârata, iii. 16782.
[2] Ibid., v. 1028.
[3] Ibid., v. 1270.
[4] Bhagavad-Gîta.

regarding me as the supreme end, are exceedingly beloved of me."[1]
"Knowing me, the enjoyer of all sacrifice and penance, the supreme Lord of all worlds and the Friend of all creatures, he attaineth rest."[2]

A Good End to the Righteous. — "The blessed Lord said, 'O son of Pritha, neither here nor hereafter is there destruction for him; never does a worker of righteousness come to an evil end.'"[3]

Worship. — "But the great-souled ones, united to godlike natures, knowing me to be the exhaustless origin of all things, worship with mind that turns to nothing else. Constant in union, with faith they worship, almost proclaiming me, striving for me with fixed vows, and bowing down to me."[4] "Whoever in love offers to me a leaf, or flower, or fruit, that given in love by the pure-hearted I accept. . . . Those who worship me in love, they are in me and I in them."[5] "Be with heart fixed on me, loving me and worshipping me; bow down to me. Thus at rest, thou shalt come, even to me the Spirit."[6]

Knowledge of God. — "Whoever knoweth him, the unborn, beginningless, supreme Lord of worlds, he among men becomes liberated from all sins."[7] "I am the source of all; owing to me all things work. Knowing this, the wise, full of love, worship me."[8]

"Arjuna said, 'Thou Supreme Being, supreme power, sacred and supreme spirit, and eternal, primeval god, unborn, all-pervading, thee thus they call . . . All that thou sayest to me I believe to be true, O Lord. Thy Majesty is indeed not known, O thou Supreme Spirit by thyself; thou knowest thyself, thou Creator of all, thou Lord of all, God of gods, and Master of the universe.'"[9]

---

[1] Bhagavad-Gîta, p. 186.
[2] Ibid., p. 102. Translated by Chatterie.
[3] Ibid., p. 45.   [4] Ibid., p. 151.   [5] Ibid., p. 155.
[6] Ibid., p. 156.   [7] Ibid., p. 159.   [8] Ibid., p. 160.
[9] Ibid., p. 162.

God. — "The splendor of this great Soul may haply be likened to the radiance of a thousand suns at once risen in the heavens."[1]

"Thou art the exhaustless, supreme goal of knowledge, thou art the supreme support of this universe, thou art changeless, the Protector of the unchanging law of righteousness; thou art the Eternal Spirit; this is my faith."[2]

"Thou art the primeval God, the ancient Spirit. Of this universe thou art the Father, and the object of veneration, the greatest of the great. There is none equal unto thee. How can there be a superior, O thou with majesty, imaged in the three worlds? Therefore bowing down and holding the body so low, O Lord, I prayed for grace. Forgive, O Lord, as forgives the father the son, the friend the friend, and the lover the beloved."[3]

"The blessed Lord spoke: 'As seen by thee, I may not thus be seen by the studies of the Vedas, nor by austere practices, nor by the making of gifts, nor by acts of worship. By self-beautifying devotion, indeed, I am known and seen in truth, and entered into. He that worketh but for me, for whom I am the supreme good, who is devoted to me, having no delight in things, and devoid of hostility, cometh unto me.'"[4]

In studying the ancient faiths one often asks, What are the enduring ideas for the human soul? When we enter that unknown spiritual life, what must be our highest thoughts? They cannot, of course, be the prevailing subjects of thought here, — the means of living, the steps of ambition, the comforts of the body, the dreams of passion, the pride of wealth; they cannot even be of the triumphs of sects or the honors of churches.

The human mind, entering that great void, must of

---

[1] Bhagavad-Gîta, p. 171.
[2] Ibid., p. 172.
[3] Ibid., p. 176.
[4] Ibid., p. 178.

necessity ask itself the Hindu questions, What is God? How can we approach him; how live in him forever; how be freed from the limitations of the body and the remembered temptations of the senses; how live eternally in purity and disinterestedness; how be prepared for the highest spiritual union with Brahma, or Varuna, or whatever be the name of the Unnamable One?

These and similar are the profound objects of reflection of the Brahman saints and poets. These questions they have striven over and over to answer. At times the Hindu seers seem, so far as human beings can, to have attained the highest inspiration in these grand themes. But no great teacher or prophet had early showed to them, by both life and words, the necessary connection of action and belief, of life and faith. Practical morality had not to many become the expression of religion. Then the natural explanations of moral problems through pre-existence and future transmigrations led them into wild theories, and pantheism had its natural influence in obscuring moral differences. Yet many in the line of Hindu thinkers are precisely in harmony with the Christian Mystics, and believed as we should all believe without the revelation of Christ. They accepted the Unknown God. The highest bliss of an endless life was to be in union with him.

Yet these the noblest thoughts and aspirations of the highest thinkers of India which we have quoted give a very imperfect and false idea of the religions of India. There was, indeed, an inspiration of the Unknown God among the people. There were no doubt considerable numbers who worked righteousness in love to him, and were acceptable to him. But no other history and no human experience is so clear a proof of the practical curse to a people which lies in a false philosophy and imperfect religion as the confused records of Hindu thought afford. The combination of pantheism and idolatry seems to be the worst possible spiritual atmosphere for a people.

The belief in re-birth, previous existence, and future transmigration became almost stamped congenitally on the Hindu mind. It overshadowed existence from the earliest moment with the deepest darkness. The devout and thoughtful worshipper saw no escape from it, except after millions of æons in the absolute cessation of personal existence by absorption in God. Pain and suffering and sin were the necessary accompaniments of conscious life through all possible existences till the soul entered into the Infinite Spirit. There was no thought of a limited spirit " doing the work " of an unlimited Being, lessening sin, relieving pain, curing sickness, scattering happiness, until at length he arrives at such a moral union with Him that he lives in his life and works his work. The mortal is simply purified and disciplined by the pains and penalties of endless transmigrations, until he is swallowed up in God and ceases any more to be himself. As various passages in the Vedas and from later poems show, there were individuals among the Brahmans who attained a much higher idea of the union with the Divine; but the other is the prevailing view. A death-shadow rested on the Hindu intellect, — the thought of sin and pain and its eternal continuance.

Then a low mythology corrupted morals, and pantheism destroyed the sense of personal responsibility for wrong-doing. Hence sprang practical social evils in India, belonging to a very low condition of human society, which have lasted to the present day.

CHAPTER XIV.

BUDDHISM.

The mission of the Lord Buddha is mercy seeking to save.
Words of a Buddhist (EDKINS).
God in the form of Mercy.
Ancient Inscription on a Statue of Buddha.

OF all religious phenomena in the history of the human mind, Buddhism has been — next to Judaism and Christianity — the most remarkable and the most wide-reaching. The prayers of this faith are uttered by as many human beings as those of Christianity,[1] and its hopes and aspirations and principles have been the consolation and support and guidance of countless millions of the human race during more than twenty-four centuries. Its leading principles and doctrines were not new even in the sixth century before Christ. They appeared in different forms for many ages in the expression of Hindu thought and in poetry, as has been seen in the chapter on

---

[1] Schlagintweit estimates the number of Christians in the world at 350,000,000, and of Buddhists at 400,000,000; but in China many are classed as Buddhists who are in reality followers of Confucius. Rhys Davids estimates the Buddhists at 500,000,000, and Christians at 327,000,000. Monier Williams, however, in his recent work on Buddhism, numbers the Buddhists at only about 100,000,000.

Hinduism. The humble and reverent among the Brahmans had long ago received the intuition of the Unknown God, the centre and source of all force and life, and the Ideal of moral perfection; they had believed that union with him brought infinite peace, and freedom from all the sorrows and passions of life, — a mystical repose in which the soul was in Brahma and was Brahma.[1] They, too, like the Buddhists, had denounced the formalism of the priests and the hypocrites; they had also uttered those ideals of Universal Love which included all castes and classes, all beings above and below, here and hereafter; they, too, had taught a divine patience, and had grasped that highest conception of sympathy which could make them say, "Love your enemies;" "Do unto others as ye would have others do unto you."[2]

Yet the Hindu monotheism had degenerated into every species of degraded polytheism and idolatry; formalism and the tyranny of caste ruled all things; selfishness, hatred, and lust prevailed; or among the higher intel-

---

[1] "As a weaver taketh out of a colored garment a piece, and weaveth a new and more beautiful form, so the spirit in death letteth this body fall and all its interests become extinguished, and prepareth itself another new form of Brahma's nature, either divine or human. . . . As he has wandered so he becomes; whoever has done good becomes a good being, whoever evil, an evil. Whoever is free from desire, whoever only desireth God, whoever hath attained desire, from his body the powers do not retreat to another body, but draw together; he becometh Brahma, and goeth to Brahma" (Oldenberg).

[2] See the Mahâ-bhârata and earlier poems.

lects a pantheism extended which extinguished individual worship and personal responsibility.

Amid all these evils, some time in the sixth [1] century before Christ, there appeared in northern India one of those great personalities who in a measure draw their inspiration directly from above. The mists of legend shroud the figure, and the peculiar Oriental extravagance of imagination has to an even unusual degree exaggerated the traits of this gentle and disinterested teacher. But it would be no more historical and reasonable to judge of the real features of Gotama Buddha from these grotesque narratives, than it would be to construct a traditional portrait of Jesus Christ from "the Gospel of Infancy" or the "Visions of Hermas."

It has been the good fortune or the inspiration of Christianity to hand down narratives of its Founder, unequalled in simplicity, terseness, and beauty. It is the misfortune or essential weakness of all other forms of religion to transmit documents of such repetition, puerility, and weakness, that the truth under them is with difficulty traced and perceived. But we see enough under the Buddhistic legends and traditions to understand the astonishing influence of this personality about whom they have gathered.

It is unfortunate again that the Hindu and Chinese defective ideas of form and of art have transmitted no suitable

---

[1] Max Müller places Buddha's birth about 557 B. C., and his death at 477 B. C. (Dhammapada, p. xxxvi.).

portrait or statue of this remarkable being; yet now and then among the innumerable representations of him are some of singular sweetness and nobleness.[1] The deep, lustrous eyes which are here pictured must have looked upon human suffering with a sympathy never equalled in the history of man except by One. When, at what we may call his conversion, or his attaining the idea of Nirvâna, he said the following words, we see a compassion almost unknown among men: —

"The fearful power of error is taken away from the soul, the sun of knowledge is arisen, the gates of the false way which leads to existences filled with misery are closed; I am on the other shore, the pure way of heaven is opened, I have stepped into the road of Nirvâna. On this road will the oceans of blood and tears be dried up, the mountains of human bones be broken through, and the host of death destroyed, as the elephant overturns the reed hut of the marsh. He who follows without distraction this way, escapeth the wheel of re-birth[2] and the revolutions of the world. He can boast to himself, 'I have done what lay upon me; I have destroyed this existence for myself; I will not again be re-born; I am free.'"[3]

---

[1] Especially is this true of the Buddha of the Jamalgiri sculptures. It is remarkable that the inscription beneath this noble figure is "God in the form of Mercy!" (See Lillie's Buddhism, p 145.)

[2] These lines well express the horror of the Hindu at re-birth:

> A weary and broken-down man,
>   With sorrow I come to thy feet;
> Subdued by the fate and the ban
>   That hides the long future I meet,
> I suffer without ceasing the pain
>   Of wonderful infinite life.
>
> Folk-Songs of Southern India, p. 39.

[3] Burnouf.

And yet we can see that the great teacher had not fully grasped the truth which can wipe away all tears. When he says, "As a mother at the risk of her life watcheth over the life of her child, her only child, so also let every one cultivate a boundless good-will towards all beings . . . above and below and across, unobstructed, without hatred, without enmity, standing, walking, sitting, or lying, as long as he be awake let him devote himself to this state of mind; this way of living, they say, is the best in this world,"[1] — when these words come to our ears, we hear something of a like voice to that which said, "Come unto me, all ye that are weary and heavy-laden." From a thousand legends and narratives we may gather that to Gotama, the Enlightened (the Buddha), the barriers of human selfishness fell away. To him the miseries of the poor, the slave, the *chândâla* (outcasts), were his own; the tears which men had shed from the beginning, "enough to fill oceans," were as if falling from his own eyes. The great pang of sorrow, piercing the heart of the race, inconsolable, unspeakable, struck to his own heart. For him the sin of the world, the unsatisfied desire, the fierce passion and hatred and lust, poisoned life, and he cared for nothing except for what would change the heart and remove this fearful mass of evils.

The legends make this wonderful pity and disinterested-

[1] Metta Sutta, Old Buddhistic Writings, Dhammapada, Max Müller, p. 25.

ness outrun all bounds of reason, as where it is related that in one of his previous existences he had given his body to satisfy the hunger-cravings of a famished tiger. Even in his final existence on earth he is related to have repeatedly refused heaven, or Nirvâna, until he had planted his truth in the world.

Under these legends, and the words which we have quoted from him, and which he undoubtedly spoke, we see arise the form of a teacher or saint such as the world has not known outside of Christianity, — a lover of man, of purity, of truth, a healer of sorrow and sin, a despiser of all luxury and wealth and power, a dreamer of a mental state where should be no pain or sin or sorrow any more.

It is but a natural poetry, that when he appeared in infant form on the earth, divine flowers fell all over the world, the dumb spake, and the blind saw, and no man thought evil of another; and when he died, the earth quaked, and the feet of the dead teacher were marked with the tears of men and of angels.

Where Gotama uttered his beautiful words ought indeed to be the place among the most sacred of the world. His relics, were they genuine, should be among the best treasures of the earth. The followers of such a teacher have not really exaggerated the value of his life. His genuine words ought to be a priceless inheritance for all succeeding times. To have listened once to those compassionate tones should have softened the hardest natures; to have heard of peace and purity and blessedness from those lips ought to have changed lives for all coming years. The world sees but few of such men, and all that belongs to them is sacred forever. We may smile at the grotesque legends and the childish exaggeration which have decked a pure and disinterested life. Yet he who said, " Let a man overcome anger by love, let him overcome evil by good, the stingy by liberality, the liar by truth; "[1] he who called the chândâla and the courtesan to forsake their sins and follow him, and was obeyed; who gave up wealth and honor and station and power for the sake of the poor and sinful and unbefriended; who pictured a future state of beatific peace which no storm shall shake and no time decay; who warned men that not in the clefts of the mountains or the depths of the sea, not in life or in death, can they escape the effects of an evil deed; whose creed is described by a disciple as resting on one principle, "Mercy seeking to save;"[2] who preached heart-purity and universal love as the conditions of future blessedness, — such a man must ever be listened to as one of the world's benefactors, or even as a prophet partly inspired by God.[3] It is scarcely to be wondered at that his most

[1] Dhammapada, p. 223.   [2] Edkins: Buddhism in China.
[3] It has been said of Buddha, "Had he been Christian, he would have been greatest in the presence of God."— Si fuisset Christianus, fuisset apud Deum maximus (quoted from Marco Polo by Beal, Catena, p. 7).

striking statue bears the ancient inscription, "God in the form of Mercy."

In one of the beautiful old stories of Buddhism which we shall quote, is the touching narrative of the death of a simple-minded Chinese believer and scholar, whose dying moments were comforted with the hope of looking hereafter on the face of "his loving and affectionate Lord." So millions of Buddhists have died, reckoning it as among the purest joys of eternity that they should look upon his features who was the earthly embodiment of infinite patience and immortal love.

Perchance some of those who have been permitted to know of a higher embodiment, may share this sentiment towards the Hindu who of all other sons of men felt the most for human sorrow. Many of us have at times cherished the not fanciful hope that in the ages of a future mysterious existence it might be graciously allowed us to see the spiritual features of the noble dead. We may have imagined the rugged traits of him who promised himself "there as here to spend his time in questioning and scrutinizing the persons to see who is wise, and who seemeth so but is not;"[1] or the high beauty of the great follower of Socrates, who said, "It is the clear view of truth, the possession of eternal beauty, the contemplation of absolute good, which makes up the life of the good and happy;" or the saintly face of the beloved disciple who

[1] Socrates: Apol., 32.

uttered the highest religious thought known to man, "God is love;" or the patient, seraphic traits of the "Angelical" artist and monk who on earth was said to have almost beheld the Father face to face. But among them all there is none of pure human birth whom so many millions will gaze upon with such unspeakable gratitude and devout affection as the Hindu saint who lived for the unhappy and the sinful, — Gotama, the Enlightened.

It must be remembered that there is something in Buddhism which is akin to the highest Christian thought, — a poetic Mysticism, which may therefore be easily misunderstood. When Christ speaks of himself "in God," and "God in him," and of his followers in both, he utters truths beyond the ordinary understanding. When John says, "God is love;" or Paul, "For us to live is Christ;" or Saint Augustine declares God "ineffable;"[1] or Justin Martyr speaks of "God as not only above all names but above all existence;" or Clement of Alexandria states that only by laying aside all finite ideas of the Divine nature can we attain to a clear idea of God;[2] or John of Damascus discourses of God as not belonging to "things,"[3] as beyond knowledge and being, — these are one and all Mystics, discoursing of truths beyond human ken, yet in the lan-

---

[1] Hoc unde scio, nisi quia Deus ineffabilis est (De Doct. Christian.).

[2] Strom., vii. 689.

[3] οὐδέν γὰρ τῶν ὄντων ἐστίν (De Fed. Orth., i. 4).

guage of men. Still, under these poetic expressions will be conveyed grand glimpses of eternal truths. So when we as Christians speak of a "God who can neither remember nor forget," because he lives in an eternal Now, and of a Being "unchangeable," who yet loves and suffers and is righteously indignant, we are no more inconsistent or contradictory than the Buddhist, who says in the words of his sacred writings, "He is ignorant who declareth that the Perfect One[1] [in his beatified existence] either goeth or cometh; for there is no place whence he should come or whither he should go; he who looketh for me through any form or sound shall never find me."[2] The Mystic of the Middle Ages says: "To God as Godhead appertains neither will, nor knowledge, nor manifestation, nor anything that we can name or say or conceive. But to God as God [Person] it belongeth to express himself, and know and love himself."[3]

So the true follower of Buddha will not admit that God can be a Person, because a person belongs to time and space, has a beginning and an end, and is thus defective. The true God must be absolute, perfect, and eternal. The Christian position that there may be an eternal manifes-

---

[1] Tathâgata. Oldenberg translates this epithet of Buddha, "the Perfect One;" the Pali dictionary (Childers), "the Sentient Being," or "the one who goes in like manner" with other beings; even as Christ called himself "the Son of man."

[2] Sutta Vajra, chap. xx. and xxvi.

[3] Theol. Germ., p. 100.

tation in a personal Being of an absolute Being, seems hardly to have occurred to the Buddhistic mind.[1]

If the reader will compare with many Buddhistic expressions the following passage from that beautiful manual of Mysticism in the Middle Ages, the "Theologia Germanica," he will see the essential character of Buddhism.

"Now let us mark, where men are enlightened with the true light, they perceive that all which they might desire or choose is nothing to that which all creatures, as creatures, ever desired or chose or knew. Therefore they renounce all desire and choice, and commit and commend themselves and all things to the Eternal Goodness. Nevertheless, there remaineth in them a desire to go forward and get nearer to the Eternal Goodness; that is, to come to a clearer knowledge, and warmer love, and more comfortable assurance, and perfect obedience and subjection; so that every enlightened man could say, 'I would fain be to the Eternal Goodness what his own hand is to a man.'"[2]

The great difference in the two kinds of Mysticism is the more distinct personality in the Christian's belief of God, and this is the key-note to the defect in Buddha's teachings. But it is on the most important dogma of Buddha's teachings that Mysticism has had its greatest power, and where uncertainty has done the most evil,— that of Nirvâna.

The early Buddhist, and probably Buddha himself, could not admit any personality in an absolute God; and

---

[1] Yet in one hymn we hear of "non-eternal thoughts coming from an eternal Thinker." (See chapter on Hinduism.)

[2] Theol. Germ., p. 28.

so in regard to a state of perfect blessedness they could not admit the limitations of personality as we see it in this life. As the follower of Tauler, in the extracts we have just given, dreams of a state where is "no desire," so the early disciple of Gotama constructs an existence where is no desire, no want, no pain or sorrow or sin. It is not a dreamless sleep. Surely it cannot be annihilation which could call forth that enraptured exclamation from Buddha when he first grasped the idea of Nirvâna, which we have quoted, where he sees "the ocean of tears and blood of humanity dried up, the mountains of human bones removed, and the hosts of death destroyed."[1] It is not nothingness which could inspire such pæans of praise and gratitude in different ages from devout Buddhists. Besides, the state of Nirvâna begins at times before death; it thus began with Gotama and some of his most sanctified followers. It is not a cessation, it is rather a consummation. It is the fruit of one life or many lives, of service to other beings, of purity, self-control, and the uttermost self-sacrifice. We shall quote great numbers of ancient texts describing this, the Buddhist's heaven. But, unlike our idea of heaven, it is not in any place or time.[2]

[1] Burnouf, p. 462.
[2] This passage from an ancient Buddhistic sermon shows how mystical was the Buddhist's idea of time as relating to future life: "Whoever, after having washed away all sins, within and without, does not enter *Time* among gods and men, who are subject to time, him they call cleansed" (Sutta Nipâta, 521). "The ascetic is freed from Time" (880).

It is a state of consciousness, a moral condition of each sentient being. When the Christian Mystic says, "If a man neither careth for nor seeketh nor desireth anything but the Eternal Good alone, and seeketh not himself nor his own things, he is in the kingdom of heaven, and he is as safe in hell as in heaven,"[1] he but describes the Buddhist Nirvâna. There is possible, as all Christians believe, such a union of the soul with the Divine, such freedom from selfishness and sensual desires, that peace surrounds it like an atmosphere; the low cares and bodily passions of life cease, hatred and malice are dried up, the heart lives in the happiness of others, and no shadow can darken the light or ruffle the surface of that beatific peace. This is the "peace passing understanding" of the Christian.

It is true that the root of Nirvâna[2] means "blowing out;" but these texts show it is the blowing out of the fires of lust and hatred and passion.

The Hindus before Buddha conceived such a beatitude as the fruit of union with Brahma. It is probable that in Buddha's mind, behind his thought of blessedness, was the idea of an Infinite and Absolute Spirit, — Âtman;[3] but whether he ever regarded Brahma as the absolute God is doubtful. It is more probable that to him Brahma and all the gods of the Hindu pantheon were grand be-

---

[1] Theologia Germanica, p. 36.   [2] *Id*, — to blow out.
[3] Oldenberg's Life of Buddha, p. 31.

ings, who began to be and should yet come to an end, who were related to time, to "becoming and ceasing;" but the condition of which he dreamed, and towards which he unceasingly aspired, had no connection with time, with birth and death. It was absolute and eternal. In this state of beatification, the curse of existence to the Indian mind — the ever-recurring birth and death — had passed away. There was everlasting rest and unsullied holiness.

But there were vital defects in this doctrine. The statements easily led the disciple towards a belief in a quietude which was equivalent to non-existence. There are texts even in very ancient Buddhistic sermons [1] which point to annihilation; but the immense majority of verses and discourses are full of faith and hope in future blessedness. The very vivid and natural presentation of Buddha's Socratic discussions with the extreme worshippers of the Vedas,[2] which we shall quote, is a remarkable proof of this. In these he demonstrates by question and answer that a union of the soul with Brahma must mean a likeness of the soul in love and truth and purity with the Divinity, who is perfect, and that Nirvâna must consist in this state of mind, for which his disputants were by no means prepared. In ancient Buddhism, Nirvâna, says Beal,[3] has four prominent characteristics, — personality,

---

[1] Davids : Buddhistic Suttas.
[2] Tevigga Sutta, in Davids' Budd. Suttas, p. 203.
[3] Beal's Catena, p. 154.

joy, purity, and permanence. In later Buddhism it often is defined as "restoration to the true condition of being." In all the reported words of Gotama, salvation, or Nirvâna, is always conditional on a change of heart in this life.

The great want in Buddha's teaching, however, was the clear and distinct presentation of God as Father. It may have lain back in his mind when he pictured the state of perfect blessedness hereafter; it seems sometimes to be assumed in his arguments, as we have noted;[1] but the lack of it is the fatal defect of Buddhism, and unfits it to be the absolute religion of mankind. In heartfelt, unselfish sympathy with the woes of humanity, and in unceasing aspirations for purity and holiness, in entire sacrifice for men, even the lowest and poorest, in a love encompassing all creatures, Gotama Buddha has but One surpassing him in human history. But some of the humblest followers of that One have stood far above the Hindu saint in the consciousness of God, and in the relation to him as an Infinite Father. It is this want which will make Buddhism less and less a power in the advancing progress of the race. Yet Gotama was undoubtedly inspired to a certain degree by the Divine Spirit; he did not for some reason accept or receive full inspiration. He was an instrument under Divine Providence to redeem millions of his own people, and of other peoples, from formalism, idolatry, and selfishness, from lust and intemperance; he has given

[1] Tevigga Sutta.

a new hope and love to countless numbers of the human race; he has healed innumerable wounds, and dried the tears of millions of the sorrowful and oppressed. Of him could be said, what was uttered ages ago by the devout Egyptian of Osiris, "His heart was in every wound"[1] of humanity. He has perhaps prepared the way for Christianity. At least, there is nothing in Buddhism to prevent the most devout disciple from rising above it to the conception of a higher Nirvâna and a more perfect Redeemer;[2] from Buddha and Âtman to Christ and God the Father.

The church of Gotama, not through his influence, fell into one great error, precisely similar to the error of the Christian church. It founded an ascetic and conventual association which indeed had its blessings. It was, as some one has said, a kind of international federation of

[1] See Chapter I. of this work.
[2] Mrs. Leonowens, who was seven years in the Court of Siam, and saw the practical action of Buddhism on the lives of the ladies of the Court, says in one of her charming books that on one occasion she read some of the Gospels to these royal ladies. They were delighted with the history of Christ. "Why, he is just like Buddha," they said: "suppose you call Christ Buddha and we will call Buddha Christ!" On another occasion a spiritualized ascetic heard her read from Saint Paul's words on Charity, "If I give my body to be burned," etc. "Ye know not the meaning of your great Teacher," he said. "Soon I shall pass on to Nirvâna, but the ashes of my unworthy body are to be scattered on the land of the poor and needy to enrich it; and yet, as he saith, even that is nothing without illimitable love." The Dhammapada utters a similar sentiment.

good will, and bound India and Thibet and China in certain bonds of fellowship. All historians agree that the faith of Buddha helped to civilize eastern and central Asia, and that, nearly at the same time with the first preaching of Christianity in Europe and Asia, it caused a development of the arts in China, and humanized the tribes of Thibet and the Mongols, and did much to prevent the fierce invasions of these barbarians over eastern Europe in the early Christian Ages. Buddhism became a religion for all peoples, and softened the habits and purified the lives of many in various nations. But the convent life sowed unnatural vices, cultivated formalism and superstition, cut off men from industry and family life, and cherished idleness among great multitudes. It has produced a character and mode of life quite the opposite to any taught by Gotama the Enlightened. These effects are not directly chargeable on the founder of this church any more than the like errors in Christian history are on the Founder of our faith.

Its teachings against intemperance (for abstinence was one of the commandments) have produced more effect among Orientals than like instruction among European races; but this may be a matter of race. Its care of animals and mercy to dumb creatures seem in advance of Christian practice. But experience in both India and Europe or America shows that mercy to animals can often be consistent with great indifference or selfishness towards human beings; as where the paths of Hindu pilgrimages are marked with pitiful forms of men and women left to suffer and die, while dogs and cats and bullocks are attentively cared for.[1]

It would however seem true that, on the whole, enlightened Buddhists are more faithful to their religion than Christians to theirs. That is, the grand words of Gotama, teaching uttermost self-denial and universal love, are more often made real in the lives of Orientals than similar and grander instructions of Christ are followed in the practical lives of European and American Christians. But in such judgments one may easily make mistakes. The few Buddhists we may know are the chiefs of their peoples, from a simple society, and resemble the saints of the Middle Ages; the Oriental masses may be sensual and selfish. On the other hand, the European and American Christian belongs to industrial races, and to a commercial age. His problem is to carry on the commercial and industrial progress of the century, and yet to live "in Christ and God" and serve mankind, — manifestly a much more difficult task than ideal living in a simple state of society. If thus far he has not succeeded in it, the fault is not with his religion.

It is claimed by many that under Buddhism there is far less sexual crime than under Christianity. Here also it is difficult to judge. The high standard of Christian peoples

[1] See Vaughan's Crescent and Cross, p. 31.

in regard to female purity tends to depress all offenders, and to make the professionally lewd even lower than they are elsewhere. It is probable that there are proportionally fewer "lost women" in Ceylon, or China, or Thibet, or Japan, or parts of India, than in Europe; but it is believed that family life is much purer under Christian inspirations than under Buddhistic teachings. Yet Gotama's doctrine of personal purity is the highest possible.

The superstition which has followed Buddhism in many countries is certainly a most depressing fact in the history of human progress; but almost equally bad effects have followed Christianity in Italy and Spain and other countries. Neither class of results is a legitimate effect of the teachings of the founders of these faiths.

The great practical contrast between the effects of the two faiths is, that under Buddhism the leading reforms of modern society, the higher position of woman, the purification and elevation of marriage, the abolition of slavery,[1] the raising up of the poor and oppressed, the liberalizing of political institutions, the doing away with cruelty[2] and violence, have all dragged slowly, or have never even

[1] Slavery, which had been an object of King Asoka's reforms (250 B. C.), still existed in the most purely Buddhistic country, Ceylon, till its abolition by the English in 1845. It is indeed true that the treatment of illegitimate children by their parents is better in Buddhistic than Christian countries; but that is partly a side result of the higher purity of the Christian races. The parents are more ashamed of the sin, and commit another sin to cover this.

[2] The exposure of children still continues in China.

begun. It is doubtful if in these respects two thousand years have brought Buddhistic countries any nearer the doctrines of their great teacher. On the other hand, the history of each Christian country is of a progress, slow but steady, towards the ideals of their religious Leader. What might be called the *Gesta Buddhæ* (the achievements of Buddha) are the weakening of priestly tyranny in India, the lessening of the power of caste,[1] the encouragement of monogamy, the improving of the position of woman, humanity to animals, the diminution of bloodshed, and above all, the cultivation of spiritual and moral life instead of ceremonial and professional religion,[2] and the employment of missionaries of religion. But the present moral and spiritual condition of India and China shows how far behind are these reforms to the *Gesta Christi* made manifest in Europe and America.

It can only be said that Christianity contains within itself the seeds of reform and progress, while Buddhism degenerates. The life and gospel of Jesus the Christ are from the Eternal Goodness, from God himself, and so must ever work towards the redemption of man. The life and law (Dhamma) of Gotama the Enlightened have an inspiration indeed from the Unknown God, but not

---

[1] Caste has endured, however, for centuries in the purest Buddhistic country, Ceylon.
[2] Yet the most extended and formal ceremonial church in the world has been planted by it in Thibet and China.

sufficiently clear and powerful to save the race. The one, Christianity, has behind it the long inspiration of the Jewish sacred writings, and the relation of the Jewish people to Jahveh, or God. No such monotheistic inspiration exists elsewhere in human history. The other, Buddhism, has for a source the lofty but confused convictions and wild fancies of Brahmanism, where too often pantheism took the place of a belief in a God of love.

Certain able writers [1] have taken the position that Buddhism is an utterly "false religion," that it does not teach the existence of the soul or the being of God, offers only annihilation to the believer, and has but little practical influence on human life. This is evidently an extreme ground, and without a fair consideration of all the facts. No earnestness in defending Christianity, or love for its Divine Author, should lead Christian writers to ignore any good features in ethnic religions, or any facts in their favor. The truth seems to be that Buddhism has passed through certain changes of belief, as all religions tend to do. Lillie [2] says that an analysis of an ancient Buddhistic writing, the Lalita Vistâra, shows three Buddhistic schools of thought: one, the earliest, where Brahma is held to be the Supreme God; the second, in later development, where

---

[1] Kellogg has written a learned and vigorous little book on this theme. — "The Light of Asia, and the Light of the World."

[2] History of Buddhism, p. 114.

Buddha becomes God; and the third, or still later metaphysical school, where annihilation is taught. In a succeeding chapter we shall quote especially from one most ancient Buddhistic writing, the Dhammapada (Religion's Path), which Max Müller believes to contain the very words supposed to be spoken by Buddha, and thus accredited to him in the Council of Asoka within one hundred and thirty years of the death of the master. This and some of the ancient sutras, or discourses, contain the oldest reported sayings and teachings of Gotama. We defy any of our readers to read candidly these words, coming down from a great antiquity, and at the same time gather the impression that the writers doubted the existence of the soul, or of God, or a future life. Some expressions there are indeed pointing towards annihilation[1] as the future destiny of the soul; but they are vastly outweighed by other and more hopeful expressions. The older the writing or tradition, the more full of hope and faith in the future. It is true that under Buddhism, as under Christianity, mystical expressions sometimes seem to exclude the existence of a personal Ego, or a personal God; but the general drift is towards a continued existence of the soul (for Karma[2] itself must mean the

---

[1] See Sutta Nipâta (1072-1075).

[2] Karma expresses a highly mystical idea, — the indestructible consequences of sin following each human soul in eternity constituting its punishment, and condemning it to continued transmigrations into lower forms of life; but apparently in such changes the memory or

moral effects of action continued with a given spiritual being), and towards a belief in an intelligent moral Power over the universe.

Lillie quotes from an ancient Buddhistic writing that there "is a place called Nirvânapura, where is neither misery nor death, but the good enjoy happiness forever;"[1] and eternal punishment in hell is threatened "to those who teach Nirvâna to be death or annihilation."[2]

Mr. Kellogg, in his excellent little book on Buddhism, wisely calls attention to the great contrast between the historical credibility of the Christian documents and those of Buddhism, the former going back to contemporary witnesses, and the latter founded on oral tradition for centuries, and put in writing several hundred years after the occurrences. But the Christian religion depends for its credibility both on the trustworthiness of its witnesses and on its essential character. Buddhism, however, rests mainly on its moral and spiritual drift. The extravagant and childish miracles which its legends have ascribed to its author give no weight to its claims, but rather weaken them. The great things to be demonstrated are, "What did Gotama teach, and what kind of man was he?" Oral tradition and great varieties of ancient documents enable

consciousness of identity may at times be lost. A poetic rendering of the idea of Karma would be, —

"Our deeds follow us from afar;
And what we have been, makes us what we are."

[1] Lillie's Buddhism, p. 123.   [2] Upham's Sacred Books, iii. 18.

the historical student or the candid inquirer to get near the true answer to these questions, even without the testimony of eye-witnesses.

The true personality of Abraham or Moses rises up before us distinctly, and yet it is doubtful if we have anything but oral tradition and later writing for an historical basis of their characters. It seems to me that we do also see with distinctness the true moral nature of Gotama Buddha, and that his teachings are definite and characteristic.

The Asoka Inscriptions. — But a new source of evidence has appeared in the past few years in regard to Buddha and his teachings, which perhaps modern objectors to this faith have not duly considered. About one hundred and twenty-five years after the death of Buddha appeared in India a king or emperor, originally of the kingdom of Magadha, but who subsequently became monarch of two thirds of the vast territory of Hindustan. His probable ancestor (possibly his grandfather), Sandrokottos, as the Greeks called him, is related to have been driven from the camps of Alexander the Great in the victorious campaign of the latter in India. He subsequently reconquered much of India. This king, surnamed Piyadasi (Beloved of the Gods), but more commonly called Asoka, became converted to Buddhism, and is considered as the Constantine of this faith. In fact, if measured by the number of human beings reverencing his name and obeying his commands, not Cæsar or Charlemagne held so great a position in the world; his influence has extended, says Davids, "from the Volga to Japan, from Ceylon and Siam to Mongolia and Siberia."[1]

Fortunately for history this great ruler, or one of his line, about 250 B. C. inscribed his edicts on rocks and pillars over a vast extent of territory. They are in Pâli dialects, and during the past fifty years have been translated by scholars. They were issued at the period of the Punic Wars of Rome; and yet no ruler of modern times has surpassed them in sentiments of lofty humanity and compassion, or in ideas of broad and noble toleration. We shall quote extracts from them in a succeeding chapter. They are evidently Buddhistic; they speak of the familiar triad of Gotama's followers, "the Lord, the Law, and the Church." They allude with deep reverence to Buddha; they exhort to the care and the preservation of his sacred writings, or of those in regard to him; but they entirely omit to teach the errors of later Buddhism. They speak reverently of God; they exhort men to goodness in view of heaven and paradise; they show unshaken faith in a life to come, and say nothing of a Nirvâna of nothingness. The learned and royal author of them speaks of ascetics as a modern Christian philosopher might do, declaring that "ascetics of all shades of belief should remain unmolested; they all seek to obtain self-conquest and purity

---

[1] Davids: Buddhism, p. 122.

of soul. People have different opinions and different attachments, and ascetics obtain sometimes all, and sometimes only a part, of what they long for."[1]

This wonderful liberality has the true ring of Buddha's teachings, and is in great contrast to the ascetic extravagancies of the holy order in later centuries. But the great similarities to Buddha's doctrine are in the remarkable humanity and compassion exemplified in these Rock Edicts of King Asoka, — a feeling and principle not only far in advance of those of any royal edicts of that day, but even of most similar proclamations and legislation of modern Christian kingdoms. The humane king proclaims that slavery and the use of torture must be abolished, — reforms that in Europe and America have only been carried out in the nineteenth century; he orders capital punishment to be done away with; and with a most enlightened humanity he commands medical aid to be furnished to men and animals, wells to be dug in dry places for the use of the people, trees to be planted to furnish shade for the tired wanderer, and others for fruit for the needy. Villages are to be built for the monks, the holy books are to be carefully preserved, *stupas* (memorial towers) are to be erected for the consolation, happiness, and advantage of men in this world and the next, and " thus to the end of time this memorial [through its relics and associations] would allow my people to gain heaven."[2]

[1] Rock Edict III., Lillie, p. 63.   [2] Edict II., p. 69.

Even the sacrifice of animals, as well as the putting of them to death, is prohibited [1] on religious grounds, in view, no doubt, of Buddha's commandment not to kill. The estimate of almsgiving and prayers is precisely that of Gotama. "Religion consists in good works; in the non-commission of many acts, in mercy and charity, purity and chastity. These are to me the anointment of consecration. . . . There is no almsgiving and no loving-kindness comparable with the alms of religion." [2] "Not that the Beloved of the Gods deemeth offerings or prayers to be of the same value with true spiritual glory." [3] The royal disciple, like his master, inculcates obedience to parents, kindness to children and friends, mercy to brutes, indulgence to inferiors, reverence to priests and sages, the suppression of anger, passion, and cruelty, or extravagance, and the cultivation of generosity and toleration and charity.

More than two thousand years ago this humane Buddhist ruler, in advance of all other princes and kings, founded a remarkable office, that of Chief Minister of Religion (Dhamma), whose duty it was to preserve the purity of the Buddhistic faith, and care for the right treatment and progress of nations and subject-races. Similar officials were appointed in the dependent courts and other governments to watch and promote the education of women

---

[1] Delhi Pillar, Lillie, p. 63.   [2] Edict IX., p. 69.
[3] Edict XII.

in harems and elsewhere in the religion of Buddha. These commands are said to have been imitated in Ceylon [1] and other Buddhistic countries. Can it be wondered at that under such an enlightened and humane ruler, a follower of Sakya Muni, his faith spread in the next five centuries as did Christianity in Europe and Asia in its early ages? The pure spirit of this disciple of the Saint of India has remained unknown for twenty centuries, until these sentences written on the rocks have come to light, declaring what at least were the ideals of this religion in ages gone by. Whether they were ever realized we have no means of knowing.

It must be remembered that Buddhism almost utterly perished in the land of its birth (India) within a thousand or eleven hundred years; so that in 700 A. D. it was scarcely known there. It probably died out through its own corruptions and could not withstand persecution. At present it seems to exist in its greatest vigor in Ceylon. The lack of definiteness of belief in a moral and intelligent Power over the universe condemns it to final extinction.

The reader of this and the succeeding chapter on Buddhism will often be struck with the apparent resemblances between this faith and Christianity in the narra-

[1] Tennent states that as early as 20 A.D. a king of Ceylon, influenced by Buddhism, caused fruit-bearing trees to be planted throughout the island (Ceylon, i. 367).

tives and the discourses of their founders. The more, however, these seeming likenesses are studied, the less forcible they appear; and the most able and impartial scholars do not usually believe in any influence of the one religion upon the other.

Many of the resemblances of the two faiths come from the modern translations of ancient Buddhistic terms. The ideas of Sakya Muni are connoted by words from Saint Paul or the Apostles; yet the two may be far apart as the poles in their real meaning. There are, it is true, remarkable similarities, as has been noticed by M. Huc and other travellers, between the ceremonial of the Thibetan and Chinese Buddhistic Order and that of some branches of the Christian Church. This not improbably may be due to the influence of the Nestorians in the sixth and seventh centuries in China.[1]

It is of course perfectly possible that the peculiar tenets of Gotama Buddha could have trickled down through Essenism on early Christianity. The world even then was bound together by many cords of commerce and intercourse, and the thinkers of one country affected the thoughtful of many other nations. But the great contrast between the Essenians on the one side and Christ and the early Christians on the other in the matter of abstinence and asceticism, shows how little the influence of the first touched the early believers socially. The same, and even

---

[1] See Mosheim, Ecc. Hist., i. 421.

more, may be said of the Buddhists. The Brotherhood of Gotama was an order of ascetics and celibates; the Church of Christ was an association of lovers of God and of men, who were to be in the world and not of it. The rules of the latter consider men and women as members of families, and carrying on the relations of life in a natural way; the manifold regulations of the former — especially in later Buddhism — regard the believers as members of a convent, in the most unnatural relations. Moreover, though the end and object of the founders of the two religions were essentially alike, that is, the purification and exaltation of the human soul, their means were entirely different. Gotama hoped for it, first by a life of utter self-denial and benevolence, then by an intellectual operation, the fixing the mind on charity and love, and restraining all desires, until a beatific peace had been attained. Jesus Christ promised salvation by love, directed to himself as a perfect Ideal, and through him to the perfect and infinite Father, whose manifestation he was. The soul was cleansed through the power of affection and duty towards a sinless and boundless Benefactor and an eternal Friend. The two methods are world-wide apart, and the one could not have influenced the other.

Christ promised an eternal conscious personal life with the Father to the believer. Buddha promised peace; but whether that of everlasting sleep or nothingness, or whether a mystical union with Àtman, the Spirit of the universe, is not perfectly clear. At all events, the two lines of belief could not have arisen from each other. The resemblances noted often arise from similar Oriental circumstances, and from the corresponding position of elevated moral teachers in such countries as Palestine and India.

When we hear of affecting conversations with outcast women " at a well," and of similes drawn from a sower and his work, and like subjects, we may be sure that in Oriental countries most teachers and reformers and prophets have had similar experiences. The impassioned words of the spiritual teacher against formalism are probably alike under all climates. The ideals of sympathy and purity and justice among the most elevated and self-denying of mankind are similar in all countries. They are all probably the expressions of a supernatural influence, a divine inspiration from the Unknown God; but in Jesus Christ they are found perfect.

CHAPTER XV.

SACRED WRITINGS OF BUDDHISM.

How fleeting all things that have together come!
Their nature's to be born and die.
Coming they go   and then is best,
When each hath ceased and all is rest.
Very ancient Buddhistic Verse.

THERE is of course a difficulty in determining amid all the legends and exaggerations of the Buddhistic sacred writings what precisely Gotama Buddha said and taught. Yet a certain harmony and consistency of statement can be found in the multitudinous expressions attributed to him, and in the reports of his many discourses and sermons. The Buddhists claim that their canon of Scriptures was settled soon after the death of Buddha, the date of which may be put at 477 B. C.[1] However this may be, many scholars agree that the sayings of Buddha were carefully gathered and orally handed down within a hundred years of his death, or at the time of the Second Buddhistic Council, 377 B. C. It is probably to this oral tradition that we owe so many of the puerile representations in the Buddhistic writings, the memorizing aiding itself by such artifices.

[1] Max Müller: Dhammapada, p. 36.

The most condensed and valuable of Buddhistic writings, the Dhammapada ("Religion's Path," or "Footsteps of the Law"), was in existence in some form at the date of the Council under King Asoka, 242 B. C., and was supposed by its members to contain the words of Buddha.[1] Max Müller, however, inclines to put the date of Asoka as early as 263-259 B. C. The Dhammapada was translated into Chinese in the third century A.D., and into Pâli in Ceylon in the fourth, and has been rendered into Thibetan and various Oriental languages. The versions seem substantially the same. It, with the ancient Suttas (sermons), now translated[2] into English, are invaluable as showing the original conceptions of this faith.

It is altogether incredible that so profound a feeling as shows itself in all Buddhistic writings in regard to the person of Buddha should have gathered around a pure figment of the imagination, a sun-myth,[3] or a hero of

---

[1] Max Müller: Dhammapada, p. 31. Sacred Books of the East.

[2] See Sacred Books of the East, Sutta Nipâta, and others. The different spelling of Buddhistic words comes from the translations in various languages.

[3] An able and learned French scholar, M. Senart, has written a very ingenious argument to prove that the whole story of Buddha is a solar myth (Essai sur La Legende du Buddha). Dr. Oldenberg answers this very convincingly. One of his strongest points is that the oldest Buddhistic records — the Southern Pâli stories and documents — are the most free from mythical features, and seem simply an historical narrative; while later poems and legends, such as the Lalita Vistâra of the northern Buddhists, seem much bedecked with fanciful and mythical features. The older the documents the more like per-

poetic fancy; and all this beginning (if scholars are correct) within a century of the reported death of its subject. Moreover, the figure shadowed forth in the legends, and around which are formed the traditions, is a harmonious conception, of the same general character in all the records and stories; and the teachings in all the earlier reported conversations and sermons are consistent with one another. They are often extremely metaphysical and mystical; they are marked by great omissions and profound earnestness; but they are like one another. The teachings of the Dhammapada, the Sutta Nipâta, and many very ancient sermons attributed to Buddha, seem to proceed from one mind, or from various minds imbued with the ideas of one teacher. They have a like character. They must have emanated from one source, or under similar influences.

It need hardly be said that they have little resemblance to the sayings of Christ. These were designed for the poor and needy, for the babes in the kingdom of heaven; they show an unequalled simplicity and directness; they have the freshness of divine inspiration, the glow of heavenly communion. Buddha's words, on the other hand, are addressed to the intellectual. They relate above all to ideal and metaphysical conceptions. They rest

sonal and real history. That some features of ancient solar myths should become attached to the lives of historical popular heroes is perfectly natural.

especially on certain great ideas in the field of speculation, which (whether true or false) are entirely beyond the grasp of ordinary men and women. Such conceptions as Karma, or the endurance of the moral effects of each life during succeeding lives without a conscious personality; or of a soul which is a bundle of faculties or sensations and perceptions where each is dissolved and yet *something* survives: or of a great, unspeakable, impersonal Spirit (Âtman) which has no relation to time or space or any term in human thought; or a mental state (Nirvâna) which at times appears to belong not to person, or time, or place, or any human condition, — such mystical ideas or imaginations, it is obvious, are not for the masses of mankind.

But the great truths which in innumerable expressions are preached in Buddhistic writings are practical, and belong to all ages and races. They are (1) the fearful existence of human suffering, (2) its cause, (3) its extinction, and (4) the path which leads to this extinction. Here are topics which must interest the human mind while the world endures.

But it must not be supposed that Buddhism, as it has appeared in human history, confines itself to these simple and grand topics. Its early history — as is true of all religions — is the more simple and more inspired with great truths. It gradually degenerates into mysticism, transcendental religion, and formalism, and it ends with building up a church, the most ceremonial and external in spirit which has ever existed, and with negations which are destroying its influence over morals and the practical life of men and women.

Dhammapada. — This remarkable book, it should be remembered, is only a small portion of the Three Pitakas (Collections), the Buddhistic Canon; but it is of the most undoubted antiquity, and may fairly be put back (at least in form) to 250 B. C.

The Maker. — "Looking for the Maker of this tabernacle, I must run through a course of re-births so long as I do not find him. Painful is birth again and again. But now, Maker of this tabernacle, thou hast been seen; thou shalt not make up this tabernacle any more! All thy rafters are broken; thy ridge-pole is sundered. The mind approaching Nirvâna hath attained the extinction of all desires." [1]

The above verse is one of the most famous and ancient of the Buddhistic texts, believed to be the words of Gotama himself on attaining the idea of Nirvâna. They are supposed by scholars not to refer to any belief in a Creator; but they seem to me consistent with Buddha's shadowy belief. Under the law of Karma the saint has run through birth after birth, but has not hitherto been fitted by suffering to leave mortality and see the Âtman, or Spirit of the Universe. But now he is emancipated; he has attained Nirvâna; he has left the body and all bodily effects; he knoweth God, and bids defiance to the

[1] Dhammapada, pp. 153, 154.

body which has imprisoned him so long. Even the Infinite One cannot replace him in the sad chain of earthly sin and sorrow. There is indeed in these strange words no sense of the Fatherhood of God. They are world wide from the words of Jesus, but they are not the words of an atheist.

The Uncreated. — "If thou hast learned the destruction of the *Sankhára* (the conformations), thou knowest the Uncreated." [1]

"If thou hast learned that all human action and faculty and thought, and all conformations of human powers, are illusions and impermanent, thou knowest the Eternal, or God himself."

Morals. — Buddha being asked what is a true Brahman, or sage, answers: "He is a true sage who hath banished all wickedness from himself, who knoweth nothing of mockery and nothing of impurity, a self-conqueror." [2]

The five great commandments supposed to be given by Buddha are: Thou shalt not kill; thou shalt not steal; thou shalt not commit impurity; thou shalt not speak an untruth; thou shalt not drink intoxicating drinks. It is often impressed on the followers of Buddha that sin is above all in the thoughts.

"Whoever speaketh or acteth with impure thoughts, him suffering followeth, as the wheel the feet of the steed; whoever acteth with pure thoughts, him joy followeth like a shadow which never leaves one. . . . If a man live a hundred years and spend the whole of his

---

[1] Dhammapada, p. 383.   [2] Oldenberg (German.), p. 120.

time in religious attention and offerings to the gods, sacrificing elephants and horses, all this is not equal to one act of pure love in saving life."[1]

Thought. — "This body of thine shall soon return to the earth, thy form destroyed, thy spirit fled; why then covet such an abode? It is the mind that maketh its own dwelling-place. From earliest times the mind, reflecting on evil ways, courts its own misery. It is thought that maketh its own sorrow."[2]

Impurity. — "The messengers of Jama (the King of Death) are close to thee; thou standest at the door of thy departure, and thou hast no provision for thy journey."[3] "When thy impurities are blown away, and thou art free from guilt, thou wilt enter into the heavenly world of the elect."[4] "What is the use of plaited hair, O fool; what the use of raiment of goat-skins? Within there is ravening, but the outside thou makest clean."[5] "He who is tolerant with the intolerant, mild with the fault-finding, free from passion among the passionate, him I call a true Brahman [sage]."[6]

The Pilgrimage of Beings. — "This pilgrimage," says Buddha, "O my disciples, hath its beginning in eternity. . . . What think ye, O disciples, whether is more, the water which is in the four great oceans, or the tears which have flowed from you, or have been shed by you, while ye strayed and wandered on this long pilgrimage? Because that was your portion which ye abhorred, and that which ye loved was not your portion. A mother's death, a father's, a brother's, a sister's, a son's, and the loss of relatives, the loss of property, — all this have ye experienced through long ages."[7]

Spiritual Worship. — "If a man repeat each month a thousand sacrifices, and go on enduring his bodily sufferings without ceasing,

---

[1] Chinese Dhammapada, p. 59. [2] Ibid., p. 73.
[3] Ibid., p. 235. [4] Ibid., p. 236.
[5] Ibid., p. 394. [6] Ibid., p. 406.
[7] Oldenberg, p. 221.

this is not equal to a moment's undivided attention to the Law."[1] "The sacrificing to spirits in order to find peace, or expecting reward after this life, the reward for this is not one quarter that man's who pays homage to the good."[2]

Destiny. — "Not in the void of heaven, not in the depths of the sea, not by entering the rocky clefts of the mountains, — in none of these places can a man by any means escape the consequences of his evil deed."[3] "He who inflicteth pain on the gentle and the good, or falsely accuseth the innocent, — this man will inherit one of these ten calamities."[4]

Spirituality. — "Sacrifices and such acts are sources of misery day and night, a continual burden. To escape sorrow a man should attend to the Law of Buddha, and arrive at deliverance from world-priests."[5] "Although a man goeth naked with tangled hair, though he clothe himself with a few leaves, or garments of bark, though he covereth himself with dirt and sleep on the stones, what use this, in getting rid of impure thoughts?"

Earnestness. — "How can ye be gay, how can ye indulge desire? Evermore the flames burn; darkness surroundeth you, and will ye not seek the light? . . . Man gathereth the flowers, his heart is set on pleasure, death cometh upon him like the floods of water upon a village, and sweepeth him away. . . . Neither in the region of the air, nor in the depths of the sea, nor if thou piercest into the clefts of the mountain, wilt thou find a place on this earth where the hand of death will not reach thee."

The Happiness of Believers. — "He whose appetites are at rest, like a steed thoroughly broken in by the trainer, he who hath put away pride, who is free from impurity, him thus perfect the gods themselves envy."[6] "The believer who dwelleth in an empty hut, whose soul is full of peace, enjoyeth superhuman happiness,

---

[1] Dhammapada, Beal, p. 87.
[2] Ibid., p. 89.
[3] Ibid., p. 93.
[4] Ibid., p. 95.
[5] Ibid., p. 97.
[6] Oldenberg, p. 222.

gazing solely on the truth. . . . Esteeming this body like a bubble, regarding it as a mirage, breaking the flower-shafts of the tempter, press on to the bourn where the monarch Death shall no more gaze upon thee!"[1] "Having abandoned lust, malice, ignorance, having broken the bonds of transmigration, entertaining no fear for the loss of life, let me walk alone, like a rhinoceros."[2]

Earnestness. — " Buddha hearing some Brahmans laughing after listening to instruction, said : 'What room for mirth, what for laughing, remembering the everlasting fire? Surely this dark and dreary world is not fit for one to seek security and rest. Behold this body in its fashions; what reliance can it afford as a resting-place, filled with crowded thoughts, liable to every disease? Oh, how is it that men do not perceive its false appearances? When old, its beauty fades; in sickness, what paleness and leanness, the skin wrinkled, the flesh withered, death and life joined together; and when the body dies, and the spirit flies away, as when a king throws away a broken chariot, so do flesh and bones lie scattered. What reliance in the body?'"[3] "No burning greater than lust, no poison worse than hate, no misery greater than the body, no joy like its destruction."[4]

Pleasure. — "It is related that four monks were giving their ideals of complete happiness. One found it in the pleasure of spring walks, another in the delight of congenial society, another in the comforts of wealth, and still another in the joy of love and marriage. Buddha said unto them : ' Let there be an end to such talk, for all these things are the source of sorrow, misfortune, and calamity; this is not the way of eternal peace. The flowers of spring fade in autumn, friends shall be scattered, wealth and the beauty of women are the cause of every misfortune; the highest bliss is to leave the world, to search after supreme wisdom, to desire nought for one's self, to aim at Nirvâna.' "[5]

[1] Oldenberg, p. 237.
[2] Sutta Nipâta, p. 19. A very ancient sermon.
[3] Dhammapada, p. 100.   [4] Ibid., p. 116.   [5] Ibid., p. 119.

The Saints. — "Who is a saint [Bhikshu]? Not he who begs regularly his food . . . but he who gives up every cause of guilt, who lives purely, who by wisdom is able to crush every inclination. Who is the wise? Not he who is simply mute while the busy work of his mind is impure, but he whose inward life is pure and spiritual. And who is the enlightened saint? Not he who saves the life of all things, but he who is filled with universal benevolence, who has no malice in his heart; and the man who observeth the law is not he who talketh much, but one who keepeth his body in subjection to the law." [1]

Life. — "What is life, but the flower or fruit which falls when ripe, but which ever fears the untimely frost? Once born, there is nought but sorrow; for who is there that can escape death? From the first moment in the womb there is nought but the bodily form, transitory as the lightning flash. . . . The body is but a thing destined to perish; there is no certain form given to the spirit connected with the body. . . . It is not the matter of one life or one death, but from the birth proceed all the consequences of former deeds, resulting in joy or misery. The body dies, but the spirit is not entombed." [2]

What is Good Fortune? — Buddha said, "He who hath faith and delighteth in the true gospel, this man is fortunate. A friend of the virtuous, holding with the righteous, always making virtue his first aim, keeping his body according to laws of purity, he is truly fortunate." He goes on to describe the believer "as temperate, pure, looking to the Scriptures, self-restrained, caring for wife and child, not giving way to idleness and self-honor, patiently continuing in the way of duty, rejoicing to see a minister of the faith, observing religious duties, and placing confidence in the teachers of religion. Such an one desireth above all things to escape birth. He is devoted to charity, and to paying due respect to Divine spirits. He is anxious to get rid of sensuality and covetousness and anger. He is full of love for all things in the

[1] Dhammapada, p. 128.   [2] Ibid., p. 168.

world, practising virtue to benefit others; such an one is indeed fortunate."[1]

Faith. — "Faith can cross the flood even as the master of the ship steers his bark across the sea; ever advancing on the ocean of sorrow, wisdom lands us on yonder shore. The wise man who liveth by faith in virtue of his holy life, enjoyeth unselfish bliss, and casts off all shackles. Faith lays hold of true wisdom; religion leadeth to deliverance from death."[2]

Selfish Good. — "Spirits [Devas] who have been good for the sake of reward, after much joy shall reap much sorrow."[3]

The four truths most dwelt upon by the ancient Buddhistic writers are, first, the reality of misery, second, its cause, third, the possibility of its destruction, fourth, the means needed for this end. An ancient verse tells us that the doctrine of Buddha was to avoid all wickedness, to do all righteousness, and cleanse the heart of all desire.[4] A very ancient poem thus states the doctrine of the faith:

> "Without complaint, without envy,
> Continue in the practice of the commandments,
> Knowing the way to moderate appetite.
> Ever joyous without any weight of care,
> Fixed, and ever advancing in virtue, —
> This is the doctrine of Buddha."[5]

The Sutra of Forty-two Sections.

This collection of ancient Buddhistic writings was known in India to the Chinese pilgrims as early as 64 A. D., and must have existed there much earlier than this.

[1] Ibid., p. 176.
[2] Chinese Dhammapada, Beal, p. 57.
[3] Budd. Scriptures, p. 98.
[4] Beal's Catena, p. 156.
[5] Sik. Tath., Beal, p. 158.

Good for Evil. — "A man who foolishly does me wrong, I will return to him the protection of my ungrudging love; the more evil cometh from him the more good shall go from me; the fragrance of these good actions always redounding to me, the harm of the slanderer's words returning to him." [1]

Charity. — "A man in the practice of religion who exercises charity from a feeling of obligation or feeling of partiality does not obtain much merit. And when we see a man giving in charity, who rejoices at it that he is thus advancing the cause of religion, he also shall obtain religion." [2]

"To feed crowds by the hundreds is not to be compared with the act of feeding one really good man;" and this thought is wrought out through a series of climaxes to the end that "feeding a thousand myriad of angelic men is nothing to feeding one Buddha and learning to pray to him from a desire to save all living creatures." On the other hand it is said, "To feed one good man is infinitely greater in point of merit than attending to questions about heaven and earth, spirits and demons, such as occupy ordinary men." [3]

These are some of the difficulties which meet the believer: "To be poor and at the same time charitable, to be rich and religious, to repress lust, to bear insult without anger, to be in the world and not set heart on it, to extirpate self-esteem, to be at once good and learned, to attain one's end without exultation." [4]

---

[1] Budd. Scriptures, Beal's Catena, p. 193.
[2] Dhammapada, p. 194.   [3] Ibid., p. 195.
[4] Ibid., p. 195.

A Charitable King. — The ancient Buddhistic records tell of a king who distributed in one day the accumulated treasures of five years. Having collected in a space called the "charity enclosure" immense piles of wealth and jewels, he first adorned the statue of Buddha, then he distributed to resident priests, then to priests from a distance, then he divided large sums among numbers of disciples, next among heretics following the ways of the world, and lastly he gave to widows and orphans, the poor and the desolate. After having thus disbursed his wealth, he gave away finally his diadem and jewelled necklace, saying with joy, "Well done! Now all that I possess hath entered into incorruptible and imperishable treasuries."[1]

Goodness. — Buddha said, "Who is the good man? The religious man only is good. And what is goodness? First and foremost it is the *agreement of the will with the conscience.* Who is the great man? He who is strongest in patience, he who patiently endureth injury and maintaineth a blameless life, he is a man indeed."

Spiritual Power. — "But once get rid of the pollution of the wicked heart, then we perceive the spiritual portion of ourselves which we knew to be from the first, although involved in the rut of life and death."

Buddhistic Golden Rules.

"For never in this world does hatred cease by hatred. Hatred ceases by love; this is always its nature."[2] "Earnest among the heedless, awake among the sleepers, the wise make progress, leaving

---

[1] Buddhistic Records of Western World, p. 233.
[2] Dhammapada, p. 29.

those behind; even as the swift steed leaveth the horse with no strength."[1] "As the bee, injuring not the flower, its coloring or scent, flieth away taking its nectar, so let the good man dwell upon the earth. He who formerly was heedless, and afterwards becometh earnest, lighteth up this world like the moon escaped from clouds."[2] "Let us live happily, then, free from ailments among the ailing; let us dwell free from affliction among men who are sick at heart."[3] "Let us live happily, not hating those who hate us. Let us live free from hatred among men who hate us."[4] "Anger, drunkenness, obstinacy, bigotry, deception, envy, self-praise, disparagement of others, high-mindedness, evil communications, — these make uncleanness, not the eating of flesh."[5]

Self-Conquest. — "One self-conquered is better than the conquest of all other people. Not even a god, not Mârâ (Satan) with Brahma, can change into defeat the victory of a man over himself."[6]

The World. — "He whose evil deeds are covered by good deeds brightens up this world like the moon when freed from clouds. . . . This world is dark, only few can see here; a few only go to heaven, like birds escaped from the net."[7]

A Parable.

"The Lord Buddha was passing over a ploughed field, when he met a husbandman toiling at his work. The husbandman said unto him bitterly, 'O priest, I both plough and sow, and having ploughed and sown, I eat; thou also, O priest, shouldst plough and sow, and then only eat.' The Blessed One said unto him, 'I, too, O husbandman, plough and sow, and then I eat.' 'But,' said the husbandman, 'we see neither yoke nor plough nor plough-

---

[1] Dhammapada, 19.   [2] Ibid., p. 172.   [3] Ibid., p. 197.
[4] Ibid., p. 223. Similar beautiful ideas are found in the Indian poem Mahâ-bhârata.
[5] Amagandha Sutta, 7, 11.   [6] Dhammapada, pp. 104, 105.
[7] Ibid. pp. 173, 174.

share, nor goad nor oxen.' The Blessed One answered unto him, 'Faith is my seed, penance the rain, wisdom the yoke and plough, modesty the shaft, mind the string, and presence of mind my ploughshare and goad; exertion is my beast who carrieth me to Nirvâna.' "[1]

Apothegms.

"The uncharitable do not go to the world of the gods."[2] "Better than ruling over the earth, better than going to heaven, better than lordship over all worlds, is the reward of the first step in holiness."[3] "Not to commit any sin, to do good, and to purify one's mind, that is the teaching of the Law of Buddha."[4] "Let us live happily, then, not hating those who hate us; let us dwell free from hatred among those who hate."[5] "Let us live happily, we who call nothing our own. We shall be like the bright gods feeding on happiness."[6] "Kinsfolk, friends, and lovers salute a man who hath been long away and returns safe from a far country. In like manner his good deeds receive him who hath done good, and hath gone from this world to another."[7] "He who holdeth back rising anger like a rolling chariot, him I call a true driver; other people are but holding the reins."[8]

Beatitudes.

II.

Not to serve the foolish,
But to serve the spiritual,
To honor those worthy of honor, —
Blessed be this.

VI.

To bestow alms and live righteously,
To give help to kindred,

---

[1] Sutta Nipâta, p. 20.   [2] Dhammapada, p. 177.
[3] Ibid., p. 178.   [4] Ibid., p. 183.   [5] Ibid., p. 197.
[6] Ibid., p. 200.   [7] Ibid., pp. 219, 220.   [8] Ibid., p. 222.

Deeds which cannot be blamed;
To abhor and cease from sin,
Abstinence from strong drink,
Not to be weary in well doing, —
Blessed be these.

VIII.

Reverence and lowliness,
Contentment and gratitude,
The hearing of the law at due seasons, —
Blessed be this.

X.

Self-restraint and purity,
The knowledge of the noble truths, —
Most blessed be this.[1]

Riches. — One of the old Suttas says: "How hardly shall the rich man instruct himself in the Way! Who shall have riches and power and not become their slave?"

The True Treasures.

The true treasure is that laid up by man or woman
Through charity and piety and temperance and self-control.
. . . .
In the individual man, in the stranger and sojourner,
In his father and mother and elder brother,
The treasure thus hid passeth not away,
Though he leave the fleeting riches of this world.
This a man taketh not with him, —
A treasure that no wrong of others and no thief can steal away.
Let the wise man do good deeds, — the treasure that follows of
    itself.[2]

[1] Lillie, p. 154.   [2] Nid. Sutta, Davids.

"I long not for death, I long not for life; I wait till the hour cometh, like a hireling who waiteth for his wage; I wait with assured and wakeful mind."[1]

"Hunger is a most grievous pain; the illusions of life are the most grievous sorrow; recognizing this as a truth, man attaineth Nirvâna, supreme happiness. . . . The wise who cause no suffering to any being, who keep their body in check, they walk to the everlasting state. He who hath reached that, knoweth no sorrow. He who is permeated by goodness, the believer who sticketh to Buddha's teaching, passeth from here to the land of peace, where transientness finds an end, where is happiness."[2]

NIRVÂNA.

Nirvâna is often spoken of as the "going out" of the fires of lust and pleasure and hatred and delusion.[3] In the Buddhistic scriptures of the Chinese it is said, "In sorrow is no Nirvâna, and in Nirvâna is no sorrow." Again, "I, Gotama Buddha, devote myself to righteousness, so that I may arrive at the highest Nirvâna."[4]

Again, says an ancient verse: —

"The heart carefully avoiding all idle pleasure,
Diligently applying itself to the holy law of Buddha,
Letting go all lust and consequent disappointment,
Fixed and unchangeable, enters upon Nirvâna."[5]

"These wise people, meditative, steady, always possessed of strong powers, attained to Nirvâna, the highest happiness."[6] "A saint

---

[1] Oldenberg: Melindapanka, p. 271. Later than the Dhammapada.
[2] Oldenberg: Dhammapada, p. 385.
[3] Davids, p. 100.
[4] Catena of Buddhistic Scriptures, Beal, p. 174.
[5] Ibid., p. 159.   [6] Dhammapada, p. 23.

who delights in reflection, who looks with fear on thoughtlessness, will not go to destruction; he is near to Nirvâna."[1] "If like a trumpet trampled under feet thou utterest not, then thou hast reached Nirvâna. Anger is not known to thee."[2] "In long-suffering is called the highest Nirvâna; no happiness like rest or quietness, and the highest happiness is Nirvâna. The way to peace leadeth also to Nirvâna."[3] "When thou hast cut off passion and hatred, thou wilt go to Nirvâna."[4] "The sages who always control their body, they will go to the unchangeable place where they will suffer no more. . . . Some people are born again on earth; evil-doers go to hell; righteous people go to the heavens; those who are free from all worldly desires enter Nirvâna. One is the road leading to wealth; another that leading to Nirvâna. If the saint, the disciple of Buddha, has learned this, he will not yearn for honor; he will strive after separation from the world."[5] "The believer who delighteth in diligence and looketh with terror on sloth, cannot fall away; he is in the very presence of Nirvâna."[6] The Buddhas declare the best self-mortification to be patience, long-suffering, but the best of all to be Nirvâna."[7] "Those who are ever on the watch, who study day and night, whose heart is set on it, their sinfulness dies away."[8] "Cut down lust, not a tree. From lust springeth fear; having cut down, with all its undergrowth, the forest of lust, become *Nirvâna'd.*"[9] "Cut off self-love, as an autumn lotus, with your hand; devote yourself to the path of peace alone, for by the blessed one hath Nirvâna been revealed."[10] "The wise man who is trained according to the commandments, seeing the force of this truth, should at once clear the path leading to Nirvâna."[11] "Bail out this boat; when bailed it will go quickly; when thou hast got rid of lust and hatred, thou shalt go to Nirvâna."[12]

[1] Dhammapada, p. 32.
[2] Ibid., p. 134.
[3] Ibid., p. 285.
[4] Ibid., p. 369.
[5] Ibid., p. 75.
[6] Ibid., p. 32.
[7] Ibid., p. 184.
[8] Ibid., p. 226.
[9] Ibid., p. 283.
[10] Ibid., p. 285.
[11] Ibid., p. 289.
[12] Ibid., p. 369.

"Temperance and chastity, to discern the noble truths, to experience Nirvâna, that is the greatest blessing."[1] "Beautiful as groves and thickets covered with bloom in the first hot months of summer, the Buddha preached for the good of all his glorious law which leadeth to Nirvâna."[2] "All earthly glory and heavenly joy and the gain of Nirvâna can be procured by these; namely, charity, piety, and self-control."[3] "As where heat is, there is also cold, so where the threefold fires of lust, hatred, and ignorance are, there must Nirvâna be sought."

"Having conceived bliss to consist in peace, let him not be indolent in Gotama's commandments."[4] "For he a conqueror unconquered saw the doctrine invisibly without any traditional instruction."[5] "Such a disciple, who has turned away from desire and attachment, and is possessed of understanding, has already gone to immortal peace, the unchangeable state of Nirvâna."[6] "And seeing misery . . . searching for truth I saw inward peace."[7]

The true disciple is spoken of as the Confessor of Peace.[8] In this world much has been seen, heard, thought. The destruction of passion and of the dear objects that have been perceived is the imperceptible state of Nirvâna.[9] Nirvâna is called the destruction and decay of death.[10] By the leaving of desire Nirvâna is said to be.[11]

"So the mendicant Suddhabra was received after baptism into the higher grade of the Sacred Order under the Blessed One, and from

---

[1] Mang. Sutta, vii.; Davids: Buddhism, p. 101.
[2] Ratuna Sutta, v 12. [3] Nidhi Kam. Sutta, v. 113.
[4] Sutta Nipâta, 933. [5] Ibid., 934. [6] Ibid., 203.
[7] Ibid., 837. [8] Ibid., 84. [9] Ibid., 1085.
[10] Ibid., 1093. [11] Ibid., 1108.

immediately after his ordination the venerable disciple remained alone and separate, earnest, zealous, and resolved. And ere long he attained to that supreme goal of the higher life [Nirvâna] for the sake of which men go out from all and every comfort to become houseless wanderers; yea, that supreme goal did he by himself, and while yet in this visible world, bring himself to the knowledge of, and continue to realize and to see face to face; and he became conscious that birth was at an end and that the higher life had been fulfilled, that all that should be done had been accomplished, and that after this present life there would be no beyond [of birth-and-death, or transmigration]." [1]

The Sutta Nipâta closes thus: —

"To the insuperable, the unchangeable, whose littleness is nowhere, I shall certainly go; in this [Nirvâna] [2] there will be no doubt for me; so know me of an untroubled mind." [3]

Buddha. — Buddha is entitled "the Elevated, the Joy-bringer, the Joy-spender, whose senses are still, whose soul is in peace, the highest Self-Conqueror, the hero who hath overcome himself, and watcheth over himself, and holdeth his senses in check. He appeareth in the world for salvation to many peoples, for joy to many nations, from compassion to the world for blessing, salvation, and joy to gods and men." [4]

[1] This passage is taken from a very ancient Buddhist writing, possibly dating to the first century after Buddha, — The Book of the Great Decease, Davids, v. 68.

[2] It is noteworthy that the translations of the term "Nirvâna" in the Thibetan always give the meaning of emancipation or state of deliverance from pain, or emancipation from pain and death (Burnouf, p. 17, Introd.).

[3] Sutta Nipâta, 1148.   [4] Oldenberg, p. 336.

His Mission. — It is related that an old monk lay sick of a loathsome disease, and no one would approach him or help him. The Lord Buddha entered his dwelling and washed and tended him till he was restored to health, saying, "The purpose of the Holy One in coming to the world is to befriend the poor, the helpless, the unprotected, to nourish those in bodily affliction, to help the orphan and the aged."[1]

Death of a Buddhist. — "The famous Chinese traveller, Hiouen Thsang, who went as a pilgrim from China to India to investigate Buddhism in the seventh century, had just finished his translation of the holy books into Chinese, when he felt his death approaching, and thus addressed his disciples: 'After my death, when ye take me to my last home, let it be in a simple and modest way. Wrap my body in a mat and place it in some quiet, secluded valley; let it not be laid in the neighborhood of a royal palace or a convent; for a body as impure as mine should not lie in such a place.' His disciples wept bitterly; but at length, his end approaching, he gave alms to the poor, and called the brethren of the convent to his bedside, to bid adieu to his impure and despised body. 'I desire to see the merit of my good deeds bear fruit with all mankind; I desire to be born in the heaven called Joyous, to be admitted among the disciples of the Loving One, and there to serve him as my tender and affectionate Lord. I desire to be born in future births, here on earth, that I may accomplish with unceasing zeal my duties to the Lord Buddha, and at length arrive at the condition of perfect wisdom, Nirvâna.' After uttering his adieus, he lay long in serious thought; then, as he sank, regretting that he had made so little progress towards the fulness of holiness, he said: 'Adoration to the Loving One, gifted with sublime intelligence, I

---

[1] Dhammapada, p. 94.

pray to be allowed with all men to behold thy face. Adoration to the Loving One! I pray to be admitted after death to thy presence and the multitude that dwelleth around thee.' In the middle of the night his disciples asked him, 'Hast thou yet obtained a new birth in heaven?' 'Yes,' he gently whispered, and breathed his last."[1]

Buddha and Confucius. — It is related by Edkins in his "Notes on Buddhism in China" that a follower of Buddha assailed the doctrine of Confucius as relating only to this present life, urging that it does not reach to the future state with its interminable results; that its motives to virtue are derived from the happiness to posterity; that the only consequence of vice is present suffering, and that the rewards of the good are merely worldly honors. On the other hand, the Buddhist claimed that the aims of Buddha are illimitable; that his one sentiment is "mercy seeking to save;" that he speaks of hell to deter from sin, and points to heaven that men may desire its happiness; he exhibits Nirvâna as the spirit's final refuge, and tells us of a body to be possessed under other conditions, long after our present body has passed away. The disciple of Confucius answered that we ought to do right for its own sake, and without reference to reward; that to praise Nirvâna is to promote a lazy inactivity; and that to dwell on the form of the body which we may attain to in a future life is calculated only to develop the love of the marvellous.

[1] Beal: Buddhism in China, pp. 113, 114.

In "Chinese Buddhism" Buddha's body is described as "co-extensive with the universe," dwelling in all time, with excellences innumerable as the dust-grains, beyond all human character, transcending all human language.[1]

Buddha's Beatification. — "On that night when the Lord attained the state of Nirvâna, angels [Devas] sang together in the midst of space a joyous song, and there rained upon earth every kind of sweet flower. . . . All fell at the feet of Buddha; there was no ill-feeling or hatred in the hearts of men, but whatever want there was, whether of food or drink or raiment, was at once supplied; the blind received their sight, the dumb spake, the deaf heard, those bound in hell were released, and every kind of being, beasts, demons, and all created things, found peace and rest."[2]

The Outcast Women. — Buddha is often spoken of in these narratives as conversing with well-known courtesans, seeking to lead them to a higher life. In one case he is said to have preferred the society of one of these women to that of nobles and princes, and she subsequently became his pure and devout disciple. In another case his disciple Ananda is said to have come to a well and to have asked for water of a chândâla woman drawing water from the fountain; and she said unto him, "How canst thou, being a follower of the Blessed One, ask water of me, a chândâla?" And he said, "I did not ask after thy caste or family, but I asked thee for water;" and she gave unto him, and became thereafter a disciple.

[1] Beal: Buddhism in China, p. 102.
[2] Beal: History of Buddha, p. 225.

The First Sermon of Buddha. — This discourse, which has come down through the centuries, is said to have been on the "Foundation of the Kingdom of Righteousness." The poetic Oriental tradition relates that on that day the angels thronged to hear the discourse until the heavens were emptied, and the sound of their approach was like the rain of a storm. All the worlds in which were sentient beings were made void of light, so that the congregation assembled was in number infinite. But at the sound of the trump of the King of Angels they became still as a waveless sea. And then each of the countless listeners thought that the sage was looking towards himself alone, and was speaking to him in his own tongue.[1]

In this discourse are brought forth "eight divisions of the noble path," which, though sounding commonplace to us, have been the inspiration and the assistance of so many million Buddhists. They are: 1. Right views. 2. Right aims. 3. Right speech. 4. Right conduct. 5. Right livelihood. 6. Right effort. 7. Right-mindfulness. 8. Right contemplation. In these ancient sermons the appeal is often put to the Master, "Show us the way to a state of union with Brahma;" and in one instance he thus replies: "Know that from time to time a Perfect One [Tathâgata] is born unto the world, a fully Enlightened One, Blessed and Worthy, happy with knowledge of the world, unsurpassed as a guide to erring mortals, a teacher

[1] Davids: Buddhistic Suttas, vi. 42.

of gods and men, a Blessed One. He by himself thoroughly understandeth and seeth as it were face to face this universe, — the world below with all its spirits, and the worlds above of Mârâ and Brahma, and all creatures and gods and men, — and he then maketh his knowledge known to others. The truth doth he proclaim both in its letter and its spirit, — lovely in its origin, lovely in its progress, lovely in its consummation. The higher life doth he make known in all its purity, in all its perfectness."[1]

The Pharisees. — In one of these sermons he proves to the pharisees of those days, the Tevigga, those who boasted of an extraordinary knowledge of the Scriptures and the Law (the Vedas) in a highly Socratic manner, that these Brahmans were not in likeness to Brahma, and therefore could not be united to him hereafter; that, though versed in the knowledge of the Vedas, they bore anger and malice in their hearts, were sinful and uncontrolled, and how would it be possible that after death, when their body was dissolved, they could become united to Brahma, who is free from anger and malice, is sinless, and has absolute self-control. "These Brahmans, while they sit down in confidence, are really sinking down in the mire, and so sinking, they arrive only at despair, thinking they are crossing over to some happier land; therefore their threefold wisdom is called a waterless desert."[2] But to the beloved disciples,

---

[1] Davids: Buddhistic Suttas, p. 186.
[2] Tevigga Sutta, or Knowledge of the Vedas, p. 185.

who are seeking simply and truly this union with Brahma, he explains in what manner they must seek to cultivate universal love. "Thus the whole wide world, above, below, around, and everywhere, does the disciple continue to pervade with the heart of love, far-reaching, grown great, and beyond measure. . . . Even so of all things that have shape or life there is not one that he passeth by or leaveth aside, but regardeth them all with mind set free, and deep-felt love. Only this is the way to a state of union with Brahma."[1] The Socratic method with the disciple is pursued somewhat thus: "'Will the disciple who liveth thus be in possession of women, wealth, and the luxuries of life?'—'He will not, Gotama.'—'Will he be full of anger?' —'He will be free of anger, Gotama.'"[2] And so the questions proceed in regard to malice, impurity, want of self-control, and yielding to the world. All these things the true disciple is shown to be free from. "'Is there, then, agreement and likeness between the disciple and Brahma?'—'There is, O master.'—'Very good, Vasettha. Then it must be that the disciple, free from all these things,— anger, malice, impurity, being pure in mind, and master of himself,— will after death, when the body is dissolved, become united with Brahma.'"[3] The disciples acknowledge themselves convinced, and betake themselves to the Perfect One as a refuge, to the Truth and the

[1] Davids : Buddhistic Suttas, p. 201.
[2] Ibid., p. 202.
[3] Ibid., p. 203.

Brotherhood. "May the Blessed One accept us as disciples and true believers from this day forth as long as life endureth."[1]

In these ancient sermons are found these beautiful words, no doubt real thoughts of Buddha, which have come down through the ages: —

"The true believer must be kind to all creatures that have life; he passeth his life in honesty and purity of heart; he liveth a life of chastity and purity; he speaketh truth; from the truth he never swerveth; he liveth as a binder together of those who are divided, an encourager of those who are friends, a peace-maker, a lover of peace, impassioned for peace; a speaker of words that make for peace, etc. . . . Whatever word is humane, pleasant to the ear, lovely, reaching to the heart, urbane, pleasing to the people, such are the words he speaketh."[2]

The Death of Buddha. — "The great Buddha, Lord of the world, having finished his work of converting the world, entered on the joy of the Nirvâna. . . . With his head to the north he lay, and thus spoke to his disciples : ' Who shall now make unto us a boat to cross over the great sea of birth-and-death; who shall light a lamp to light us through the long night of ignorance?' . . . When the Holy One was about to die, a brilliant light shone round about; men and angels were cast down, and together showed their sorrow as they spake thus one to another : 'Now the great Buddha, the world's Lord, is about to die. The happiness of men is gone, the world hath lost its support.' Then said Buddha, ' Say not the Holy One hath gone forever, because he dieth; the body of the gospel endureth forever, unchangeable. Put away all sloth, and without delay seek for the emancipation of the world.' . . .

[1] Davids : Buddhistic Suttas, p. 203.
[2] Buddhistic Suttas, Kula Silam, p. 190.

"Then the heavenly host, bearing exquisite divine flowers, sang through space the praises of his sacred nature, each in full sincerity of heart offering his full sacrifice of worship. . . . His mother, the queen Maya, fainted, till once again she said in loud accents, 'The happiness of men and gods is departed, the world's eyes are put out, all things are desert, without a guide.' Then by the holy power of the Perfect One the golden coffin of itself opened, spreading abroad a glorious light, and he with hands crossed and sitting upright saluted thus his loving mother: 'Thou hast come down from afar; thou who livest so holy needest not be sad.' Whereupon his beloved disciple, Ananda, suppressing his grief, said unto him, 'What shall I say hereafter, when they question me?' The Lord answered, 'Say, when Buddha died, his loving mother, Maya, from the heavenly courts descending, came to the grave, and Buddha preached the Law for her sake.' Strange marks appeared on his feet; Ananda said, 'What be these?' And they answered unto him, 'When first he died, the tears of men and gods, falling on his feet, left these marks.'"[1]

The Death of Buddha (another account). — "At last Buddha arrived at Kusinara. 'Go, Ananda,' saith Buddha, 'and prepare a bed for me between two sâka trees,[2] with my head to the north. I am tired, Ananda; I shall lie down.' . . . Heavenly melodies," says the legend, "were sounding in the air in honor of the Holy One; but to the Holy One belonged another honor, another glory. . . . 'Whosoever, Ananda, male or female follower, liveth in the truth and walketh according to the commandments, these bring to the Holy One highest honor and praise.' . . . But Ananda went into the house, and weeping said, 'I am not yet free from impurities; I have not yet reached the goal; and my master, who taketh pity on me, hath not yet entered into Nirvâna.'[3] . . . But Buddha said unto him, 'Not so, Ananda; weep not, sorrow not! Have I not ere this said to thee, Ananda, that from all that man loveth

[1] Buddhistic Records of Western World, Beal, ii. 39, 40.
[2] Shorea robusta.   [3] Oldenberg, p. 201.

and from all that he enjoyeth, from that he must part? ... How can it be, Ananda, that that which is born, groweth, and is subject to decay, should not pass away? That must be. ... Thou hast done well, Ananda; only strive on; soon wilt thou be free from impurities!'

" Shortly before his departure Buddha said: 'It may be, Ananda, that ye shall say the world hath lost its master; we have no master more. Ye must not think this. The Law and the Truth which I have taught and preached unto you, these are your master when I am gone hence!' And unto his disciples he said: 'Hearken, O disciples; everything that cometh into being passeth away. Strive without ceasing!' These were his last words. His spirit then rose from one state of ecstasy to another, up and down through all the stages of rapture, until he passed into Nirvâna. The earth quaked and thunder rolled. At the moment when Buddha entered Nirvâna, Brahma, the Eternal, spake these words: 'In the worlds at some time all beings put off their bodily frame; at this very moment Buddha, the prince of victory, the supreme master of all worlds, the mighty Holy One, hath entered into Nirvâna.'"[1]

Death of Buddha (still another tradition). — "Ananda sent messengers to all the disciples that the Blessed One was dead; and when they heard this saying, they, with their young men, their maidens, and their wives, were grieved and afflicted and sad and troubled at heart. And some of them wept, dishevelling their hair, and some stretched forth their arms and wept, and some fell prostrate on the ground, and some reeled to and fro in anguish at the thought. 'Too soon,' they cried, 'hath the Blessed One died! Too soon hath the Happy One passed away! Too soon hath the Light gone out of the world!'"[2]

---

[1] Oldenberg, p. 203.

[2] This description is from ancient Buddhistic sermons, dating back probably to the fourth century before Christ (Davids: Buddhistic Suttas, vi. 24).

This ancient Buddhist "Book of the Great Decease" closes its touching narrative of Buddha's departure with:

"Bow down with clasped hands! Hard, hard is it to meet with a Buddha through ages of ages!"[1]

A Modern Buddhistic Liturgy. — The world is so fortunate as to possess a complete form of a modern Buddhistic liturgy, compiled originally by a pious Chinese emperor in 1412 A. D., though probably existing much before that time. It is to be found in Beal's "Catena."[2] After many directions as to forms and ceremonies, the liturgy piously says: —

"But if at the time of prayer there be no devotional thoughts, but only a confused way of going through external duties, and if there be after worship indifferent conversation, gossiping, and babbling, hurrying to and fro, lounging or sleeping, just as on ordinary days, . . . what benefit or assistance can we look for from our religious exertions? . . . Finally, let all worshippers strive after a firm faith, and excite in themselves an earnest intention, and so having purified thought, speech, and action, and engaging in this worship in a spirit of entire devotion, they shall obtain an answer to their prayers."[3]

Chant. — "In close heart communion we adore the eternal Buddha, the eternal Law, the eternal Church (Order)."

One portion of the service closes with this grand expression: —

"So through endless ages yet to come, discharging these sacred duties, all sentient creatures, united at length with the Divine essence, shall obtain supreme wisdom, — the state that admits of no birth, the wisdom of Buddha himself.'[4]

---

[1] Davids: Buddhistic Suttas, p. 136.
[2] Catena, p. 398.   [3] Ibid., p. 400.   [4] Ibid., p. 402.

The great object of worship in this liturgy is Kwan-Yin, who is elsewhere described as the Offspring of the Eternal Light,[1] the Redeemer of the world, or Word of God,[2] a manifestation of God himself, and one form of the beloved Buddha. The liturgy continues: —

"Oh, would that our own teacher [Buddha], and our merciful Father and Lord, would descend to this sacred place and be present with us who now discharge these religious duties. Would that the great, illimitable, compassionate Heart, influenced by these invocations, would now attend and receive these our offerings. May the omniscient and omnipotent Redeemer . . . now come among us and remove from us impurities of thought, speech, and action."

Chant.

Hail, thou ever present Redeemer, who hast perfected righteousness and art possessed of great mercy, who art manifested throughout the universe for the protection and defence of all creatures, and who leadest to the attainment of boundless wisdom,[3] . . . who dispellest all troubles, even diseases and ignorance, who art able always to answer prayer, . . . who removest all doubt, . . . possessed of infinite spiritual power, beyond the capacity of language to express; we accordingly adore thee and worship thee with one heart and one mind.[4] All hail, great, compassionate Redeemer! . . . may I soon attain the eyes of Divine wisdom, may I soon pass over the sea of sorrow, may I quickly attain holiness, may I reach Nirvâna.

> Though I were cast on the mountain of knives,
>   They should not hurt me;
> Though thrown into the midst of the lake of fire,
>   It should not burn me.

[1] Amitâbha.
[2] Catena, p. 385.
[3] Ibid., p. 403.
[4] Ibid., p. 404.

> Though hurled to the lowest hell,
>   It should not hold me;
> Though hungry ghosts surround me,
>   They should not touch me.
> Though exposed to the power of wicked spirits,
>   Their malice should not reach me.
> Though transformed among the lowest forms of life,
>   I should attain to the highest wisdom.[1]

Confession.

We and all men from the very first, by reason of the grievous sins we have committed in thought, word, and deed, have lived in ignorance of the Enlightened Ones [the different manifestations of Buddha], and of any way of escape from the consequences of our conduct. We have followed only the course of this evil world, nor have we known aught of supreme wisdom; and even now, though enlightened as to our duty, yet with others we still commit heavy sins, which prevent us advancing in true knowledge. Therefore in the presence of the Redeemer and the Buddhas we would humble ourselves and repent us of our transgressions.[2]

The worshipper then, after a complete prostration, humbly says: —

"We and all men from the first, from too great love of outward things, and from inward affection to men, leading to sinful friendships, having no wish to benefit others, or to do good in the least degree, have only strengthened the power of the sources of sin and added sin to sin; and even though our actual crimes have not been so great, yet a wicked heart hath troubled us within; day and night without interval or hesitancy have we continually contrived how to do wrong. There hath been no desire after knowledge, no fear of misery, no alarm, no heart-chiding; we have gone on heedless of consequences. Now therefore believing from the bottom of the

---

[1] Catena, p. 405.   [2] Ibid., p. 407.

heart in the certain results of sin, filled with fear and shame and great heart-chiding, we would thus publicly repent us of our sins. We would cut off our connection with worldly objects, and aspire to the heart of knowledge; we would separate ourselves from evil, and pursue good; we would diligently recount all our past offences, and earnestly pursue the path of piety, ever remembering the blessedness of heaven, and the power of all the Buddhas to deliver and rescue us and all men from evil. Hitherto we have only gone astray, but now we return; oh, would that the merciful Redeemer [Kwan-Yin] would receive our tears of amendment."

The end of the Service is as follows : —

"I pray for all men that they may attain perfection of wisdom; I pray that all men may be deeply versed in the wisdom of scriptures, and acquire perfect knowledge. I pray that all men may agree in the principles of truth, and maintain peace, and reverence the sacred Order." [1]

It should be noted that Kwan-Yin is called Redeemer because he has taken oath to save all that breathes.

The Earliest Texts of Buddhism.

KING ASOKA'S ROCK EDICTS (250 B.C.).

"Confess and believe in God, who is the worthy object of obedience." [2] "I have appointed religious observance, that mankind having listened thereto shall be brought to follow in the right path and give glory to God." [3] "All the heroism that the Beloved of

---

[1] Catena, p. 409. The remarkable resemblance of this liturgy to Christian prayers and praise may possibly be due to the early influence, in the sixth and seventh centuries, of Nestorian Christians in China. But if so, this proves the great kinship of the ideas at the root of both religions. (See Mosheim : Ecc. Hist., i. 421)

[2] Edict I., Lillie, p. 58.   [3] Edict VII.

the Gods has exhibited is in view of another life; earthly glory brings little profit, but on the contrary produces a loss of virtue. To toil for heaven is difficult for peasant and for priest, unless by a supreme effort he gives up all."[1] "Whoso doeth this is blessed of the inhabitants of this world, and in the next world endless moral merit resulteth from such religious charity."[2] "May my loving subjects obtain happiness in this world and in the next."[3] "A small man who exerts himself somewhat can gain for himself great heavenly bliss; and for this purpose this sermon hath been preached."[4] "Confess and believe in God. I acknowledge and confess the faults that have been cherished in my heart."[5] "This is true religious devotion, this is the sum of religious instruction, that it shall increase the mercy and charity, the truth and purity, the kindness and honesty of the world."[6] "The precious maxims of the Beloved of the Gods comprise the essence of learning and spiritual knowledge; namely, dutiful service to father and mother, to spiritual teachers, the love of friend and child, charity to kinfolk, to servants, to Brahmans that cleanse away the calamities of generations. Further, also, unceasing perseverance in all these things is fame."[7]

Tolerance. — "A man should honor his personal creed, but not blame that of his neighbor.... He who acteth otherwise, impaireth his own creed and injureth that of others. The man, whoever he be, who possesseth his own creed and blameth that of others, saith, 'Let us set up our own religion in full light;' that man, I say, doeth much injury to his own creed, wherefore religious harmony alone is good."[8] "I pray with every variety of prayer for those who differ from me in creed, that they following my proper example may with me attain unto eternal salvation."[9]

[1] Edict X., Lillie, p. 61.
[2] Edict XII.
[3] Second separate Edict, Burnouf.
[4] Rupnath Rock. Lillie. p. 62.
[5] Delhi Pillar.
[6] Delhi Pillar, Edict VIII.
[7] Delhi Pillar, Edict XIII.
[8] Rock Edict XII.
[9] Delhi Pillar, Edict VI.

"The Beloved of the Gods does not esteem glory and fame as of great value, for it may be got by crafty and unworthy persons; to me there is no satisfaction in worldly pursuits; the most worthy pursuit is the prosperity of the whole world; my whole endeavor is to be blameless toward all creatures, to make them happy here below, and to enable them to attain heaven."[1]

[1] Alabaster, Wheel of the Law, Preface, xxxiv. (quoted from Edicts).

CHAPTER XVI.

REVIEW.

IF the reader will cast his eye over the preceding chapters, he will see that all the great and leading families of races in the world's history have at some time received the inspiration of the Unknown God. They or their ancestors have no doubt during their earliest periods of development deified natural and lifeless objects, and worshipped stocks and stones as fetich. Then they have adored the great powers or appearances of Nature, such as the storm, the thunder, the light, and above all, the sky, or heaven. Next they have risen to the conception of the Heaven-God, luminous, resplendent, eternal, bringing light and life, yet perhaps only one out of many intelligent powers or deities. At that stage of development the Sun is the great personification of Deity. He rises glorious over the desert sands or the illimitable waters, and night shadows flee, and the world, seemingly in death, wakes to life, and a new existence of joy and activity begins. With his coming not only darkness departs, but moral shadows, and he becomes the emblem of truth and justice and beneficence. The magnificent orb is the impersonation of a Power, glorious, unspeakable, benevolent, which causes and governs all. This is the Heaven-God, and soon the Day-Father, the Father in heaven.

This is the usual and natural development among masses of men. The myth-making fancy attaches itself to these ideas, and changes and remoulds them endlessly. And where the imagination is stronger than the reason or the moral faculty, and under control of the sensual feelings, we have the phenomena of polytheism, idolatry, and all its degrading effects, even down to the most cruel and licentious rites of worship.

But during this development of religion from the lowest stage of animalism, there will always be individuals, and sometimes races, with the capacity for the highest inspiration. Men will arise to whom the intuition of God, as the One all-causing, all-loving, ever-enduring, will come home as the most real thing in the universe,— men who at once know its truth, who live for it and die for it, and to whom all other human beliefs are as nothing in the balance. These men are the prophets and inspired leaders of the world; and if their intuition be of a God of righteousness, or a God who is Father, they necessarily lead the moral progress of their race and of mankind. We have seen that the most ancient race in human culture, the Hamitic family, grasped this grand thought of monotheism, and with it attained to the connected truths of a moral judgment to come and an immortal life for the soul.

The Egyptian faith at one period seems only another form of the highest belief; it is one aspect, apparently, of the Absolute Religion. But the race which received the highest intuition of the Divine, or of a "God of righteousness," was the Semitic, in one branch the Hebrews, and in another (probably) the ancient Akkadians of the valley of the Euphrates.

With the Jews, this revelation was probably very ancient, and was handed down in its purest form, yet in every age obscured by much animalism and human ideas of the divine, so that only a chosen few retained the truth in its simplicity. These few, however, have led all races, and the thoughts and imaginations and ideals of that roving tribe of Oriental herdsmen now guide and control all advancing civilization. Their related people — the Chaldean Akkadians — have indeed probably transmitted much to their kinsmen the Hebrews; but otherwise they have passed out of human history.

Passing over to the Aryan races, we find many of its leading peoples recognizing at some period of their development the One God. Far back in Grecian tradition and poetry appears a grand figure, the spiritual Zeus, and in Latin memories the Omnipotent Jove, the "Best and Greatest;" though the belief in the Roman Jupiter is earlier obscured by polytheism and myth than a like faith among the Greeks. This wonderful Aryan tribe transmit this grand faith through the Mysteries, and through the great thinkers, Socrates and Plato, and above all by means of the most heroic and religious school of thought known to antiquity outside of Christianity, — the Stoics.

Looking farther, to the Oriental Aryans, we find the Iranians rising to the highest and purest faith (in many respects) ever granted to man. The Heaven-God, pictured by the luminous and resplendent sky, and by the sun itself, is the Being of infinite moral Light, of Truth, and Purity. He is Truth itself. He is Ahura Mazda, or the Lord All-knowing. Certainly if man should ever take any material object as representing or picturing the mysterious Existence which is unknowable, he would naturally choose the life-giving, glorious sun, bringing splendor and beauty, and driving away darkness and death. And if things created could possibly contain or express him, what altar or temple could for a moment be so fittingly conceived to be his dwelling, as the infinite expanse of the sky and the boundless, luminous ether? The Sun-worship and the adoration of Light might well have gone down through the ages as one of man's many defective efforts to grasp the infinite and to know the unknowable. But the ancient Iranians, or Persians, attempted to explain the problems of existence by the supposition of another and evil Power in the universe.

The modern intellect does not even claim to explain the origin of moral evil. It takes refuge in its own limitation. It knows that the human mind can see but a small segment of an infinite circle. It finds enough, as did also the Greek intellect, in the structure of the moral universe to justify confidence and hope. But the theory of two gods, though so attractive, and explanatory of so much that is mysterious in the world, leads to endless confusion and discouragement. Even if, as under the Zoroastrian faith, the Good Spirit (or Ormazd) finally overcomes the Evil (or Ahriman) and becomes the One Unknown God, still his omnipotence is shaken, and the Father of all is but one Victor among many spirits warring during the ages of eternity. Such a faith cannot feed the human soul, and dies out at last. Yet the Iranian conceptions of the life beyond the grave, and the moral retributions connected therewith, and of the spirits unseen associated with man, and the future Redeemer who shall take away the sting of death and save the world, have survived, and united with the Jewish faiths and inspirations. In this form they have become the eternal property of the human race, and the expression of its highest hopes. Socrates had apparently heard of the Persian faith in a Redeemer, when he said that at length one would arise even among the barbarians, who could charm away the fear of death.[1] Probably all the higher races have at times felt this hope. The revelation of Christ has only confirmed this dim expectation and dream of humanity.

Another branch of the Aryan family, the Hindus, are

[1] Phædo.

found in their ancient hymns to have conceived a Deity who is the Life and Source of all things, Varuna, or οὐρανός (Heaven). Human language cannot express more loftily or clearly the idea of One who made all things and is contained in no temple built by hands, and is worshipped not by external rites, but by purity of heart and beneficence of life, than do these Vedic hymns. When these grand ideas have penetrated the soul, and the worshipper is ready to say, "I am in thee, and thou art in me, and all things are in thee," the step is easy to the thought, "All things are God." The individual is nothing. God is "the all in all." He moves all things. The will of man sinks into his will, not by voluntary action, but of necessity. There is no free will, no choice of purpose, no good or evil, in man's actions. All things are God and come from him. He is the source of evil and the source of good. Man is only a bubble on the torrent of eternity. He comes forth from the Eternal One and returns to him and is lost in him. The human instrument has no character; he can expect no retribution, he has no destiny. He is but a broken fragment of the vast, passionless Infinite Being. This is Hindu pantheism. But when this could not satisfy the soul, the imagination of the people took hold of polytheism and idolatry. And according to the best observers, nothing in the moral results of misdirected religion can ever equal in horror and sensuality the effects of pantheism materialized by idolatry. Man is given up to the vilest animalism, and attempts to believe that this is God. It need not be said that such a religion tends to the utter destruction of human society. But in India there were saving elements. The ancient Vedic faith taught the Unknown God, and the truths of utter self-denial and absolute integrity and love, embracing all creatures. The popular belief added future retribution as a moral sanction. And finally there became stamped on the Hindu mind as a solution of the problem of moral evil the profound and hopeless conviction of transmigration, or re-birth. All sin and pain and evil were the consequences of previous existence, and must go on to create other sin and wrong and suffering in future lives. Re-birth, ever recurring, was the black horror before the Hindu intellect. It was a pessimism without hope or change. The evil that had been should be again, and always bring its own punishment. Not Brahma nor Mârâ — not God nor Satan — could lessen the consequences of an evil deed. Yet it was a pessimism based on eternal righteousness. It contained the seeds of life everlasting. The reform came in a peculiar direction, and was itself, with all its defects, full of divine inspiration. As Tennyson in his wonderful poem makes Lucretius say: —

> "The gods, who haunt
> The lucid interspace of world and world,
> Where never creeps a cloud, or moves a wind,
> Nor ever falls the least white star of snow,

Nor ever lowest roll of thunder moans,
Nor sound of human sorrow mounts to mar
Their sacred everlasting calm ! and such,
Not all so fine, or so divine a calm,
Not such, nor all unlike it, man may gain,
Letting his own life go."

Such a peace of Nirvâna was conceived by a great Hindu personality, where the pains of re-birth, and the storms of passion, and the pangs of sorrow, and the torture of sin and selfishness should cease by "letting one's own life go." The believer was to so fill his mind with love to all beings above and below, here and hereafter, so free his soul from all sensuality and passion, so consecrate himself to human service and the cure of human ills, that a peace like that which bathed the gods of Lucretius should settle upon him. He would escape the horrors of re-birth, the stings of wild desire, the sense of sin, and the agony of sorrow. In the view of many of Buddha's followers he would be in eternal union with Brahma himself; he would be in a heaven which no time or event could reach or change.

This strange mystical belief was conditioned by the most elevated morality and the highest sympathy and benevolence. There could be no Nirvâna without lives of labor for humanity, and the utmost purity and truth. Buddha's religion was "compassion seeking to save." This alone has given it a life of nearly twenty-five centuries. But the want of a direct faith in God as Father and of sure hope in life eternal has doomed it to final extinction. Despite its noble morality and its divine compassion, it must pass away.

The Unknown God is there, for "God is Love," but not through a revelation sufficiently clear, or an inspiration so overpowering, as to lead humanity through its long and weary wanderings in coming ages. Yet it is an incredible satisfaction that to so many millions of human beings the invisible things of the unseen Creator were made manifest through many centuries, even his everlasting power and his divinity or beneficence.

CHAPTER XVII.

HEATHEN INSPIRATION AND THE SCRIPTURES.

There was the true Light which lighteth every man as he cometh into the world. — JOHN i. 9.

IT is important at this point to ask what is the view of the Christian Scriptures as to the non-Christian religions, and the belief in God among the " nations," or heathen.

In the Old Testament there are allusions which would show that the heathen attributed to their gods what really belonged to Jahveh. Thus Isaiah (or his successor) says of Cyrus that he was guided and led towards justice and righteousness by Jahveh, though he knew it not; the inscriptions showing that he attributed his own inspiration to Merodach (the Assyrian god), as if the Divine Being gave men inspirations which they attribute to false gods.[1] And in one passage the prophet Micah seems to believe that a heathen nation in the happy times coming may walk righteously in the inspiration of its own deity, while the Jews live in the fear and love of their own God. "They shall beat their swords into ploughshares and their spears into pruning-hooks. Nation shall not lift up

[1] Isaiah xlv. 4, 5, and Sayce, Ancient Mon., p. 156.

sword against nation, neither shall they learn war any more; . . . for all the peoples will walk every one in the name of his god, and we will walk in the name of Jahveh for ever and ever,"[1] — the idea perhaps being that under a perfect humanity the nations will worship the same Being, though under different names.

In the New Testament we have first the remarkable expression of John in the opening of his Gospel: "There was the true Light which lighteth every man coming into the world" (or, "as he cometh into the world").[2] That is, the light from God, which was most of all manifested in Christ, has visited every human being, of whatever race or creed or rank. The human soul is constituted to receive divine inspirations, and everywhere is touched by them. But though this Light was in the world and the world was made by him, the world knew him not.[3]

As a whole, the world did not receive and follow these inner inspirations. Wherever the Jews, or the "nations," opened their souls to this spiritual influence, we may call them "inspired" in greater or less degree. This inspiration may be defined as a supernatural elevation of the moral and spiritual faculties;[4] not, except indirectly, a strengthening of the judgment or wisdom or intellect, but a power is given the persons inspired to see moral truth

---

[1] Micah iv. 3, 5. This passage, however, may be susceptible of another interpretation.
[2] John i. 9   [3] John i. 2   [4] Morell.

more distinctly, and better to know God. Such inspirations may visit all men, of every degree of civilization; but they will probably be most powerful among tribes in close contact with Nature, and where solitude, with not too grinding toil, opens the soul to grand impressions.

Every human being can recall occasionally in his experience moments when sudden and grand visions of truth, not to be accounted for by any apparent causes, burst upon his mind. Such may be Divine inspirations, perhaps not miraculous, but from the ever-acting Spirit of God, working through the laws of the human soul.

This principle of the universality of Divine influence came home early to the mind of Christ's apostles; and Peter, when he has discovered that in God's sight no man is common or unclean[1] because he is a Gentile or heathen, is compelled to utter the great truth of charity, "Of a truth, I perceive that God is no respecter of persons; but in every nation he that feareth him and worketh righteousness is acceptable to him."[2]

The Apostles were surrounded by Greek and Latin Stoics, the believers in the spiritual Zeus, the Egyptian worshippers of Xoper and followers of Osiris, the disciples of Zoroaster and perhaps of Buddha, and divers others of various creeds. They did not class all these as believers in devils or evil spirits. Some they held as worshippers of "dead gods" ($\theta\epsilon\hat{\omega}\nu$ $\nu\epsilon\kappa\rho\hat{\omega}\nu$), as the "Teachings of the

---

[1] Acts x. 28.   [2] Acts x. 34, 35.

Twelve Apostles" call them;[1] but others, they see, are "fearing God" and "working righteousness," and are "acceptable to him." They did not the less exalt Christ and his gospel, that they acknowledged those who worshipped under heathen names as true believers in God.[2]

So Paul finds "disciples" in Ephesus who had never even heard of the existence of the Holy Spirit, and probably not of Jesus Christ, but who had repented of sins and waited for a Redeemer,[3] as so many non-Christians have done in all ages.

But the great sermon of Paul at Athens (of which unhappily we have such a brief report) should be the model and lesson for all Christians who speak and write of the faiths of non-Christian peoples. These are his words: —

"Ye men of Athens, in all things I perceive that ye are exceedingly religious. For as I passed along, and observed the objects of your worship, I found also an altar with this inscription, 'To the Unknown God.' What therefore ye worship in ignorance, this set I forth unto you. The God that made the world and all things therein, he, being Lord of heaven and earth, dwelleth not in tem-

---

[1] Teachings of the Twelve Apostles, p. 135.

[2] The words of Christ that "no one cometh unto the Father but through me" (John xiv. 6) seem at first opposed to this view. But may not these be interpreted, "No man can come into union with God except through the spirit in me, through self-sacrifice and love"? for "God is Love." Accordingly those who have never heard of Christ — the heathen and the unfortunates in Christian lands — may by their humility and unselfishness and devotion be inspired by that "Comforter" spoken of by Saint John (John xiv. 26), even the spirit of Christ, and so "come unto the Father."

[3] Acts xix. 1-4.

ples made with hands; neither is he served by men's hands, as though he needed anything, seeing he himself giveth to all life, and breath, and all things; and he made of one every nation of men for to dwell on all the face of the earth, having determined their appointed seasons, and the bounds of their habitation; that they should seek God, if haply they might feel after him and find him, though he is not far from each one of us: for in him we live, and move, and have our being; as certain even of your own poets have said, For we are also his offspring. Being then the offspring of God, we ought not to think that the Godhead is like unto gold, or silver, or stone, graven by art and device of man. The times of ignorance therefore God overlooked; but now he commandeth men that they should all everywhere repent; inasmuch as he hath appointed a day, in the which he will judge the world in righteousness by the man whom he hath ordained; whereof he hath given assurance unto all men, in that he hath raised him from the dead." [1]

This great preacher does not begin his message of a new religion by denouncing the old. Amid a crowd of the most beautiful structures for worship or the expression of poetical fancy ever erected by man he merely notes the profound religious sentiment beneath them; he observes that the people of Athens are in all things (not "somewhat superstitious," which is inconsistent with his argument, but) "exceedingly religious" (which is equally true to the Greek words). He adroitly mentions, among the innumerable altars and temples which had attracted his attention, an altar inscribed, "To the [2] Unknown God (Ἀγνώστῳ

[1] Acts xvii. 22-32.

[2] "The" is equally correct with "an," and agrees with the argument better.

θεῷ), built, we may suppose, by pious Greeks to gain the protection of some foreign god, or by some genuine worshipper of the "God of All." Some of his audience had no doubt worshipped the Spiritual Zeus, the God of their poets, the Being adored in the secret worship of the Mysteries, and to whom noble praise had been rendered by the Stoics. The great Apostle does not denounce this worship, or deride the idea of Zeus, though it had been so much corrupted by mythology. He only offers with a gentleness like that of his Master to "set forth" that Being whom they had "worshipped in ignorance." He pictures him even as the great Stoical poets and philosophers, both Greek and Roman, had pictured him,—as One who had created all things, Lord of heaven and earth, dwelling not in human temples,[1] nor needing aught from men, who had given them all things, and had made all races and nations one.

Before this assembly of the intellectually *élite* of the ancient world this strange and barbarous Jew is found announcing a higher spirituality and more perfect humanity than even the greatest Stoics had known. This Oriental preacher tells them also that the Unknown God had so formed all the races of men that they should search for him and feel after him and find him, though he was always near them; and then with a large liberality he quotes what the Stoics had said of Zeus, "For in him we

---

[1] A thought often dwelt upon by Stoics.

live, and move, and have our being," and also what Aratus and Cleanthes had written of Zeus, "For we are his offspring."[1] To him for the moment Zeus represented the idea of God, — the One, spiritual, omnipotent, all-wise; and from this basis the Apostle argues to the higher ideal of God in Christianity, and to the direct message of Christ of repentance, and the hope offered by him of resurrection.

Following out these ideas, the Apostle reasons in the Epistle to the Romans[2] that the nature of the true God has always been revealed to the heathen; that they could always see his "everlasting power" and his "divinity," his purity and love and truth, in nature; and that in consequence their violations of his law "had no excuse." And after a terrible picture of the sins of men, especially of the heathen, he still offers a door of escape. "For when Gentiles which have no law do by nature the things of the law, these, having no law, are a law unto themselves; in that they show the work of the law written in their hearts, their conscience bearing witness therewith, and their thoughts one with another accusing or else excusing them."[3] He apparently teaches here that there is

[1] Ἐκ Διὸς ἀρχώμεσθα τὸν οὐδέποτ' ἄνδρες ἐῶμεν
ἄρρητον· μεσταὶ δὲ Διὸς πᾶσαι μὲν ἀγυιαὶ
πᾶσαι δ' ἀνθρώπων ἀγοραί· μεστὴ δὲ θάλασσα
καὶ λιμένες· πάντη δὲ Διὸς κεχρήμεθα πάντες·
τοῦ γὰρ καὶ γένος ἐσμέν.
     Aratus of Soli (from the poem Φαινόμενα).

[2] Romans i. 20, 21.   [3] Romans ii. 14, 15.

among the heathen a faculty, God-given, the conscience, which shall acquit or condemn; that is, there is from nature such a knowledge of its Creator, and such a sense of truth and justice and love, granted to all men, that the mind through its feeling for right can give the sentence of acquittal or condemnation.

Paul in one place avows himself "a debtor of the Greeks." There are so many passages in his Epistles strongly resembling words of leading Stoics, that treatises have been written to show his indebtedness to Seneca and others. However this may be, in one eloquent passage it seems to me he had in view the noble and humane sentiments of the Greek and Roman thinkers around him; and though he offered his followers in Philippi something higher than Stoicism, yet he could speak thus: "Finally, brethren, whatsoever things are true, whatsoever things are reverend, whatsoever things are just, whatsoever things are pure, whatsoever things are lovely, whatsoever things are gracious, if there be any virtue or any praise, think on these things."[1] The hope of immortal life and the absorbing love of Christ could not blind him to the beauty and grandeur in the teachings of non-Christian scholars, and he held all this, too, to belong to Christian life and doctrine.

In another passage[2] he speaks of the gospel as having been "preached to every creature under heaven"

[1] Philippians iv. 8.   [2] Colossians i. 23.

at a time when in fact only a few Jews and heathen had heard it. Saint Augustine, whether led by this passage or others, declares that the truths at the basis of Christianity had been known to the ancients from the beginning, and that "it was called Christianity in our day, not as having been wanting in former times, but as having in later times received this name."[1] Again he says: "We bring you good tidings, that ye should turn from these vain things unto the living God, who made the heaven, and the earth, and the sea, and all that in them is, who in the generations gone by suffered all the nations to walk in their own ways. And yet *he left not himself without witness*, in that he did good, and gave you from heaven rains and fruitful seasons, filling your hearts with food and gladness."[2] So with other Apostles. When John says, "Beloved, let us love one another, for love is of God; and every one that loveth is begotten of God, and knoweth God,"[3] he gives one of those definitions of religion which must have included many a humble heathen who had never even heard of the existence of Christ, but who loved the Unknown God, and "worked righteousness," waiting for light.

Christ and the Apostles frequently allude to the Divine instruction and training of the ancient Jews as being adapted to their low moral condition; as if there were evils among them which God "overlooked" or permitted because they had not grown up to higher ideas. Among

[1] Op., i. 12.   [2] Acts xiv. 15, 16.   [3] 1 John, iv. 7.

these were plainly hatred of enemies, blood-revenge, freedom of divorce, concubinage, polygamy, and slavery. Take these passages: "That ye turn from these vain things unto the living God, who made the heaven, and the earth, and the sea, and all that in them is, who in the generations gone by suffered all the nations to walk in their own ways;"[1] "The times of ignorance, therefore, God overlooked, but now he commandeth men that they should all everywhere repent;"[2] "Moses for your hardness of heart suffered you to put away your wives,"[3] — these and similar words contain commands approved of Jahveh in ancient time, but supplanted by higher maxims of Christ. Again Christ, in picturing the future life, says: "And they shall come from the east and west, and from the north and south, and shall sit down in the kingdom of God; and behold, there are last which shall be first;"[4] as if outside of the apparent kingdom of God on earth there would be many within the final kingdom of heaven.

[1] Acts xiv. 15, 16.

[2] Acts xvii. 35. "Ye have heard that it was said to them of old time, Thou shalt not kill; and whosoever shall kill shall be in danger of the judgment (Matt. v. 21). . . . Ye have heard that it was said, Thou shalt not commit adultery; but I say unto you etc. (27, 28). . . . It was said also, Whosoever shall put away his wife, let him give her a writing of divorcement; but I say unto you, etc. (31)

[3] Matt. xix. 8. [4] Luke xiii. 29, 30.

CHAPTER XVIII.

THE CONVERSION OF THE NON-CHRISTIAN NATIONS.

THE question now comes up whether we can reasonably expect that this inspiration of the heathen will culminate in Christianity. The apparent obstacles before our missionaries and churches in non-Christian lands are certainly not nearly so great now as they were to the Apostles and their successors in the Roman Empire. The Christian religion leads the progress of the world, and has all the prestige which belongs to the faith of the most moral, powerful, cultivated, and scientific peoples of the world. Persecution cannot alarm its followers, and the rewards of this world follow the confession of its truths. Yet many persons are disturbed at its slow advance among Oriental and non-Christian races, we think without reason. The progress of our faith in the last hundred years among barbarous or pagan peoples has been a wonderful phenomenon. Still, to hopeful minds the advance of the cross against pagan banners seems astonishingly slow.

Undoubtedly the one great obstacle to the spread of Christianity in the world is the lives of its professors.[1] So

---

[1] The following words were spoken to Mr. Terry, the first English missionary to India, 1616: " Christian religion! Devil religion! Chris-

long as the rumseller, the slave trader, the dishonest merchant, the drunken sailor, or licentious soldier represents the Christian religion to Eastern peoples, the followers of Mahomet or Buddha or Confucius or Brahma will prefer their own teacher, or prophet, or deity to any which this faith may offer. They will justly say, "By their fruits shall ye know them;" and whatever missionaries and teachers may preach, they will reject the religion exemplified by such lives as they have long known.

The great counteracting argument is the sight and experience of the best fruit of the teachings of Jesus, — a pure family life in a Christian home. Therefore it seems to us an error (as has been done) to urge celibate and monastic establishments by Europeans in Oriental and African countries. Nor should the success of a missionary

tian much drunk, Christian much do wrong, Christian much beat, Christian much abuse others" (Modern India, p. 236).

A distinguished Hindu Brahman, Chunder Sen, converted to Deism, made these interesting statements in a speech in England. "It appears to me, and has always appeared to me, that no Christian nation on earth represents fully Christ's idea of the kingdom of God. I do believe, and I must candidly say, that no Christian sect puts forth the genuine Christ as he was and as he is; but in some cases the mutilated, disfigured Christ, and, what is more shameful, in some cases a counterfeit Christ. Now I wish to say that I have not come to England as one who has yet to find Christ. When the Roman Catholics, the Protestants, Unitarians, Trinitarians, Broad Church, Low Church, and High Church, all come around me and offer their respective Christs, I desire to say to one and all, Thank you; I have my Christ within me; though an Indian, I can still humbly say, Thank God that I have my Christ" (Hist. Relig. Thought, p. 506).

be tested alone by the number of his nominal converts. It may well happen that his best influence has been the silent one coming out from a disinterested Christian home and family life, teaching integrity, industry, kindness, and brotherly love as fruits of the spirit of Christ. It is not reported that Livingstone ever made a convert; and yet Africa is full of the influence produced by his humane, truthful, noble spirit, devoted to Christ and his cause.

Another very great obstacle to the conversion of the heathen lies in the divisions of the Christian Church. These weaken all missionary efforts. Until sufficient unity is secured to combine without opposition or jealousy in works aiming at the conversion of the non-Christian world, but little effect will be produced.

We do not concur in much that has been said in recent years as to the incapacity and self-indulgence of missionaries in foreign countries. Certainly from America have been sent out many very able and scholarly men who have added to the treasures of knowledge of the world, — men, too, of heroic, self-denying natures, who left many luxuries and distinguished careers at home, and have devoted whole lives to the humble work of teaching distant races the religion of Jesus. It seems ungenerous for those of us who are " at ease in Zion " to criticise the labors of these noble and heroic men. But there is an advance in human thought; and it may well be that these devoted workers for religion and humanity have not kept up with the best wisdom of the day in regard to their methods of instruction. For instance, have our missionaries in China and Japan and India kept in mind, in their teachings, the great model for all mission work, Saint Paul's speech on Mars Hill at Athens? Should not an American missionary addressing a Buddhistic audience stand, as Paul did, on what they both believed? Should he not, as the great Apostle did towards the Greeks, show his respect and admiration for their sacred writings, and for the spirit of the saintly Gotama, and taking the texts of the Dhammapada, and the life of Buddha, argue from them to the higher manifestation of God in Christ and his gospel? Or in India could he not quote the sublime texts of the Vedas, and lead the hearers up, above idolatry and polytheism, to a higher conception than that of Brahma,—to that of the Infinite Father and his incarnation in Jesus Christ? A Christian orator could admit that his audience had often worshipped an Unknown God; but he could offer to set forth a higher God, and thus win their minds to hear further of the truth.

If Buddhism has gained such amazing conquests over Oriental nations, could not Christianity, with a similar but far superior humanity and self-sacrifice, and with the true Son of God to present, gain still greater victories? There seems nothing to prevent an Oriental who has hung on the words of Buddha from listening even more intently to the words of Christ. But he will not be induced to do so by denunciation of such a sweet and loving soul as Gotama.

The preacher must arm himself with the best of Buddha's truths, and then show the higher in the teachings of Jesus. He must offer the Fatherhood of God, which the Hindu saint never mentally grasped, and the hope of a conscious, living immortality, which the great Mystic may not fully have attained.

May we not imagine a Christian scholar, gathering his little audience of devout Buddhists in some village of Ceylon, or China, or Japan, thus addressing them: —

Supposed Christian Sermon to Buddhists.

"Brethren in humanity, I have been among your gorgeous temples and the humble shrines of your poor, and I see that you are an extraordinarily religious and reverential people. But as your great teacher and saint has said, 'If a man live a hundred years, and spend the whole of his life in religious observances and offerings to the gods, this is not equal to one act of pure love;'[1] or, 'If a man repeat each month a thousand sacrifices, and go on enduring his bodily sufferings without ceasing, this is not equal to a moment's undivided attention to the Law;'[2] or, 'the sacrificing to spirits in order to find peace, or expecting reward after this life, the reward for this is not one quarter that man's who pays homage to the good.'[3] The great

---
[1] Dhammapada, p. 59.   [2] Ibid., p. 87.   [3] Ibid., p. 89.

Unknown God is to be worshipped best by self-sacrifice and love to all mankind, as the Lord Buddha has taught you. You agree with him that the crown and aim of human life is to be in union with God; but as he taught the pharisees of old, the worshippers of the Vedas (Tevigga), this union is only possible to the pure and loving of heart, because, as you admit, God is alone perfectly pure and loving. How will you attain this purity? Your teacher has grandly said, 'Not in the void of heaven, not in the depths of the sea, not by entering the rocky clefts of the mountain, can a man escape the consequences of an evil deed;' but we offer you an escape.

"The Lord Buddha has also taught you to meditate on love to all, above and below, to those here and those far away, now and forever, and that thus you will enter into the state of universal charity which fits you for union with Brahma. But we present you One, the Son of God, the Incarnation of his Spirit, the Embodiment of his love, who is as it were the Elder Brother of Buddha. He lived, as Gotama lived, for the poor and outcast and sinful; for all men. He did more; he died for them. He taught what your prophet taught, but in simpler and more vivid way,— humility, purity, self-denial, patience, truthfulness, love for all creatures, now and evermore. He taught higher things; he showed all men that God was a Father, and he made manifest the Eternal Goodness. He gave the hope that the sin which seemed to your pure teacher unforgivable and unforgettable, is, through the Divine Love set forth in the life and death of his Son, washed away and utterly cleansed. We offer you a Redeemer higher than Kwan-Yin. You will find that faith in him and love for him will purify you from evil, and through him your diseases of soul will be healed. More than this: He offered not alone a Nirvâna of peace, but a living immortality in the bosom of the Father, a life of activity and blessedness and purity, forever scattering blessings through the universe of God. His great servant, Saint Paul, has spoken words of the heavenly life, which we offer you, — words such as your loving saint has spoken of Nirvâna: 'Eye hath not seen, nor ear heard, neither have entered into the heart of man, the things which God hath prepared for them that love him.'[1]

"When you bring your beloved ones to the funeral pyre or the open grave, you can only look forth into the darkness and say, ' Perchance, after ages of transmigrations, we shall be so purified that we may be deemed worthy to be in the same heaven with those we have loved. We may there be permitted even to look upon the face of Buddha the Blessed; but all is uncertainty. We know not that memory or hope or love will survive with us. We know not that the Best of all human beings will live to look upon us or to be looked upon by us. We only know that blessedness comes through self-sacrifice and pain and

---

[1] 1 Corinthians ii. 9.

death. Nirvâna may be joy; it may be nothingness.' But we, as Christians, in the name of our Blessed One, offer you assured hope, immortal joy, and perfect union with the Infinite Father. As he arose from the dead, so shall you. As he liveth, so will you live.

"It is true our Lord does not offer to explain the origin of evil, but neither does the Lord Buddha succeed in doing this by means of the baseless theory of previous existence. He does not attempt to do away with transmigration, for there is no evidence of its reality. He only offers God as love, and Christ as his incarnate Son, and eternal life through the knowledge of and faith in him. This is the new Dhamma, or Gospel, we offer; the fresh Dhammapada, or Religion's Path. The sight of and love for this One, higher than Buddha, is the means of preparing you for union with the true Brahma, or God the Father.

"Had Gotama, the Enlightened, but known or heard Jesus Christ, he would have been perhaps the highest of his followers. In heart he served the same ideals, though our Lord was the Son of God, and nearer to the Father.

"In the spirit and love of Buddha we offer you a better Redeemer than Sakya Muni, even the LORD CHRIST."

CHAPTER XIX.

CONCLUSION.

THE long search sketched in this volume for the traces of Divine inspiration previous to and outside of Christianity, in human history, brings with it a great reward. The ways of God to men appear somewhat justified. The distant past is not alone dark with superstition and idolatry and bloody rites and sensual practices under the name of religion, but over the black waves is a long pathway of brilliancy from the great Pharos of the ocean of humanity, — the " Light which lighteth every man," the Spirit of God. Under this heavenly glow are the sweet and unknown virtues and sentiments of human history; the little acts of disinterestedness, the pure aspirations, the heroic deeds of quiet life, the sweet affections, the humble prayers, the unseen patience under suffering, the faithfulness which no dangers could shake, and the love which the waters of death could not quench, — all that is best in human life, and which no historian or poet has ever recorded. All these have been stimulated among the non-Christian races by the faith in the Unknown God, and union with him. Morality has received its greatest impulse from religion.

"Our little systems have their day;
   They have their day and cease to be;
   They are but broken lights of Thee,
And thou, O Lord, art more than they."

Prayer.

O Thou Unknown God! No powers of man can grasp Thee! In Thy fulness thou art unknowable. We pass away; Thou art eternal. To Thee belongeth not time or space. Thou changest not, and yet thy being is full of eternal waves of thought and feeling. From the nature which Thou hast given us, and from thy universe, we know that we are in thy image. Thou hast revealed thyself in Christ thy Son. As he is, such art Thou. We thank Thee that Thou hast also made Thyself known in all ages, to all men, of every race and tribe. We bless Thee that thy creatures in ancient days have seen thy face. We thank Thee that in all their ignorance and animalism they have known thy loving-kindness, which is better than life. We thank Thee that amid impurity they have felt thy purity; that where so much was selfish around them they have seen thy unchanging beneficence. They have only known Thee in part; but who hath known Thee wholly? They have served Thee blindly; but who hath seen all the ways of the Lord? They have given up thought and heart and life to what they conceived thy will. If they have erred, who of us is free from error? They have called Thee by various names; but what are names to Thee? We thank Thee that Thou hast come nearest to us and all men in Jesus Christ thy Son. In him we know Thee as Father. In him we see thy face. We bless Thee that he is leading the progress of mankind. We cannot conceive a higher manifestation of Thyself. But if it be thy will that he "come again," and we receive a higher revelation, we know that the God of our fathers is still our God; that the Spirit made manifest to Abraham and Moses, and appearing to Egyptian priests and Chaldean shepherds, to Greek believers in Zeus and followers of Ahura Mazda, to worshippers of Varuna and disciples of Buddha, and incarnated in the Lord Jesus, is the Spirit Eternal, the All-Father who belongeth to all ages and races and nations of men. We too, O Thou *Theos Agnōstos*, would join with feeble voices the great acclaim of praise and honor and glory which ariseth to Thee from all tribes and countries of men, and would humbly offer our lives in service to Thee, whom we shall yet see face to face.

APPENDIX.

THE UNKNOWN GOD AS REVEALED TO THE ANCIENT PERUVIANS.

"O PACHAMAC, thou who hast existed from the beginning and shalt exist unto the end, powerful and pitiful, who createst man by saying, 'Let man be,' who defendest us from evil and preservest our life and health, art thou in the sky or in the earth, in the clouds or in the depths? Hear the voice of him who implores thee, and grant him his petitions. Give us life everlasting, preserve us, and accept this our sacrifice."[1]

[1] Prayer of the ancient Peruvians, preserved by De Ore, and quoted by Brinton in his "Myths of the New World," p. 298 (earlier, 1868, edition), who accepts it as undoubtedly genuine.

INDEX.

ABBOTT'S TRANSLATION, 94.
Abraham: era, 5, 11, 66; father of monotheism, 52; exodus, 55; prayer, 65; call, 67; influence, 72, 73; existence denied, 75-77; family idolatry and personal inspiration, 173; national ideas, 174; historic figure, 247.
Acts, Book of, quoted, 66, 92, 134, 174, 301-303, 307, 308.
Æschines, quoted, 91.
Æschylus, quoted, 90, 91, 95-103.
Africa, 310, 311.
Ahriman: rank, 184-187; in diseases, 185; in demons, 186; in lies, 185, 187; conquered, 188, 194, 195, 294.
Ahura Mazda: character, 183-187, 293, 294; light and truth, 187; obscured, 188; creator, 189; conqueror, 189, 194; converse with his prophet, 197. (See *Ormazd*.)
Akkadian People: name, 51; origin, 51, 52; civilization, 52; mixture with Semitic nations, 55; brutality, 67; relation to Assyrians, 68; discoveries, 72; traditions about creation, 75; records, 76, 77; cuneiform inscriptions, 171; leaders, 174; ancient faith transmitted, 177.
Akkadian Religion: chapter, 51-77; ancient, 52; seven evil spirits, 52, 53; invocations, 51-58, 61, 62; deities, hymn to fire-god, 54; Hebrew resemblances, 55; penitential psalms, 56, 57; prayer for the king, 57; for the soul, 58; death, 59; sin, 59, 60; mediator, 60-62; psalms of worship, 62-64, 66; sun-god, 63, 64, 69, 70; original sin, 64; prayer to the God of Ur, 65; sorrow, 66; human sacrifice, 67; chief god, 68; prayer to Assur, 68, 69; immortality, 69; Istar's Descent, 69; connection with Jewish history and religion, 70; revolt in heaven, 70, 71; monotheistic inscription, 71; inspiration, 72, 174; moon-god, 73; the unknown God, 74; little known, 171; two strata, 172; elemental worship, 173; pantheism, 174; comparison with the Bible, 175; elevation, 292.
Alexandria: Hebrew influences, 8; school of thought, 171.
Amenti, 19, 22, 29, 30, 35, 42, 43.
Ammon, 11-17.
Amulets, 10, 30.
Ananda, 277, 282, 283.
Ancient Monuments, 61, 62. (See *Sayce*.)
Angessi, quoted, 32, 44, 48.
Animal Magnetism, 134.
Animal Worship, in Christian Symbols, 6.
Annihilation, 245. (See *Nirvâna*.)
Apap, 20, 31, 35.
Apostles: monotheism, 7; surrounding influences, 301, 302. (See *Paul*.)

Apothegms, 269.
Apuleius, quoted, 83, 84.
Aramaic, 50.
Aratus, quoted by Paul, 93, 123, 305.
Archæology, relation to religious study, 5, 6.
Archilochus, quoted, 90.
Aristophanes, quoted, 86.
Aristotle, quoted, 83, 93, 98, 101, 102.
Art, a revealer of religion, 6.
Aryan Race: low images of deity, 11; ideas of God, 292-294; Hindu branch, 294, 295.
Asceticism, 235, 253.
Asha: defined, 183, 189; law, 193.
Asia: degraded religion, 174; spread of Buddhism, 240; Light of, 244.
Asoka, King: council, 245, 256; inscriptions, 247-249; career, 247-251; rock-edicts, 287-289.
Assur, 68-71.
Assyria: kings, 52; deities, 54, 58; Abraham, 77.
Assyrian People, Semitic origin, 172.
Assyrian Religion: mediator, 60; divine light and truth, 63; immortality, 69; scriptures, 76; a chief god, 299.
Atharva Veda, 206, 210, 214.
Atheists, in appearance, 127.
Athenians, golden rule, 99. (See *Greek, Paul.*)
Âtman, 236, 239, 253, 258, 259, 297.
Augustine: on Jove, 104, 105; indebtedness to Stoics, 163, 164; on deity, 232; on basis of Christianity, 307.
Aurelius, Marcus: among the Stoics, 125; imperial saint, 128; on Christian obstinacy, 136; maxims, 143; writings, 152-160; right living, 152; harmony with nature, 152, 157; manhood, political ideals, quick-passing opportunity, 153; readiness for death, 154, 158; charity of opinion, city of Zeus, 154;

day of death, simple prayer, contentment, transitoriness of life, 155; Stoic's view of the universe, self-questioning, 156; happy death, Stoic's prayer, 157; destiny, according to nature, self-respect, 158; man worthy of the universe, deity, future life, 159; all the gift of God, eternity, life a drama, 160; appeal to Epictetus, 161; vague hopes, 165.

BAAL, names, 61.
Babylonia: race, 51; long history, 76; Abraham, 175.
Babylon, name, 68.
Babylonian Religion, not enduring, 170. (See *Akkadian.*)
Baptism, Greek, 85.
Baur's Works, quoted, 134.
Beal's Catena, 237, 265, 271, 276, 277, 284-287.
Beatitudes, 269.
Beauty, eternal, 114.
Bhagavad-Gîta, 198, 208, 212, 213, 217-220. (See *Rig* and *Vedas.*)
Bible: phrases in Seneca, 135; literary superiority, 175; honesty, 176; comparison with heathen worship, 299-308; inspiration of false gods, 299; true light, 300, 301; Stoics and apostles, 301-304; Paul, 304-308; Romans, 305, 306; sins, 307, 308. (See *Acts, Old Testament, New Testament, Paul,* etc.)
Biblical Archæology, 54, 69, 71.
Birch, Samuel, quoted, 16, 24.
Boissier's Works, 134.
Bonzyges, 99.
Book of the Dead: 9, 11, 14, 17, 20-37; described, 19, 40.
Book of Origins, 75-77.
Bossuet's Works, 125.
Boston Art Museum, 12.
Boulaq Museum, 13, 20.

Brahma: nature, 212, 217, 218, 221; repose, 225; union with, 236, 278, 279; superior god, 244; true followers, 260; preferred, 310; incarnation, 312.
Brahmanism: pantheistic, 199, 200; questions, 200; wild fancies, 244; pharisees, 279.
Breaths of Life, quoted, 30.
Bridge's Babylonian Life, 59, 60, 65, 66, 69, 70, 76.
Brinton's Works, 321.
Brotherhood of Gotama, 253.
Brugsch, on Egypt, 9-12, 15, 16, 18, 40.
Buddha: teachings, 210, 255, 260, 261; statue, 224, 267; parables, 225, 268, 269; often misrepresented, birth, 226; conversion, sculptures, 227; the Enlightened One, partial truths, 228; legends, 228, 229; unselfishness, 228, 232; cradle, 229; value of life, 229, 230; almost Christian, 230, 239; saint, 232; name, 233, 274, 275; next to Jesus, 238, 257; church, 239; achievements, 243; deification, words preserved, 245; moral nature, 247; death, 255, 281-284; sun-myth, 256, 257; ancient sermons, 257, 281; five great commands, 260; true disciples, 273; mission, helpfulness, 275; relation to Confucius, 276; universal body, 277; aid to outcast women, 277; first sermon, 278; eight divisions, 278, 279; Socratic method, 280; preferred, 310; best truths, 313; something better, 313-316.
Buddhism: chapter, 224-254; widespread, 224, 240, 249; formalism, 225; compassion, 227; idea of heaven, 228; in China, 230, 277; stories, 231; poetic mystics, 232-234; divine personality, 234, 235; future life, 235, 236; defects, 237-239; asceticism, 239, 240; temperance, 240, 241; sexual purity, 241, 242; superstition, 242; reforms, 242-244; not wholly false, three schools, 244; underlying beliefs, 245; early converts, 247; triad, edicts, 248; liberality, 249; worship and sacrifice, 249, 250; humanity, 250, 251; decay, close, resemblances to Christianity, 251; ceremonies, 252; variations from Christianity, 253; peace, 253, 254; steps of progress, 290-293; myth-making, intuition, 291; moral elements, 297, 298; temporary, 298; amazing conquests, 312.
Buddhist Writings: sacred, 246; Asoka's teachings, 248-250; chapter, 255-289; canon, 255, 259; value, 256; legendary centre, 256, 257; unlike the Bible, 257, 258; great truths, 258; degeneration, 258, 259; famous verse, 259; Nirvâna, 259, 260, 271-274, 297; morals, 260; thought, impurity, pilgrimage of beings, 261; spiritual worship, 261, 262; destiny, happiness of believers, 262; earnestness, 262, 263; pleasure, 263; saints' life, good fortune, 264; selfish good, faith, four great truths, 265; Sutras, 265-267; charity, and good for evil, 266; benevolent king, goodness and spiritual power, 267; golden rules, 267, 268; self-conquest, the world, 268; parable, 268, 269; apothegms, 269; beatitudes, 269, 270; riches, 270; true treasures, 270, 271; true disciple, 273, 274; modern liturgy, 284-289; chant, 284, 285; confession, 286, 287; earliest texts, rock-edicts, 287-289; tolerance, 288.
Buddhists: literature, 217; numbers, 224; formalism, 225; hope in death, 231; councils, 255, 256; spelling of words, 256; southern, 256; re-

lation to apostles, 301; supposed sermon to, 313-316.
Burnouf's Works, 227, 235, 274, 288.

CÆSAR, 247.
Callimachus, 81.
Canaan: invaded, 66; Abraham's occupancy, 77.
Capital Punishment, abolished, 249.
Carter's Version, 144.
Caste, 242, 243.
Cave-dwellers, 2.
Ceylon: religion, 240, 248; slavery, 242; caste, 243; humanity, 251; missionaries, 313.
Chabas, translations by, 13, 19, 38, 40.
Chaldea: magic, 52; Jews, 55, 191; Story, 63; bricks, 66; bloody records, 67; invasion, 76. (See *Akkadian*.)
Chaldean Religion: Ur, 64; ancient monotheism, 71; immortality, 85; source, 106; sacred books, 175; charitable king, 267; charity, 192, 239, 266.
Charlemagne, 247.
Chastisement, value of, 137.
Chatterie's Translations, 219.
Chedorlaomer, 66, 76.
Childers's Dictionary, 233.
China: religion, 224, 240; defective ideas, 226; arts, 240; lost women, 243; children neglected, 242; formalism, 243; Nestorian influence, 252, 287; pilgrims, 265; scriptures, 271; great traveller in, 275; missionaries, 312, 313.
Christendom: sexual impurity, 241, 242; divisions, 310, 311.
Christian Church, legends, 178.
Christianity: suppositional picture of its end, 5, 6; unfairly judged, 68, 74; Abrahamic influence, 75; church mysteries, 78, 85; relation to rationalists, 108; moral heights, 116, 117; pre-Christian revelations, 119; similar ideas elsewhere found, 133; contact with Seneca, 134; not grasped by scholars, 135; indebtedness to Stoicism, 163-166; permanence, 170; qualities, 170, 171; errors, 173; Hindu ideas, 218; nearness to Buddhism, 229, 251, 253; bad effects, 242; seeds of progress, 243; Judaic background, 244; mysticism, 245; better results, 246; spread, 251; truths old as mankind, 307; progress, 309-313; fewer obstacles, 309.
Christians: called Atheists, 127; held in contempt, 136; fearlessness, 165; numbers, 224; ascetic errors, 239, 240; bad characters, 309, 310; homes, 310.
Christmas Chant, 7.
Chrysostom, 122.
Chunder Sen, lecture, 310.
Cicero, quoted, 83, 84, 102, 127, 131, 132, 163, 164.
Cleanthes: quoted, 81, 90; verse, 120; hymn, 123, 124; cited by Paul, 305.
Clemens of Alexandria: quoted, 82, 83, 85, 90, 92; a mystic, 232.
Colebrooke's Translations, 208.
Comforter, the, 302.
Confucius: followers, 224; relation to Buddhism, 276; preferred, 310.
Conscience, after death, 192.
Constantine, 247.
Contentment, 155.
Cosmogony, verse, 209.
Croswell's Translations, 81, 123.
Cyril, quoted, 82.
Cyrus, reign of, 61, 62.

DANTE, 69.
Darius, 189.
Darmesteter, on Persian religion, 183, 186, 188, 189, 192.
David's Psalms, 55, 66, 123, 176.

Davids, Rhys, on Buddhism, 224, 237, 248, 271, 273, 274, 278-280, 283, 284.
Day of Account of Words, 27-29.
Deacon, definition, 132.
Death: psalms, 58-60; Plato and Socrates, 117; Seneca's view, 140-142; readiness for, 154, 158; day of, 155; happy, 157; Christian view, 164-166; with conscience personified, 192, 193; of the wicked, 193; prayer for the dying, 213-215; leader, 215, 216; Buddhist view, 231, 275, 282-286.
Decalogue, 45, 46, 50.
De Horrack, on Egypt, 30.
Delhi Pillar, 250, 288.
Delitzch, on the Akkadians, 51.
Demons, 186. (See *Ahriman*.)
Dendera Temple, 11, 18.
Denis's History of Moral Ideas, 103.
De Rougé, on Egypt, 10, 20, 29, 40.
Destiny, 158, 262.
Devéria, on Egypt, 25, 32, 33.
Dhammapada, 226, 228, 230, 239, 243, 245, 250, 255-274, 312, 313, 316; Chinese, 265.
Dillman, Dr., quoted, 70.
Diodorus: on Egypt, 7; Mysteries, 80, 85.
Diogenes Laertius, 130, 162.
Dio Chrysostom, 94.
Disease, attributed to Satan, 185. (See *Ahriman*.)
Döllinger, on the Mysteries, 85.
Dourif, on Stoicism, 134.
Drug, or Satan, 189, 195.
Duality, 190. (See *Zoroastrianism*.)
Duncker, on the Persian faith, 189.
Dyer's Translation, 53.

EARNESTNESS, 262, 263.
Ecclesiastes, Book of, 43, 44.
Edfu Temple, 18.

Edkins's Translations, 224, 230, 276.
Egypt: oldest civilization, symbolism, 5; historians, 7, 8; buildings, 11; Denkmäler, 17, 19; borders, 77; inscriptions, 209.
Egyptian People: kings, 21, 40; confusion of persons in history, 32; relation to Jews, 41-50; cultivation, 41, 42; caste, 43; garments, 44; intellectual superiority, 168.
Egyptian Religion: monotheistic, 1-40; temple inscriptions, 1, 5; misunderstood, 6; better known to-day, 8; unseen God, 8-10; spiritual rise, 11; deities, 11-17, 68; intuition, triad of deities, 12; résumé of belief, 17; dearest deity, 19, 20, 26; priests, 22; love, 23; Anubis, 27; Day of Account, 27-29; bodily resurrection, 29, 30; pictures of the unseen, 37-39; highest point, 38, 50; prophecy of light, 40; elevated conceptions, 40, 89; emblems, 42; secrecy, 44, 49; decadence, 46, 47; wide-spread, immortality, 49; priestly mysteries, 79, 80, 85; goddess, litanies, 84; oracles, 106; excelled, 116; relation to Moses, 171; barren results, 170; faults, sacred literature, 175; almost absolute, 292; influencing the apostles, 301.
El, 68.
Elamite Invasion, 66, 76.
Eleusinian Mysteries, 80-83. (See *Mysteries*.)
English People: their deity, 74; poetry, 74, 75; Puritan element, 76, 77. (See *British Empire*.)
Ennius, 104.
Enoch, death of, 48.
Epictetus: views, 124, 165; Stoicism, 125, 132; divine love, 128, 129, 130; Jews called Christians,

136; physique, maxims, 143; writings, 144-151; life, 161.
Esne Temple, 16.
Essenism, 252.
Eternity, 160.
Euripides, quoted, 97-100.
Eusebius, quoted, 80, 82, 84, 101.
Evil: origin of, 187; endless consequences, 296. (See *Sin*.)
Ewald, 75.

FAITH: power and perseverance, 169; Buddhist, 265.
Fatherhood of God: not always discovered, 167; wanting in Buddhism, 259, 260. (See *God*.)
Fire-god, hymn, 54. (See *Sun-god*.)
Flint Age, 2.
Flood, 5, 70.
Freedom, in Stoicism, 151.
Future Existence: punishment, 31; idea of Stoics, 159, 160; inevitable conclusion, 169; Buddhist idea, 230, 235, 253; not taught by Confucius, 276. (See *Immortality*.)

GALLIO, 134.
Genesis, Book of: Jehovah, 50; Agade, 51; Elam, 66, 73; Abraham, 75-77. (See *Book of Origins*.)
God: Egyptian idea, 1-50; moral action, 1; one will, 2, 148; one power, 4; flowing locks, 6; plurality of gods, 6, 7; unseen in stars, 8, 9; high spiritual images, 11; behind all forces, 12; life and truth, 14; creator, 15, 25, 149, 193, 194, 259; weaver, 15; Babylonian idea, 51-77; purity, 67; names, 68, 207, 208; national limitation, 74; mysteries, 80-82. Greek idea, 78-105 (see *Zeus*); Socrates and Plato, 106-119; as love, 106, 298, 302; impartation of moral life, 108. Platonic idea, 110-113, 117; idea of Stoics, 120-181; pattern for imitation, 121; beyond evil, 122; within, 127; habitation in virtue, 130; moral governor, 136-138; profound belief in, 143; son of, 144; master, 145, 151; fatherhood (*q. v.*), 146, 149; to be praised, 146; union with, 147, 194; friend, 150; universal source, 160; far away, 162; of Stoicism, 166; righteousness, 168; spiritual personality, 173, 233-236; self-existent, 179; like his universe, 181. Persian idea, 182-197 (see *Zoroastrianism*); garment, 194; Om, 208. Hindu idea, 198-223; supremacy, 216; known and unknown, 219, 303, 304; great soul, 220; defined, 221. Buddhist ideas, 224-289; uncreated, 260. Chinese idea, 285; primitive notions, 290, 291; intuitively known, 291. (See *Ahura Mazda, Brahma, Jahveh*.)
Golden Rules, 267, 268.
Good for Evil, 266.
Good Fortune, 264.
Goodness, 217, 266.
Grassman's Translation, 207, 214.
Grébaut's Translation, 13.
Greece: remote from Egypt, 5, 8; great thinkers, 107; Stoics (*q. v.*), 125; traditions about deity, 292; belief in God, 294.
Greek Mysteries: chapter, 75-89; great gift, 78; difficult to understand, 79; symbolic and dramatic scenes, 79, 80, 84; hymns, 80-82; darkness, 80; humanizing effect, uncertain testimony, 83; relation to Hebrew views, 84, 85; sacred truths, 85; rules, 86; divine ideal, 87, 88; contemned, 88, 89; misunderstood, degenerate, 89; enduring

influence, 171; national source, 177.

Greek Religion: origin, 106, 171; ideas of deity, 106; Socrates and Plato, 108; superior to Egyptian, 116; not permanent, 170; divine confidence, 177-180. (See *Plato, Socrates, Stoicism, Zeus.*)

Greeks: as religious historians, 5, 6; errors about Egyptian worship, 22; beauty, 72; poetry, 74, 94; ancient beliefs, 90; moral power of art, 93; Bonzyges, 99; pantheism, 161; intellectual superiority, 168; habits, 177; apostolic indebtedness, 306.

HADES, 20, 23, 33, 35, 36, 69, 79, 87-89, 107.
Halévy, J., 51.
Happiness of Believers, 262, 263.
Harris's Translations, 13, 14.
Heaven: in pictures, 7; entrance, 36, 37; described, 37, 38; revolt, 70, 71; Zoroastrian, 183, 184; Hindu, 210-212.
Hebrew Poetry, 191. (See *David.*)
Heliopolis, 19.
Hell, 183, 184. (See *Hades.*)
Heraclitus, 99.
Hercules, 99.
Hermes, Vision of, 226.
Herodotus, 5, 7, 8, 188.
Hesiod, 92, 93, 178.
Hesychus, 99.
Hibbert's Lectures, 54, 65.
Higginson's Revision, 144.
Hindu People: before the advent of Buddhism, 236; Aryan branch, 294, 295.
Hindu Religion: powers of nature, 198; moral questions, 199, 221; one deity or many, 200, 207, 208; origin of evil, 201; hymns, 201, 205-210; morality, 202, 223, 296; divine absorption, 203; soul of nature, 204; three gods, 208; cosmogony, 209; heaven, 210-212; prayer and death, 213-216; supreme spirit, 216; lord of righteousness, 217; goodness, 217-219; redemption, 218; worship, 219; soul, 220; speculations, 222; mythology, 223; containing Buddhism, 224, 225; degeneracy, 225; defective ideas, 226, 227; re-birth, 227, 297; pantheism, 295.

Holy Spirit: struggling with soul, 107; view of Seneca, 135; not in Stoicism, 161.
Homer, 92, 100, 102, 178.
Hommel, on Semitic Races, 66, 75.
Huc, Father, 252.

ILON, 67-69, 71.
Immortality: Egyptian view, 8, 17, 27, 28, 106; earliest belief, 80, 85, 87, 89; Plato and Socrates, 113-115; sure, 118. (See *Future Life, Heaven, Hell.*)
Impurity, 261. (See *Purity.*)
Increaser, the, 186, 194.
Independence, 144.
Indra, 92.
Iranians: view of universe, 182, 183; of deity, 183, 184, 294; literature, 175. (See *Zoroastrianism.*)
Isaiah, 43, 62, 70, 176, 261.
Isis: temple, 1, 45; amulet, 10; and Osiris, 10, 21, 23, 87; faith, 86.
Isocrates, 78, 99, 101.
Istar, 53, 56, 59, 63, 64, 66, 69, 170.

JAHVEH: name defined, 12, 41-50; revered, 46; faith in, 47, 48, 177; righteousness, 48, 176; allusions, 55, 62, 64; national deity, 74, 244, 300; resemblance to Zeus, 90, 91; Psalmist's feeling, 123; nature,

168; subordinate powers, 174; commands, 308.
Jama: allusions, 207, 210; hymn, 215; leader, 215, 216; King of Death, 261.
James the Apostle, 9.
Japan, missionaries, 312, 313.
Jesus Christ: biographical facts not in ancient histories, 6; myths and traditions, 7; texts, resemblance to Osiris, 27; era, 56; profile, 94; Gospel of the Infancy, 226; mystical truth, 232; nearness to Buddha, 238, 239, 314; message from God, 243; perfect inspiration, 254; Samaritan woman, 254; sayings contrasted with Buddha's, 257; elder brother, 314-316. (See *Increaser, Messiah, Osiris.*)
Jewish People: relation to Egyptians, 8, 41-50, 171; Platonized, 8; leaders, 44, 45, 72; profound faith, 47-49; general influences, 50; Semitic origin, 54; human sacrifices, 67; progenitors honored, 73; annals filled out, 76; identified with Christians, 136; superior inspiration and inferior intelligence, 168; grand ideas in history, 173; agriculturists, great words, 175; hopes of redemption, 179; Persian contact, 190; relation to deity, 299; ancient training, 307; defects, 307, 308.
Jewish Religion: names of deity, 11, 12; priestly dress, 44; immortality, 48, 58; sources, 52; sense of sin, 64; psalms, 66, 75, 174; sacrifices, 67; superiority, 70, 197; supposed late monotheism, 73, 74; Abrahamic traditions, 75; influence of Egyptian rites, 84; solemn figure, 90; fountain of faith, 172; permanence, 170, 175; inspiration, 174, 176; nearness to Buddhism, 224; background for Christianity, 244; highest, 292; survival, 294.
Job, 30, 32, 34, 48, 173, 176.
John of Damascus, 232.
John's Epistles, 307.
John's Gospel: logos, 10; Alexandrian thought, 171; God and Christ, 178; mysticism, 232; teachings, 300, 302.
John the Baptist, festival, 7.
Josephus, 84.
Joshua, 55, 56.
Jove, 103-105.
Jowett's Translations, 114.
Jude, 70.
Judgment: Egyptian view, 8, 27-29, 37, 39, 43, 106; day, 169.
Judith, Book of, 55.
Jupiter, 102, 104.
Justification, 10.
Justin Martyr: quoted, 10, 82, 100; mysticism, 232.

KARMA, 245, 246, 258, 259.
Kellogg, on Light of Asia, 244, 246.
Keph, 12.
Kerneter, or Hades, 20.
Kronios, 81.
Kuenen's Objections, 73, 75.
Kwan-Yin, 285, 287, 315.

LAFERRIÈRE, on the Stoics, 131.
Latin Race: poetry, 74; religion, 103, 104; idea of deity, 292. (See *Roman.*)
Lenormant, on Akkadians, 60, 61, 68.
Leonowens, Mrs., 239.
Life: transitory, 155, 264; a drama, 160; right, 152.
Lillie's Buddhism, 227, 244, 246, 249, 250, 287.
Livingstone's Travels, 311.
Logos, 27, 111. (See *Thoth, Word.*)

Long's Version, 152.
Louvre Manuscripts, 25, 32, 33.
Love: in religion, 23; divine nature, 225, 298, 302. (See *God*.)
Lucan, the poet of Stoicism, 130, 164.
Luke's Gospel, 308.
Lyon, on the Akkadians, 51.

MAGI, 188.
Magic, 52, 65.
Mahâ-bhârata, 210-225, 268.
Manhood, 153.
Marco Polo, 230.
Mariette, on Egypt, 20, 21, 24, 25.
Marriage, 242.
Martyr, defined, 132.
Mason's, Miss, Translation, 115.
Maspero's Writings, 40.
Matthew's Gospel, 308.
Maury, on Zeus, 99.
Maximus Tyrius, 91.
Maya, 282.
Mediator, 60, 61. (See *Jesus*.)
Memphis, inscriptions, 12, 19.
Menander, 100, 101.
Mercy, 138, 224, 227, 276.
Merodach, 60-62, 299.
Messiah, expected, 169.
Messiahship, 179. (See *Jesus*.)
Metempsychosis, 83, 88.
Meyer, E., quoted, 11, 30, 76.
Micah's Prophecy, 299, 300.
Middle Ages, 233, 241.
Milton, John, 71.
Mind, personified, 111.
Miramar, on Egypt, 35.
Missionaries, 313-316.
Monotheism: Egyptian, 1-44 *passim*; highest point, 38; elevated, 40; in Judaism, 45, 168; the father of, 52; late, 73, 74; early, 75; in Greek Mysteries, 85, 89; among the Stoics, 125; general yet narrow, 173; line of great teachers, 173; indistinct, 174; in Hinduism, 198, 200, 207, 208; degraded, 225. (See *God*.)
Moon-god, 59, 69, 73, 76.
Morals, obscurity, tradition of a great benefactor, 3.
Morell's definition, 300.
Mormonism, 135.
Moses: era, 5, 11, 40; influenced by Egypt, 43-45, 171; idea of deity, 46; sublime conviction, 50; wide influence, 72, 73; Pentateuch, 76; law, 308.
Mosheim's History, 252, 287.
Muir's Sanskrit Texts, 204, 208, 212, 214.
Müller, Max: on Hinduism, 205, 208; on Buddhism, 226, 228, 245, 255, 256.
Musæus, 88.
Mysteries: behind things seen, 2; of universe, 4; Egyptian, 8, 79; worship, 304. (See *Greek*.)
Mystery Plays, 79.
Mysticism, 232-236.
Myth-making, 178, 179.
Mythology: Jahveh independent of, 46; taking possession of religion, 107; along the Euphrates, 173; coexistent with high spirituality, 178.

NATURE: deity unseen in, 8, 9; harmony with, 152, 157, 158; the all-giver, 158; religion of, 172; influencing Zoroastrianism, 182, 183; Hinduism, 198; Hebraism, 301.
Nestorian Religion, 252, 287.
New Testament, relation to other religions, 300. (See *Bible*, *Jesus*, *John*, *Paul*.)
Nirvâna: explained, 212, 227-229, 234-240, 258, 259, 271-277, 281, 283, 285, 297, 315; omitted in Asoka records, 248.

Nirvânapura, 246.
Non-Christian Nations: how to be converted, 309-316; progress of Christianity, 309; greatest obstacle, 309, 310; influence of homes, 310, 311; divisions among Christians, 311; character of missionaries, 311, 312; future conquests, 312; sermon to Buddhists, 313-316.
Novatus, 134.

OLDENBERG'S TRANSLATIONS, 225, 233, 236, 256, 260-263, 271, 275, 282, 283.
Old Testament, connection with other religions, 299. (See *Bible, David, Isaiah, Job*.)
Opinions, charity for erroneous, 154.
Opportunity, quick-passing, 153.
Orelli, 104, 105.
Oriental Races: magic, 52; the number *seven*, 53. (See *China, Hindu, Persia*.)
Original Sin, 64. (See *Ahriman, Evil, Sin*.)
Ormazd, 183. (See *Ahura Mazda*.)
Orpheus, 10, 88.
Orphic Mysteries, 79-81; hymns, 81, 82, 178.
Osiris: legend, 7; definition, 12; part of one deity, 15; deification, 18; chapter, 19-40; dear to Egypt, 19; qualities, 19, 20; prowess, 20; special name, 20, 24, 25; mythical birth, 21; national service, 21, 22; mysteries, 22, 23; embodiment of love, 23; sufferings and death, 23, 24; liturgies, 24-26, 33; union with soul, 26; day of judgment, 27-29; resurrection, 29-33; judge, 32, 39, 50; spiritual body, 33-35; future life, 35-38; father, 35; guardian, 36; offspring of deity, 39; forgotten, 170; defects of this cult, 171; compassion, 239; relation to apostles, 301.
Ounnofer, 20, 24, 25.

PANTHEISM, 161, 170, 174, 199, 200, 222, 295.
Papyrus of the Dead, 18. (See *Book*.)
Parsees, 189, 191. (See *Persia*.)
Paul: *mysteries*, 78; citations from Greek writers, 93, 123, 129; unknown god, 103; relation to Seneca, 133, 134; theology, 178; mysticism, 232; charity, 239; Buddhist words, 252; preaching in Athens, 302-304, 312; method of reasoning, 304-306; supposed quotation by missionary, 315.
Paul's Epistles, 305-307, 315.
Pausanias, 92, 102.
Pelasgians, 178.
Pentateuch, 76. (See *Moses*.)
Persia: conqueror, 62; messianic hope, 179; religion, 188, 294. (See *Parsees, Zoroastrianism*.)
Personality of God: Oriental idea, 199, 233-235; apparently excluded, 245, 246. (See *God*.)
Peruvian Religion, 321.
Pessimism, 296.
Pharisees, 279, 280, 314.
Phidias, 93, 94.
Phocion, 159.
Phoenicians, 168.
Phonograph, 74.
Pierret's Pantheon, 19, 31, 40.
Piety, of the Stoics, 150, 151.
Pilgrimage of Beings, 261.
Pindar, 83, 91, 100, 101.
Plato: Egyptian influences, 8, 171; on beauty, 72, 82; Phædo, 82; Greek Mysteries, 88, 89; Zeus, 91, 98-102; religion, 106-119, 179, 180; motto, 106; ideas, 107; breadth, 108; not a theologian, 110; nor a pantheist, 111; moral conclusions,

113-115; inferences, 117; immortality, 118; sin, 119; basis of faith, 121; ante-Christian churches, 177; messianic hope, 179, 180; dreams, 180.
Pleasure, 263.
Pliny, 105.
Plutarch: on Egypt, 5, 7, 8, 10, 21, 23, 171; Greek Mysteries, 78, 86-89; crime, 162.
Pluto, 22.
Poetry, preserved, 74, 75.
Political Ideals, 153.
Polytheism: in the time of Abraham, 55; Akkadian, 70, 75, 173, 174; Hindu, 225.
Porphyry, 83.
Prayer: usefulness, 102; defined, 103; idea of Stoics, 127, 157; simple, 155; to Ormazd, 195; about death, 213-215; proper mood for, 284; to the unknown God, 318, 319.
Prince Ptahhotep's Teachings, 18.
Proclus, 88.
Prophets, on future life, 48.
Psalms of David, 48, 174. (See *David*.)
Ptah, 12, 15.
Punishment, 117. (See *Hades, Judgment, Retribution*.)
Puritans, 76, 77.
Purity, 196.
Pythagoras, 102.
Pythian Games, 100.

QUINTUS VALERIUS, 104.

RA: heart, 11; rank, 12, 15; hymn, 13; description, 18; father, 25. (See *Ammon*.)
Ragozin, 63, 66.
Records of the Past, 24, 30, 56-59, 63, 64, 66. (See *Birch*.)
Redeemer, Chinese, 287. (See *Increaser, Jesus, Mediator, Saviour*).

Religion: defined, 1; development, 2; great leap, 3; purest ideals, 4; Egyptian, 5-19; divorced from morality, 105; of Socrates and Plato, 106-119; progress, 290-298. (See *Akkadian, Buddhism, Egyptian, Greek, Hinduism, Jewish, Zoroastrianism*.)
Renan, on Jahveh, 50.
Renier, on inscriptions, 105.
Renouf, on Egypt, 40.
Resurrection, 29-35. (See *Future, Heaven, Immortality, Judgment*.)
Retribution, 106. (See *Punishment*.)
Revelation, Book of, 70.
Revelation, defined, 1. (See *Bible*.)
Riches, 270.
Righteousness, 10, 168, 177, 180, 181.
Rig Veda, 198-216 *passim*. (See *Bhagavad-Gita, Vedas*.)
Roman People: remote from Egyptian civilization, 5, 8; allusions to Christianity, 5, 6; errors about Osiris, 22; law, 72, 131, 163; Mysteries, 79, 80; thinkers, 89; despondency, 125, 126; pantheism, 161; milder opinions, 162; influenced by Egypt, 171; habits not affected by religion, 177.
Rome, City of, Paul and Seneca, 134.

SABBATH, 71, 78.
Sacrifice: human, 6; Osiris, 20.
Saints, 264.
Sakya Muni, 251, 252.
Samothracian Tribes, 85.
Sargon the Great, 52, 66.
Satan, 185, 189, 190, 194-196, 199. (See *Ahriman*.)
Saviour: the Increaser, 186; serpent-destroyer, 187, 194, 195; Hindu, 217, 218. (See *Jesus, Messiah, Redeemer*.)

Sayce's Lectures, 51, 54, 56, 61, 62, 66, 76, 77, 299.
Schlagintweit, on Buddhism, 224.
Schrader's Writings, 50, 53, 56, 63, 66.
Sebák, 12.
Seinecke's Writings, 75.
Self: examination, 148, 156; respect, 158; conquest, 268.
Selfish Good, 265.
Semitic Races: spiritual impressions, 4; self-existent God, 10, 11; enslaved, 42; Egyptian influence, 48, 49; herdsmen, 47; Assyrians, 51, 52, 68, 172; Hebrews, 54; Akkadian mixture, 55; sin, 64; influences, 67; deity, 68; common origin, 70, 174; revolt in heaven, 71; tribal movements, 77; branches, 168; sun-worship, 173.
Senart, on Buddhism, 256, 257.
Seneca: quotations, 33, 130; immortality, 118, 162; imitation of deity, 121; monotheism, 125; Stoicism, 133–143, 161; common law of race, 131; age and career, 133, 134; unfaithfulness to principles, 139; death, 140–142; sin, 142, 143; character, 165; relation to Paul, 306.
Sensuality, defended, 162.
Serapis, 18.
Serpent, destroyed, 187. (See *Satan*.)
Seti, 23, 40.
Seven, sacred number, 53.
Severus, 153.
Sextus Pyrrhus, errors, 162.
Siam, 239, 248.
Signet-rings, 77.
Simonides, 100.
Simplicius, 120, 124, 130.
Sinai, 45, 46.
Sin: sense of, 59; atoned, 63; Seneca's view, 142, 143; Hindu idea, 202, 203. (See *Evil, Original, Satan*.)

Sky-god, 95. (See *Zeus*.)
Slavery: illustration, 42, 43; relation to Buddhism, 242, 249.
Smith's Translation, 93.
Social Evil, 241–243, 277.
Socrates: death, 72, 116, 161; mysteries, 84, 89; doctrines, 89; religion, 106–119, 179, 180; relation to Plato, 107; philosophy, 108; good fighting, 109; morals, 113; conclusions, 117; immortality, 118; citizenship, 129; Egyptian influence, 171; follower, 231; method, 237, 280; Persian influence, 294.
Solon, 90.
Son of God, a, 144.
Sophocles, 94–97.
Soul, prayer for, 58.
Spiegel, on Zend-Avesta, 194, 196.
Spirit, one great, 14. (See *God*.)
Spiritual Body, 33–35.
Spirituality: manifestation, 3; continuity, highest form, 4; in worship, 261; power, 267.
Spiritualism, 134.
Stade's Writings, 75.
Stanley, Dean, 75.
Star, prayer to, 195.
Stoa, 133.
Stobæus, 93, 124.
Stoics: monotheism, 89, 90; disciples of Plato and Socrates, 118; views, 120–181; principles, 121, 122; spirituality, 123; last saint, 124; popular estimate, 125–127; submission, 125, 126; churches, crown, 127; imperial saint, 128; motto, relation to deity, 129; father of, on virtue, 130; harshness, 131; human brotherhood, 131, 163; enthusiasm, 132, 138; deacons and martyrs, 132; faith, 133; great doctrine, 136; relation to Christianity, 136, 164–166; principles not carried out, 139; death, 140; writings, 144–

166; Epictetus, 144-151; independence, 144; a son of God, 144; divine master, 145, 151; suicide, 145; divine fatherhood, 146, 149; divine praise, 146; survival of the best, wealth, divine union, 147; self-examination, the divine will, 148; creator, 149; pious friends of deity, 150; freedom, 151; universe, 156; prayer, 157; failure, 161; defects, 161, 162; heroes, 162; influence gone, 163; effect upon Augustine, 163, 164; curious study, 166; unsatisfactory, 180; follies, 181; influence over apostles, 301; over Paul, 304, 306; familiar thought, 306.
Suicide, 145, 161.
Sun: symbol of deity, 17; boat, 26, 37; worship, 173, 293; prayer, 195; early idea, 290.
Sun god: message, 11; Osiris, 26; prayer, 36, 69, 70; Merodach, 61; hymn, 63, 64.
Sun-myths: added to original story, 3; in Christianity, 7; in Buddhism, 256, 257.
Superstition, wrongly attributed to Christianity, 6.
Survival of the Best, 147.
Sutra, 265.
Symbolism: Egyptian, 5, 6; Christian misunderstood, 6; carried to extremes, 8.

Tacitus, 135, 136.
Talbot's Translation, 71.
Tauler, 235.
Taylor's Translation, 81, 88.
Teaching of Twelve Apostles, 302.
Teletai, word used by Paul, 78.
Temperance, among Buddhists, 240.
Tennent, on Ceylon, 251.
Tennyson's Poetry, 125, 167, 296, 297, 318.

Terpander, 90, 91.
Terry, on India, 309, 310.
Theban Inscriptions, 12, 13, 19.
Theism, cold, 161.
Theologia Germanica, 233-236.
Theon, 88.
Thibet and its Religion, 240, 243, 252, 274.
Thoth: texts, 9; existence, 10; manifestation of God, 11; figure, 12; deific rank, 15; logos, 27; divine spirit, 30; life-giver, 33, 34.
Thought and Sorrow, 261.
Tiele's Writings, 75.
Time and Space, mystically viewed, 235.
Tolerance in Religion, 288.
Transmigration, 199, 222.
True Treasures, 270.
Truth: symbolized, 10; divinity, 14; essence of life, 17; Osiris, 19.
Tum: tongue, 11; defined, 12; praised, 16.
Turanian Race, 51.
Typhon, 22, 23, 30.

Uhleman, on Egypt, 24, 25, 50.
Ulpian, on freedom, 131.
Upham, on Sacred Books, 246.
Upanishad, 208, 209, 216.
Ur of the Chaldees, 64, 65, 73, 76.

Varro, on Jove, 104.
Varuna, 204-207, 221, 295.
Vaughan's Crescent and Cross, 241.
Vedas: hymns, 198, 201; divine unity, 200; morals, 202; date, 210; should be quoted by missionaries, 312.
Virtue, personified, 164.

Wealth, 147. (See *Riches*.)
Weber, on Brahmanism, 209.
Wellhausen's Writings, 75.

336 INDEX.

Williams, Monier, History of Religious Thought, 200, 201, 209, 215, 224.
Wisdom, personified, 111. (See *Logos*.)
Woman: elevation, 242; education, 250.
Word of God: Egyptian and Scriptural view, 9-11; in Chinese worship, 285.
World, 268.
Worship: true, 219; Buddhistic, 284-287. (See *Liturgies, Prayer*.)

XENOPHANES, 92.
Xenophon, 112, 113.
Xerxes, 189.
Xnum: defined, 12; deific rank, 15.
Xoper: defined, 10; rank, 44; relation of worshippers to Christian apostles, 301.

ZELLER, on Stoicism, 129.
Zend-Avesta, 182-197 *passim*; meaning, 188; childishness, 191.
Zeno, 127, 128, 130, 131.

Zeus: allusions, 81-83, 105; hymns, 81-83, 95, 96, 123, 124; spiritual deity, 90-103, 301; attributes, 90; eye, 92; fatherhood, 93, 149, 188; face on coins, 94; prayers, 94, 95, 102, 103, 155; all-in-all, 98, 99; governed by fate, 106; mind of the universe, 111; not responsible for sin, 119; to be followed, 121, 122; desires for humanity, 124, 128; human ideal, 126; city, 129, 154; kindred, 147, 148; conscience-giver, 155; will, 164; forgotten, 170; ideal lowered, 178; heaven-god, 188; Greek poetry, 208; old idea, 292; influencing Paul, 304, 305. (See *God*.)
Zoroaster: divine conversations, 192-197; character, 197; disciples influencing apostles, 301.
Zoroastrianism: literature, 175; purity, 180; chapter, 182-197; the Increaser, 186; original deity, liturgies, 188; struggle between good and evil, 189, 294; duality, 190; morals, 189; revelations, 191; charity, 192; conscience, 192, 193; creator, 193, 194; lust, 196; the Saviour, 194-196.

www.ingramcontent.com/pod-product-compliance
Lightning Source LLC
Chambersburg PA
CBHW030321240426
43673CB00040B/1241